FOCUS ON SUCCESS

...

Scott Amundsen

University of North Carolina Wilmington

Kendall Hunt
publishing company

Cover and interior photos provided by University of North Carolina Wilmington and are used with permission.

Kendall Hunt
publishing company

www.kendallhunt.com
Send all inquiries to:
4050 Westmark Drive
Dubuque, IA 52004-1840

Copyright © 2009 by Scott Amundsen

ISBN: 978-0-7575-6400-0

Printed in the United States of America
10 9 8 7 6 5 4 3 2 1

CONTENTS

■ Pre-Course Survey

1. **Gender**

   ☐ Male

   ☐ Female

2. **Age:** _____ (Please fill in)

3. Are you a transfer student?

   ☐ Yes

   ☐ No

4. **Ethnic Group**

   ☐ White American

   ☐ African American

   ☐ Hispanic/Latino

   ☐ Asian

   ☐ Native American

   ☐ Pacific Islander

   ☐ Multiracial

5. **Classification:**

   ☐ Freshman (0–29 hours)

   ☐ Sophomore (30–59 hours)

   ☐ Junior (60–89 hours)

   ☐ Senior (90 hours and above)

6. Did you transfer from a community college?

   ☐ Yes

   ☐ No

   ☐ Other (please list)

7. Where do you live?

   ☐ Campus residence hall

   ☐ Private home

   ☐ Private apartment

   ☐ Campus apartment

   ☐ Greek housing

8. If you commute to and from campus, how long does it take to make the round trip?

☐ Do not commute

☐ Less than 1 hour

☐ 1–2 hours

☐ 3–4 hours

☐ More than 5 hours

☐ Other (please list)

	Strongly Agree	Agree	Neutral	Disagree	Strongly Disagree
9. My college education will enable me to attain my career and life goals.	☐	☐	☐	☐	☐
10. I feel that I am part of a social network on campus.	☐	☐	☐	☐	☐
11. I have decided on a major.	☐	☐	☐	☐	☐
12. I feel comfortable contacting my professors outside of class.	☐	☐	☐	☐	☐
13. I always feel prepared for class.	☐	☐	☐	☐	☐
14. I feel there is at least one university employee who cares about my welfare (i.e., instructor, advisor, staff member).	☐	☐	☐	☐	☐
15. I know what occupation I want to pursue.	☐	☐	☐	☐	☐
16. I am committed to completing my degree.	☐	☐	☐	☐	☐
17. I am involved in activities on campus.	☐	☐	☐	☐	☐
18. I know how to concentrate in class.	☐	☐	☐	☐	☐
19. I know my academic strengths.	☐	☐	☐	☐	☐
20. I know what resources are available to me as a student.	☐	☐	☐	☐	☐
21. I feel the climate at my college allows me to freely express my opinions and views.	☐	☐	☐	☐	☐
22. I ask for help from others when needed.	☐	☐	☐	☐	☐
23. I balance school and other responsibilities effectively.	☐	☐	☐	☐	☐
24. I have a clear picture of my long-term goals.	☐	☐	☐	☐	☐
25. I know how to study for different types of tests.	☐	☐	☐	☐	☐
26. I am confident in my ability to succeed.	☐	☐	☐	☐	☐

CHAPTER 1
Making the Transition to UNCW

You are finally here. The classroom is a little different. The students around you are different. The teachers are obviously different. The campus, city, and even the state or country may be different. This new environment may be very different from what you are used to, but the biggest difference you will find between your high school experience and the university experience is what is expected of you now that you are here.

As a first year student, you will soon realize you have more independence. With this expanded freedom to make decisions, plan schedules and choose new habits and friends, there comes a greater need for responsibility in your personal and academic lives. Like most first year students, you may be living away from home for the first time.

You are now responsible for many of the daily and weekly tasks that your parents and family members may have done for you in the past. You are now responsible for getting yourself out of bed on time, doing your own laundry, deciding when and what to eat, when to sleep, who to hang out with, and when and where to hang out. Even if you are not living away from home, you will soon realize that you have more social freedom than ever before, and finding the right balance between social and academic life can be one of the hardest things for college freshmen to do. One of the main goals of this course is to equip you with the knowledge and tools you need to find that balance and succeed in both your academic and personal lives.

You have probably noticed that UNCW is a very diverse institution. Here, we have students, faculty, and staff from around the world who bring a variety of backgrounds, heritages and identities to our community. One of the goals of a university is to equip students with the skills necessary to be responsible community members by strengthening their awareness of the diversity around them. With such a diverse campus community, UNCW is able to provide students with opportunities to encounter and experience a variety of people, cultures, ideas, beliefs, and practices. Whether you come from a big city or a small town, North Carolina or California, the United States or Bangladesh, you will inevitably encounter people who are very different from you at UNCW. You will appreciate and relate to some people easier than others. Remember, the same freedom that allows you to live, think and believe as you do allows others to live, think and believe differently than you. Learn to respect and appreciate the diversity around you even when aspects of this diversity do not match your preferences or meet your expectations.

■ High School vs. College

You will soon find that life in general at UNCW is different from what you experienced in high school. One of the biggest differences you will find is the role of the college professor compared to that of your high school teachers. In high school, many teachers assumed responsibility for reminding you about assignments, due dates, upcoming tests, and the material you will review and study for those tests. Many high school teachers assigned paper topics for you, often telling you what your project would be about rather than allowing you to decide on your own. Though you were expected to do the work and complete the assignment, you were often coached through the process using many ideas that may not have been your own. Most high school teachers monitor your grades and performance closely for you, often informing you and sometimes your parents of your progress, and the changes that need to be made for improvement.

If you missed class or a test in high school, you were often allowed to make up the work and sometimes retake tests for a better grade. In high school, your parents and school officials monitored your attendance. Your textbooks were also provided by the school system and were usually easy to replace if lost. Most of these characteristics of high school life were there to assist you in maintaining organization and achieving satisfactory grades. Though you may have felt you had complete control of your high school years, most of your routines and decisions were preplanned and out of your control. Whether you like it or not, you have now left behind the high school safety net. The difference between high school teachers and college instructors is essentially the amount of responsibility they place on students. College instructors expect students to attend every class, although attendance is not always mandatory. Since most classes meet no more than three times per week, you may have days when you have no classes at all. Keeping track of this new schedule is the responsibility of the student. Instructors expect students to read all assigned texts and handouts before each class and to use this information in class discussions. They also expect students to read the course syllabus and keep track of all assignments and due dates. Most instructors do not remind you of important dates the way your high school teachers did. They expect you to remember assignment directions and determine the resources and time you will need to complete them. Instructors expect students to turn in assignments on time.

Few instructors provide review resources to help prepare you for an exam or quiz. You are expected to take notes and save completed assignments to use for test preparation. If you do poorly on an exam or quiz, you will probably not get a chance to retake the exam for a better grade. Instructors expect you to study. In high school you may have studied as little as three hours per week. In college, it is generally expected that for every hour of class attended, students should study one to three hours outside of class to better understand the lecture, text material, and commit it to memory. In high school, you may never have had to study on the weekends. In college, full-time students soon learn that some weekend time must be devoted to studying.

Student Responsibilities

- Students are expected to know and adhere to UNCW's Academic Honor Code.
- Students are responsible for knowing and adhering to attendance policies given by their instructors as listed in the course syllabus and announced by the instructor.
- Students are responsible for initiating requests to make up work missed when absent. Students are expected to familiarize themselves with material covered in class while absent. The decision to allow a student to make up late or missed assignments, including tests, is made by the instructor.
- Students are responsible for making appointments with instructors rather than just dropping by their offices to ensure they receive quality attention.
- Students are responsible for monitoring their own academic progress with instructors and advisors. Students are responsible for maintaining academic good standing with the University. UNCW does not issue grade reports by mail. Students can view and/or print a copy of their grades at the end of each semester by accessing the SeaNet website from the UNCW homepage.
- Students are responsible for knowing and meeting all academic and application deadlines listed in the course schedule guide for each semester, the undergraduate catalog and academic calendar for each year.

Instructor Responsibilities

Although you are now responsible for many areas your high school teachers were responsible for previously, UNCW instructors are here to help you and want you to succeed academically.

- Instructors are responsible for setting reasonable rules for class attendance as appropriate for class content, organization, methodology, and size.
- Instructors are responsible for announcing their attendance policy as well as including it in their course syllabus.

- Instructors are required to give each student a copy of the course syllabus, or post it on the blackboard. It usually includes the material to be covered in the course along with important test and due dates, course attendance policy and the instructor's office hours, and contact information.
- Instructors are responsible for maintaining class attendance records and executing appropriate penalties for unsatisfactory attendance, including lowering a student's course grade or dropping them from the course.
- Instructors are expected to cover the material listed in the course syllabus.
- Instructors are required by the University to post and maintain regular office hours in order to provide students with the opportunity to ask questions or discuss issues relative to class outside regular class time.
- Instructors are expected to begin and end each class on time and notify students in advance, if possible, when class is canceled.
- Instructors are expected to inform students of their progress upon request without violating confidentiality.
- All University faculty and staff are expected to adhere to all University policies and regulations.

■ Faculty: Students' Most Valuable Asset

As a new student you may feel that instructors ask too much of you. You may feel they have given you too much responsibility. As you adjust to this shift in responsibility you should begin to see faculty as your most valuable asset in academic life. Developing an appropriate interpersonal relationship with instructors is essential to your academic success. Instructors are here to instruct you and encourage your learning. Understanding and meeting their expectations can only help you succeed in the courses they teach. The first step in building a quality relationship with your instructors is taking responsibility for your own learning. Instructors want to see that you have a desire to learn and are genuinely interested in their courses and your major. If you begin to experience academic difficulty in a course, instructors expect you to discuss this with them and access the academic resources available to help you learn and understand the material covered in class. If you receive tutoring in a particular subject, let the instructor know so they see you making a genuine attempt to succeed.

Class attendance is crucial for developing a quality relationship with your instructors. If you miss class repeatedly and never have a legitimate reason for your absences, you will not have a quality relationship with the instructor. If you have a legitimate reason, tell the instructor. If they ask for documentation to confirm your reason, provide it. If you know in advance that you will not be able to attend a class, ask the instructor in advance if you can get any assignments or notes that you will miss. Instructors are not required to allow students to make-up missed assignments.

Always arrive on time or earlier when possible. Be in the classroom and ready to begin class before the instructor arrives. Most instructors arrive on time and begin class the moment they step into the room. Arriving late shifts attention from the instructor to your entrance, and any attention or response it prompts from the instructor will probably not be positive. If you arrive late, quietly find the nearest seat when you enter the room and sit down. Instructors expect you to take an active role in your learning. The best way to do this is to participate in class discussion. If you know an instructor expects you to read the material before coming to class, read it. If an instructor frequently asks questions throughout a lecture to see how familiar you are with the material, be ready to answer questions. Many instructors include class participation in your final grade. If you know a particular instructor does not like you to blurt out information or interject comments during a lecture, then refrain from doing so until he or she asks for your viewpoint. If

you are asked to hold questions until the end of class, write down your questions and wait to ask them at the appropriate time. Avoid talking with other students while the instructor is speaking. Learn to read each instructor's classroom personality, and adhere to their individual preferences for class participation.

Along with class participation, the quality of the work you submit for a grade will definitely influence your relationship with an instructor. Do your best to fully understand assignments and the criteria on which they will be graded. Find out what instructors are really looking for in an assignment. If the directions are not made clear, ask for clarification. If you are not able to ask for clarification in class, contact the instructor as soon as possible outside of class for more information. When you don't understand, it is best to be honest and ask for help. Always do your best work and turn in assignments on time. If you are turning in a written assignment, it is preferred and often required that it be typed. Always take time to proofread. If you are not putting the required time and effort into your assignments, instructors may think you do not care about their class.

An obvious lack of effort can never benefit the student/instructor relationship. One of the best ways to build relationships with instructors is to meet with them outside of class. If you are concerned about your progress in a course, have questions about material covered in class, need advice relative to the subjects they specialize in, need suggestions for further reading, or help with an assignment, make an appointment with the instructor during his or her posted office hours. Arrive early for the appointment and be prepared to discuss the issues or questions you have. Write down your questions ahead of time. Do not waste your time or theirs. Get to the point of your visit as soon as possible without being rude. Write down the answers or information you are given. This lets the instructor know you are interested and attentive to what they have to say. Make sure your questions are answered clearly before you leave. If you need to meet with an instructor and are unable to make an appointment, try visiting them during their posted office hours. If you can't come in person, call or e-mail the instructor.

Always take time to thank instructors for making time for you and your concerns. You will soon find out that cultivating professional relationships with instructors will contribute to your academic success.

■ Academic Integrity

Academic integrity is fundamental to a successful academic community. UNCW subscribes to the fundamental values of The Center for Academic Integrity (CAI): honesty, trust, fairness, respect, and responsibility. According to Donald L. McCabe of Rutgers University, founder and first president of the CAI, over 75 percent of students admit to participating in some form of cheating. A study conducted in 2000–2001 of almost 4,500 students at 25 schools, suggests that cheating is also a significant problem in high school. Of these respondents, 74 percent admitted to one or more instances of cheating on tests, and 72 percent admitted to cheating on written assignments.

At UNCW, cheating is defined in the new UNCW Student Academic Honor Code as . . . "deception implying that work in fulfillment of course or degree requirements represents a student's own level of knowledge when it actually does not." Cheating includes but is not limited to unauthorized copying from the work of another student, using notes or other materials not authorized during an examination, giving or receiving information or assistance on work when it is expected that a student will do his/her own work, or engaging in any similar act that violates the concept of academic integrity. Cheating may occur on an examination, test, quiz, laboratory work report, theme, out of class assignment or any other work submitted by a student to fulfill course requirements and presented as solely the work of the student. Facilitating academic dishonesty includes acts that may not directly benefit the accused, but assist other students in violation of the policy. In either case, the students involved could face penalties ranging from a grade of F on an assignment to expulsion from the University.

Plagiarism is defined in the new UNCW Student Academic Honor Code, "a form of cheating, is the unacknowledged submission of another person's work, usually written, as one's own. Plagiarism is doubly unethical, since it deprives the true author of his or her rightful credit and then gives that credit to someone to whom it is not due." Plagiarism may occur on any paper, report, or other work submitted to fulfill course requirements. This includes submitting work done by another, whether a commercial or non-commercial enterprise, including websites, as one's own work. Many cases of academic dishonesty go unnoticed. Students may choose not to report other students they witness cheating because they do not want to get a classmate in trouble, or feel responsible for any consequences the cheating student may face. Whether you choose to ignore it or report it, cheating diminishes the overall academic integrity of the University and can directly affect your grade in a course if a grading curve is used to determine final scores.

■ The Five Core Values of Academic Integrity

Honesty

An academic community of integrity advances the quest for truth and knowledge by requiring intellectual and personal honesty in learning, teaching, research, activities, and service. Cultivating honesty lays the foundation for lifelong integrity, developing in each of us the courage and insight to make difficult choices and accept responsibility for actions and their consequences, even at a personal cost.

Fairness

An academic community of integrity establishes clear standards, practices, and procedures, and expects fairness in the interactions of students, faculty, and administrators. For students, important components of fairness are predictability, clear expectations, and a consistent and just response to dishonesty. Faculty and staff also have a right to expect fair treatment, not only from students but also from colleagues.

Trust

An academic community of integrity fosters a climate of trust, encourages the free exchange of ideas, and enables all to reach their highest potential. Only with trust can we believe in and rely on others and move forward as a community. Within an environment of trust, we can collaborate with individuals, sharing information and ideas without fear that our work or property will be stolen, our career stunted, or our reputations diminished. Through trust, our communities can believe in the social value and meaning of an institution's scholarship and degrees.

Respect

An academic community of integrity recognizes the participatory nature of the learning process, honors and respects a wide range of opinions, ideas, and cultures.

Responsibility

An academic community of integrity upholds personal accountability and depends upon action in the face of wrongdoing. Every member of an academic community—each student, faculty, and staff member—is responsible for upholding the integrity of the community.

■ Reference

The Center for Academic Integrity: http://www.academicintegrity.org/index.asp

■ Exercise 1: Adjusting to Life at UNCW

1. Your new roommate practices a religion unfamiliar to you. She has several small statues in your dorm room that she prays to each day and burns incense as an offering throughout the week. Though the two of you get along well and share many of the same interests as nursing majors, you find yourself very uncomfortable with her religious practices and beliefs. How will you handle the situation?

2. Parking is a nightmare. You have been late to your 9:00 am MW class twice already because you couldn't find a parking place. You bought a commuter day pass thinking this would allow you to park near your classes, but so far, it's just not working out. If you continue to be late, your grade will definitely suffer. How will you handle this situation?

3. It is the second week of the semester and you're beginning to feel pretty lonely. You've met a lot of people these first few days but you don't really know anyone yet. You had plenty of friends in high school and never had trouble finding ways to get to know other people, but now it is harder to find ways to get to know those around you. What will you do?

4. You received a D on the paper you thought you did so well on in your English 101 class. You feel the instructor graded your paper unfairly. What will you do?

5. During your Sociology 105 mid-term exam, you witnessed another student copying answers from a cheat sheet. When the exam grades were posted, you saw that with the curve, the cheating student got an A, while most of the class got a C or lower. What should you do? What will you do?

6. After your Biology 201 lab class, your lab partner e-mails you and asks to see a copy of your lab report to compare with his. Your instructor has repeatedly emphasized that you are not to collaborate on the written reports, but your lab partner is not doing as well as you are in the class. He is a good friend and you want to help him, but you are afraid your reports will look too similar. What will you do?

7. Your history professor assigns a take-home mid-term exam and asks that you not use any outside sources other than your textbook to complete the essay questions on the exam. While researching a paper topic earlier in the semester, you discovered a really useful journal article that would really be more helpful than the textbook for answering some of the questions on the exam. You want to do well on the exam to bring your grade up to an A. What will you do?

CHAPTER 2
Academic and Campus Resources

Edited by Rebecca Stultz and Michelle Vliem

Cornerstone

I am an engaged learner in constant search of knowledge.
I foster human dignity through acts of civility and respect.
I maintain a distinguished character based on truth, honesty, and integrity.
I pursue inner peace by recognizing the significance of spirituality.
I demonstrate honorable citizenship through acts of civic engagement.
I embrace community by active involvement and service.
I lead a lifestyle that advances physical health and emotional well-being.

University Statement on Academic Expectations for Students

In choosing UNCW, you have become a part of our community of scholars. We recognize that the UNCW learning experience is challenging and requires hard work. It also requires a commitment to make time available to do that hard work. The university expects you to make academics your highest priority by dedicating your time and energy to training your mind and acquiring knowledge. Academic success in critical thinking and problem solving prepares you for the changes and challenges you will encounter in the future. Our faculty and academic support resources are readily available as partners in this effort, but the primary responsibility for learning is yours.

■ Academic Support Services

Academic Advising

University College
Westside Hall
910.962.3245
www.uncw.edu/uc

All new freshmen entering UNCW begin their academic careers in the University College, where they are provided academic advising and other academic support until they enter their majors, usually in the sophomore year. The University College is responsible for many programs and services that help students make a successful transition to university life.

As part of the university's commitment to excellence in undergraduate education, the University College was created to provide academic advising and support to UNCW students from the time of their admission until they declare their majors. Picking courses and making a class schedule is only one part of academic advising. Your academic advisor works with you to ensure that you will

- make a successful transition to UNCW;
- identify and declare an appropriate major;
- make an educational plan and set academic goals;
- understand college regulations and graduation requirements; and
- have the support and information necessary should you find yourself in academic difficulty.

Through its advisors and academic support programs, the University College works with students in their formative semesters to assist them in developing their interests, skills, and talents to the fullest extent.

Academic Records

Registrar's Office
James Hall
www.uncw.edu/reg

The Registrar's Office is primarily responsible for maintaining the university's academic records. This office can assist you in adding and withdrawing from courses and obtaining academic transcripts, enrollment verification, and academic exceptions.

Academic Support and Tutoring Services

University Learning Center
Westside Hall, first floor
910.962.7857
www.uncw.edu/ulc

The University Learning Center's mission is to help UNCW students become successful, independent learners. Academic support programs are free to all UNCW students and include Writing Services, Learning Services, Supplemental Instruction, and Math Services.

Writing Services
Westside Hall, first floor

Writing Services provides assistance for all UNCW students as they develop and improve their writing skills. Consultations are led by faculty-recommended and trained peer tutors. Consultations are non-evaluative; instead, tutors help students identify areas to improve and develop specific revision plans. Students will build writing skills as the tutor guides them through the revision process.

Writing tutors will help students with course papers, cover letters, and application essays at any stage of the writing process. Short papers or sections of papers can be submitted online for response (see website for details). Drop-ins are welcome if a tutor is available, but appointments are encouraged.

Learning Services
Westside Hall, first floor

Learning Services offers UNCW students free tutoring and assistance in developing the skills necessary to become successful, independent learners through tutorial assistance and study skills consultations. Tutoring is offered in all Basic Studies courses as well as select upper-level courses (see website for details). Students meet for up to two hours each week with trained peer tutors to increase comprehension in course content and hone study and test-taking skills.

Assistance in general study skills is also provided by Learning Services in individual and group settings. Any UNCW student may schedule an appointment to meet individually with a study skills consultant to discuss academic goals and develop strategies to achieve them. To request a tutor or a consultation, stop by the University Learning Center to complete a request form.

Supplemental Instruction

The Supplemental Instruction program provides a series of peer-assisted group study sessions several times a week to help students in historically difficult courses. In recent semesters, Supplemental Instruction has been offered for a variety of courses, including chemistry, biology, physics, and math. Supplemental Instruction leaders are trained to work with students on both course content and study skills application. All leaders have successfully completed the course they support and "retake" it with the students they tutor by routinely attending and observing the class.

Students enrolled in supported courses will be introduced to the Supplemental Instruction leader at the beginning of the semester. Leaders will provide a schedule of sessions within the first two weeks of the semester. There is no registration and no fee for Supplemental Instruction—students simply show up for sessions on a voluntary basis. Early and frequent attendance is encouraged in order to gain the most benefit from these sessions.

Math Services
Westside Hall, first floor
910.962.7857

Drop-in tutoring is available in the Learning Lab for Math and Statistics courses. Math tutors will help students with problems, concepts, test preparation, and problem-solving skills. Math tutors help students make the transition to college mathematics as well as supporting students in upper division math and statistics courses.

Disability Services
Westside Hall, first floor
910.962.7555
www.uncw.edu/stuaff/sds/disability

Disability Services provides assistance to students with special needs in pursuing their educational goals. As a liaison between the student and the university departments, Disability Services provides information, encourages self-advocacy, and interfaces with advisors, administration, and faculty to implement strategies that will enable the student to master course content. Students with disabilities are encouraged to inform their academic advisors and professors of their needs for consideration in planning an education program in the most integrated setting possible.

University Testing Services
Westside Hall, first floor
910.962.7444
www.uncw.edu/testingservices

University Testing Services provides secure and professional testing services for the UNCW campus and the local community. Services include test administration and examination proctoring for a variety of programs. Computer-based and paper-based testing services are available for admissions, distance education and enrollment management, and professional licensing and certification. The Testing Center has accommodations for those testing candidates that have special needs or conditions. Available testing programs include CLEP, GRE, LSAT, MAT, HESI, PCAT, PRAXIS I & II, and TOEFL. Please refer to the website for the most comprehensive and up-to-date listing. Each testing program has registration or appointment requirements and a fee schedule.

Honors Opportunities

The Honors Scholars Program
Randall Library, second floor
910.962.4181
www.uncw.edu/honors

The Honors Scholars Program at UNCW provides academically talented students with a variety of innovative and unique educational experiences, both in and out of the classroom. This program encourages curiosity, critical thinking, and independent work skills by offering exciting academic and cultural activities as well as the opportunity for close working and social relationships with the faculty.

In their first two years, honors students take honors seminars and honors sections of basic studies courses. As juniors and seniors, students do honors work in their majors culminating in departmental honors—a six-credit senior honors project.

Students may enter the program as beginning freshmen, as sophomores, or as juniors/seniors in departmental honors. Depending on GPA and the number of hours completed, transfer students may be eligible for Honors Program classes at the 100/200 level or may join the program in their last two years to do departmental honors only.

Students applying for departmental honors must have at least 74 semester hours credit with a quality point average of 3.2 or better on all college work attempted (including transfer hours). At least 30 semester hours of work with a 3.2 or better quality point average must have been completed at UNCW. Academic departments or schools may require a higher grade point average for eligibility for Departmental Honors in their discipline.

Honors Program participants will receive numerous benefits, including priority class registration, chances for merit scholarships, an option to reside in the Honors House, and smaller class sizes, as well as involvement in special cultural enrichment opportunities.

Library

William Madison Randall Library
910.962.3760
library.uncw.edu

The William Madison Randall Library provides access to an extensive range of print, electronic, microform, and multimedia resources to support the instructional, research, and general informational interests of the UNCW community. Experienced staff members are available to help students identify and locate information sources relevant to their research needs. Special services, such as interlibrary loan and librarian-mediated computer database searching, are also available to students. Instruction in the effective use of information resources is provided in many academic courses and through drop-in clinics offered several times each week.

The library provides a comfortable and welcoming atmosphere, with seating for 1,000 readers. The collection includes more than 500,000 volumes, more than 4,000 serial subscriptions, and approximately 10,000 media items. The library serves the southeast region of the state as a resource for both United States and North Carolina government documents. Access to electronic subscription databases is extensive, including services such as Lexis-Nexis, EBSCOHost, and ProQuest Direct. A large body of periodical articles is available in full-text online.

The library's online system provides the catalog to the library's resources and serves as a gateway to many other databases, including general periodical indexes and specialized subject index and abstracting services.

Study Abroad

International Programs
Westside Hall, first floor
910.962.3685
www.uncw.edu/intprogs

UNCW offers a variety of opportunities for students to study abroad and to interact with international students. Programs are offered in the summer, and regular semester and academic year opportunities are available in countries throughout the world. Students receive academic credit for course work successfully completed abroad. In many cases, the price of study abroad programs is not much more than on-campus costs. Students are encouraged to consider these opportunities because having an international experience is a significant advantage in the job market and is a life-enriching experience.

■ Student Support and Services

Bookstore

UNCW Bookstore
Fisher Student Center
910.962.3188
www.uncw.edu/bookstore

The UNCW Bookstore offers textbooks, academic supplies, UNCW apparel, and gift items. The bookstore also provides services such as ordering class rings, graduation caps and gowns, and special gift ordering.

Textbooks can also be ordered online. A list of required and optional textbooks is generated from the class schedule. Once placed, the order will be available for pickup at the bookstore.

Campus Living

Office Of Housing And Residence Life
Office of Housing and Residence Life (one-story building beside Schwartz Hall)
910.962.3241
www.uncw.edu/housing

The Office of Housing and Residence Life is responsible for the development of educational, cultural, and social programs to enhance student life on campus. The goal of the Housing and Residence Life program is to create an environment conducive to academic pursuits and the personal growth of resident students. More than 82 Residence Life staff members are responsible for the supervision of resident students in the residence halls, on-campus apartments, and suite-style buildings. The Residence Life program offers opportunities for student employment and leadership positions through hall governance.

Once students have secured on-campus housing, they may remain on campus continuously throughout their academic career.

Research indicates that residential (on-campus) students, especially first-year students, are more likely to perform better academically, have higher GPAs, have higher retention rates, be more involved in campus activities, clubs, and organizations, and have a greater sense of connection to the university.

Campus Dining
www.uncw.edu/dining

UNCW offers one dining hall, eight other dining locations, and three convenience stores. Wagoner Hall is the main dining hall for the UNCW campus. Conveniently located in the center of our on-campus housing, it offers all-you-can-eat dining, featuring an exhibition station, produce market with vegetarian and vegan options, bakery, Italian kitchen, grill, sandwich shop, and "home cooking" station. The Hawk's Nest is a food court show-

casing individual locations such as Jolé Molé (Mexican), The Tuscan Oven (pizza and breadsticks), Hawk Wok (Asian), Varsity Grill (hamburgers, hot dogs, American fare), Tsunami (sushi), Freshëns, Salad Creations, Chick-fil-A®, and Quiznos®.

Commuter and Non-Traditional Student Services

The Seahawk Perch
Fisher Student Center Lobby (1012)
910.962.7371
www.uncw.edu/seahawkperch

All campus programs, services, and facilities are available to commuter students. Commuter and Non-Traditional Student Services provides support to this student group and assists them in becoming involved in campus activities. The Seahawk Perch consists of both a **Resource Center** and a **Lounge Area** in the Fisher Student Center, room 1012. The Resource Center is staffed by student assistants who can assist in acclimating to the university, finding off-campus housing, getting involved with student organizations, and meeting other off-campus or non-traditional students. The lounge area has been designated specifically for off-campus and non-traditional students, and features comfortable seating, dining and study areas, a TV/VCR, a refrigerator, a microwave, a coffeemaker, and a computer for short-term use. Students may also check out a laptop from the nearby Information Center for use in the commuter lounge.

Shuttle Service
910.962.3178
www.uncw.edu/ba/parking_trans/maps/shuttle_brochure.pdf

The **Seahawk Shuttle** operates along a variety of fixed routes. The shuttle routes run Monday–Thursday 7 a.m.–9:30 p.m. and Friday 7 a.m.–6:30 p.m. while classes are in session, during the fall and spring semesters.

Students who live within one mile of campus and students assigned to the Park-and-Ride parking zones are encouraged to ride the Seahawk Shuttle. Shuttle service is free with a UNCW One Card. A valid UNCW One Card also allows students to ride free on all local WAVE bus routes. Shuttle maps and Wilmington Public Transit guides are available at Auxiliary Services in Warwick Center or the Fisher Student Center information desk or at the above link. All routes are subject to change.

Choice of Major and Career Planning

Career Services
University Union 2035
910.962.3174
www.uncw.edu/career

Career Services provides career development programs for every stage in UNCW students' pre-professional life, from the freshman year to after graduation. From choosing a major through transforming the major into careers, the center offers numerous workshops and individual career counseling sessions to facilitate students' decision-making processes. Programs include self-assessment workshops and interests, skills, and values assessments, along with college major exploration. Web-based job listings are available in Career Services for students seeking work experience while attending school. Internships, job fairs, and on-campus recruiting are additional services available through this center.

Dean of Students

Office of the Dean of Students
University Union 2017
910.962.3119
www.uncw.edu/stuaff/doso

The Office of the Dean of Students (ODOS) is committed to student growth and development of personal responsibility by serving as a student advocate and a central resource for addressing student issues and concerns. Through collaboration with the university and Wilmington community, assistance is offered to all students, faculty, and staff through policy clarification, conflict resolution, grievance procedures, confidential consultations, and crisis intervention.

In addition to advocating for students, the ODOS develops opportunities for campus involvement through Greek Affairs, Commuter and Non-Traditional Student Services, and Values Education. Community standards are communicated through the Code of Student Life, and the ODOS adjudicates academic and behavioral violations through the campus judiciary. At the core of judicial proceedings is the education of the individual student balanced with consideration of the welfare of the university community.

Diversity and Inclusion

Office of Institutional Diversity and Inclusion
Alderman Hall 120
910.962.3137
www.uncw.edu/diversity

The Office of Institutional Diversity and Inclusion is comprised of three departments—the Upperman African American Cultural Center, Centro Hispano, and the Multicultural Center—all engaged in coordinating the university's diversity initiative by helping foster an educational climate that promotes intellectual interactions across campus and between the campus community and surrounding areas. The office provides avenues for inclusion for minority and non-minority faculty, staff, students, and community members and facilitates collaborative efforts to provide relevant programs and services throughout the year.

Upperman African American Cultural Center

University Union 2021
910.962.3832
www.uncw.edu/upperman

The Upperman African American Cultural Center (UAACC) provides students, faculty, staff, and those in the greater Wilmington community the opportunity to experience the rich heritage of African Americans from artistic, historic, and other perspectives. In support of this mission, the UAACC maintains videotape, periodical, research, and popular materials for use in the center. Videotapes are also available on a loan basis in the Upperman Center, and a sizable collection of books on the African American experience is available. Additionally, a collection of Upperman Center books is also available for loan in UNCW's Randall Library. Upperman Center programs and activities such as Heritage School, workshops, and Black History programs are offered to the university and the region. These events are provided to promote a greater appreciation and understanding of African Americans and their cultures.

Centro Hispano

University Union 2021
910.962.2621
www.uncw.edu/centrohispano

The Centro Hispano creates a responsive educational environment for Hispanic students and others interested in Hispanic cultures. The Centro supports the research, teaching, and service components necessary for the training and preparation of global citizens and informs, guides, and leads UNCW's engagement in the region on issues critical to Hispanic constituencies.

Women's Studies and Resource Center

Randall Library, 2053
910.962.7870
www.uncw.edu/wrc

The Women's Studies and Resource Center strives to create an interdisciplinary community of scholars working in the areas of sex, gender, and women's issues. The Center offers research, programming, education, and advocacy to promote gender equality, both locally and globally. The Center also provides information and referrals for a variety of UNCW and community services and resources.

Multicultural Center

University Union 2021
910.962.4274
uncw.edu/multiculturalism

The mission of the Multicultural Center is to promote the appreciation of the Asian/ Pacific Islander and Native American cultures and the awareness of issues affecting Lesbian, Bisexual, Gay, Transgender, Queer, and Questioning students.

The Multicultural Center provides programs and services that support the academic mission of the university by enhancing the educational, cultural, social, and personal development of students within these populations.

Finances

Office of Scholarships and Financial Aid

Warwick Center
910.962.3177
www.uncw.edu/finaid

The Office of Scholarships and Financial Aid administers programs of financial assistance designed to help meet the needs of students who have been fully accepted as degree-seeking. Financial "need" is determined by U.S. Department of Education formulas, based on the student's and family's income and assets.

Once eligibility is established, students may be awarded self-help aid, such as Federal Work-Study or loans. If the need is great enough and they meet any additional criteria that may be involved, they may be awarded some gift aid, such as scholarships and/or grants. Awards may vary greatly between schools, depending upon funding available. Because funds are limited and there are many steps in the financial aid process, students and families are encouraged to begin the annual application process by early February for the following academic year.

Student Accounts/Cashier's Office

Warwick Center
Student Accounts—910.962.3147
Cashier—910.962.4281
uncw.edu/ba/finance/StudentAccounts

Payment of tuition and fees is handled through the Student Accounts office and are processed through e-bill. Students are encouraged to set up a profile, which is necessary for receiving many of the benefits of e-bill, such as e-mail notification when payments are due, setting up authorized users, and payment scheduling.

Students with an outstanding balance will receive an e-mail notification to their UNCW e-mail account stating that their e-bill is available to view and print. Currently enrolled students who have a balance due will receive an e-mail notice from e-bill@uncw.edu that the e-bill is available for viewing. Upon receiving the notice, bills can be accessed via the link included in the e-mail or via SeaNet. Students are responsible for checking their UNCW e-mail for electronic bill notification and for making payments on time.

Students may pay online, forward the statement to parents or a third party, or print a copy of the statement and mail the payment. An e-bill reflects the charges and credits applied to the account as of the date the bill was created. To view the most current student account information, click Current Activity. Classes are cancelled due to non-payment each term. Students should refer to the schedule of classes for important payment due dates and cancellation dates.

The UNCW One Card

Warwick Center—Auxiliary Services
910.962.3178
www.uncw.edu/onecard

The UNCW One Card is the official form of identification at UNCW and allows students access to campus facilities and services, such as Randall Library, the computer labs, the health center and pharmacy, athletic events, recreational facilities, and campus activities. It also serves as a meal card and door access card. The UNCW One Card is administered by Auxiliary Services. While it cannot be used as a debit card off campus, it does give students Seahawk Saving$ discounts at participating off-campus vendors.

Seahawk Buck$

The Seahawk Buck$ account is a flexible spending prepaid account that is available to all students. Seahawk Buck$ turn your UNCW One Card into a debit card, which can be used at any point-of-sale location on campus. Seahawk Buck$ virtually eliminate the need to carry cash on campus. With each use, the amount is automatically deducted and the remaining balance is displayed. The Seahawk Buck$ account is automatically activated with a zero balance. Funds may be deposited by cash, check, or credit card.

Health and Wellness

Abrons Student Health Center
Westside Hall, second floor
910.962.3280
www.uncw.edu/healthservices

The Student Health Center (SHC) provides confidential services designed to promote and maintain health and wellness with attention to quality, access, efficiency, and cost.

A wide range of services are provided, including general and acute care, gynecology, health education, immunizations, allergy injections, laboratory tests, physical examinations to meet degree requirements, and referrals for specialized care when necessary. Surgical and critical medical conditions are referred to an appropriate specialist or to one of the two nearby hospitals for treatment. A pharmacy is available for both prescription and over-the-counter medications.

The SHC staff includes physicians, a physician assistant, nurse practitioners, registered nurses, and other professional staff who are able to care for students' medical needs. All are licensed and certified in their respective fields.

Visits to the Student Health Center are covered by the student health fee. Laboratory tests, medications, and comprehensive physical exams are available at an additional nominal charge. Students taking six or more credit hours are automatically charged the health center fee and are eligible for unlimited office visits and consultations at the SHC. During the summer, the health fee is included in the fee bill. Students taking fewer than six credit hours during the school year and students remaining in Wilmington over the summer without taking classes may utilize the health center by paying a health fee.

Supplemental health insurance is recommended to cover services such as hospitalization or specialty care, which are not provided by the health fee. A Student Group Health Insurance Plan is available through the university; students interested in this plan may get additional information at the Student Health Center or on the Student Health Center website.

Pharmacy
Westside Hall, second floor
910.962.3016
www.uncw.edu/stuaff/healthservices/pharmacy.htm

Students may get prescriptions filled at a reduced rate at the UNCW pharmacy, which is located in the lobby of the Student Health Center. A variety of over-the-counter medications are available for purchase as well. The pharmacy fills prescriptions written by either a Student Health Center or off-campus provider. Students may wait for or drop off prescriptions, which will be filled by our licensed pharmacist. Students with current prescriptions are encouraged to call in their refill requests a day ahead so they can be ready for pickup the next day. Payment can be made by cash, check, credit card, or UNCW One Card, or charged to a student account (ID required).

Health Promotion Services

Student Recreation Center 104
910.962.4135
www.uncw.edu/healthpromotion

Health Promotion Services is the central campus resource for health education programs and opportunities. This comprehensive approach to wellness promotes, supports, and affirms a healthy balance among all members of the campus community.

A health educator and a registered dietitian staff Health Promotion Services as well as peer educators. Health Promotion Services offers programming on sexual health, cancer risk reduction, stress management, women's health, men's health, and achieving a healthy balance. Nutrition topics include sports nutrition, weight management, vegetarian diets, and healthy eating on campus. The Hundley Health Education Resource Center provides current books, software programs, videos, handouts, and brochures on a wide range of health and nutrition topics.

CARE: Collaboration for Assault Response and Education

Westside Hall, second floor
910.962.CARE (2273)
910.512.4821 for after hours or crisis calls
www.uncw.edu/care

CARE: Collaboration for Assault Response and Education is the campus office dedicated to relationship education and violence prevention. This office provides information and programs promoting healthy relationships. When relationships are abusive or violent, the CARE office supports and connects individuals to the most appropriate resources, and frequently collaborates with both on-campus and off-campus professionals. CARE is for those affected by violence. Whether you are concerned about yourself or someone you care about, the office is a safe place for confidential consultation. In response to sexual assault, relationship abuse, stalking, or harassment, members of the UNCW campus community will receive information and non-judgmental clarification of options. Through interactive trainings and events, the female and male professional staff and peer educators at CARE work to raise awareness and support a campus environment of violence prevention and intervention.

Counseling Center

Westside Hall, second floor
910.962.3746
(after-hours crisis consultation service via UNCW Police dispatch)
www.uncw.edu/counseling

Successful academic progress is impacted by a number of personal, social, and academic factors. To assist this progress, the Counseling Center offers a variety of services, including individual personal counseling, group counseling, outreach programs, and personal development workshops. Services are confidential, free, and accessible. Common counseling concerns include loneliness, depression, anxiety/stress, sexuality, homesickness, relationships, family issues, and grief. In addition, assistance is available for students with concerns related to sexual assault, substance abuse, and body image. Referrals to off-campus professionals are provided when other counseling resources would better serve a student's needs.

The Counseling Center staff includes counselors, psychologists, a consulting psychiatrist, and supervised graduate students, all of whom have experience working within a university setting.

CROSSROADS: Substance Abuse Prevention and Education Program
Westside Hall, second floor
910.962.4136
www.uncw.edu/crossroads

CROSSROADS, the Substance Abuse Prevention and Education Program, is the campus resource for materials, programs, and educational services related to prevention of substance abuse problems. The program provides educational support and resources for students who are affected by their own substance abuse or by the substance abuse of someone close to them. Current information about effects of alcohol, tobacco, and other drugs is available through a variety of media and materials, presentations, programming, and training provided by the substance abuse prevention and education staff and student peer educators. Inquiries are handled in confidence. Additionally, the Counseling Center provides confidential assessment, intervention, and counseling for students who may be dealing with substance abuse issues.

Police and Parking Regulations

University Police
5126 Lionfish Drive
24 hours a day, 7 days a week
910.962.2222
911 emergency
Anonymous crime tips 962-TIPS (8477)
www.uncw.edu/ba/police

The primary objective of the University Police Department is to provide a safe and secure environment within which students, faculty, and staff can live, learn, and work. The department is comprised of three divisions—**Community Services**, **Investigations**, and **Patrol**. The 30 officers who staff these divisions are duly sworn, certified, armed, and empowered with the same authority as other local law enforcement officers in the State of North Carolina as regulated by the North Carolina Department of Justice.

Other services offered by University Police include bicycle registration, Police and Community Networking (PAC'N), and Rape Aggression Defense (RAD) training. RAD self-defense classes are offered several times a year. Emergency call boxes are placed throughout campus for instant access to University Police.

Parking and Transportation Services
Warwick Center, Auxiliary Services Office
910.962.3178
www.uncw.edu/parking

Parking and Transportation Services manages the university's parking resources and facilitates the use of alternative transportation methods, including providing shuttle services to, from, and around campus.

Residents:

Resident students are assigned permits by zones based upon their campus housing assignment.

- ■ Resident students may park in faculty/staff or commuter zones between the hours of 4 p.m. and 7 a.m. Monday–Friday and on weekends only, unless the lot is otherwise reserved.

Commuters:

- Commuter students are assigned permits by zones within the commuter area. They are restricted to their commuter zones Monday–Friday, 7 a.m. to 4 p.m. Commuter zones are not enforced for permit holders after 4 p.m. and on weekends. Permit holders may park in any commuter zone after 4 p.m. and on weekends.
- Commuter students cannot park in residential zones at any time.

One-Mile Radius Rule

- Undergraduate students living within one mile of campus are prohibited from parking their vehicles on campus or in the Park-and-Ride lot from 7 a.m. to 4 p.m.
- One-mile radius appeals for parking permits will be reviewed for students who have special circumstances, such as disabilities that limit access.

Nighttime Commuter Students:

- Night permits are encouraged for those who participate in extracurricular activities on campus (i.e., labs, Recreation Center, meetings, etc.) and students taking classes after 4 p.m.
- Vehicles registered with nighttime permits will be allowed to park on campus on weekends and from 4 p.m. until 7 a.m. Monday–Friday with the exception of campus resident areas.

Important Information to Know

- Decals for vehicles must be affixed and clearly visible on the outside bottom left rear windshield or left rear bumper. Decals on motorcycles must be affixed in a manner so as to be readily visible. A vehicle is not registered until the decal is affixed to the vehicle.
- Lost or stolen decals must be reported to University Police. Replacements will be issued at Parking and Transportation Services. A police report is required to obtain a replacement decal.
- Disabled vehicles must be reported to University Police in person or by phone.
- If you receive a ticket and have a valid appeal with documentation, you may appeal within seven calendar days. Written appeals to the Parking and Traffic Board are filed at Parking and Transportation Services. All decisions of the board are final.
- Sitting in your car waiting for a parking space is called queuing and is a $25 violation.
- Students with parking decals cannot park at parking meters. Students are permitted to park ONLY in the white spaces within their assigned commuter or resident zones.
- Note: Enforcement for parking decals will resume 48 hours after classes begin for the semester/term.

Bicycle Registration

Registration is required for all bicycles. University Police will register your bicycle free of charge.

Postal Services

Postal Service/Seahawk Mail
Fisher University Union, first floor
910.962.3750
www.uncw.edu/ba/postal_services

Seahawk Mail is a full-service post office. Students have access to mailboxes during the Union's operating hours. USPS, UPS, or FedEx packages can be picked up during window service hours. Fax and free notary services are also provided. Seahawk Mail is open year-round except for university holidays.

Printing Services

Printing and Copying Services
Fisher University Union, first floor
910.962.3083
www.uncw.edu/ba/printing_services

Dittos, The Copy Spot, is a full-service copy center. Dittos provides high-speed copying, color copies, color transparencies, binding services, copyright approval services, laminating, a Kodak photo printing kiosk, and resume packs. Cash, checks, and Seahawk Buck$ are accepted.

Personal copies can be made in several locations on campus. Randall Library, Warwick Center, Cameron Hall, Dobo Hall, Friday Annex, and the Education Building are equipped with copiers that will accept Seahawk Buck$ or coins.

iPrint is UNCW's easy, convenient, and reliable printing program for students. Students may print from any networked computer and pick up their documents from any iPrint release station across campus. At the beginning of each semester, each student will automatically receive $8 of free black-and-white prints on his/her UNCW One Card. After using these prints, future printed pages are debited from the student's UNCW One Card at eight cents per page.

Technology Assistance

Information Technology Systems Division (ITSD)
Randall Library, 1037
910.962.HELP (4357)
www.uncw.edu/tac

The Information Technology Systems Division (ITSD) is committed to providing a technologically progressive environment for students, faculty, and staff. This division is dedicated to leading, collaborating, and supporting with cost-effective services that promote the mission of the university. ITSD is also committed to promoting and sustaining a powerful learning experience by responding to students' needs through student survey feedback, student engagement with the division, and collaboration with other constituent groups across campus.

ITSD provides an array of services to students, including the following:

- Technology Assistance Center (TAC) in Randall Library (UNCW's help desk)
- Free antivirus software (www.uncw.edu/virus)
- Laptop checkout program in Randall Library and the Fisher Student Center
- Wireless access across campus
- SeaPort campus portal

- Blackboard course management system
- Multimedia classrooms
- UNCW Student Laptop Initiative for computer purchases
- B1nar1es, The Warranty Service Center (for computers purchased through Laptop Initiative) and Technology store with ink refill station in Fischer University Union
- Residence hall computer labs
- ResNet (residential networking service)
- Residence hall access including wired and wireless Internet, cable TV, phone/E911, and voice mail

Students should call, email, or come to the TAC for any computing or technology questions or problems. The TAC provides support via phone, e-mail, and a walk-in area as well as a large student center for project/collaborative work. Services provided by the TAC include, but are not limited to, assistance with virus removal, spyware or malware issues, e-mail questions or problems, scanning, CD creation/duplication, software questions, video editing, and file conversion.

ITSD offers UNCW e-mail to all students to keep them connected with the university community, their professors, and each other. ITSD also provides students with their one-stop campus portal—SeaPort. Through SeaPort, students have access to their UNCW e-mail, calendar, class information, online registration, Blackboard, and additional student services. Furthermore, students may access various educational tools, such as computer-based training courses and podcasts, through this UNCW portal. ITSD supports online learning through its learning management system, Blackboard Vista. Instructors may utilize this tool to deliver fully online courses or as a supplement to traditional face-to-face courses.

■ Student Involvement & Activities

Fisher Student Center
Information Center, Fisher Center Lobby
910.962.3841

UNCW's out-of-classroom (co-curricular) learning opportunities make a valuable contribution to the overall educational experience of students. Students are expected to become involved in campus life and to seek leadership experiences.

Student life at UNCW is enriched by a broad spectrum of activities, many of which occur in or around the Fisher Student Center and the Fisher University Union. These facilities are seen as the living rooms of the campus, and are home to a number of valuable services for students. Both facilities offer places to meet, eat, study, view art exhibits, and gather for informal or scheduled activities. Located in the Fisher Student Center, Sharky's Game Room is a great spot to take a break between classes to watch TV or hone skills in billiards or table tennis. Ticket sales and distribution for campus events will be handled through the box office associated with the movie theater and Sharky's Game Room. The Fisher Student Center houses the Campus Activities and Involvement Center (CAIC), as well as additional meeting rooms, lounge spaces, Einstein Bros. Bagels Café, and the Information Center. The Information Center is an excellent source of both campus and local information, including campus maps, bus schedules, and brochures from businesses and services.

Athletics
Nixon Annex
910.962.3232
www.uncw.edu/athletics

UNCW has held membership in the National Collegiate Athletic Association since 976-77. The athletic department sponsors nine NCAA Division I programs and is a member of the Colonial Athletic Association and the Eastern College Athletic Conference. Varsity intercollegiate teams are fielded for men in baseball, basketball, cross country, golf, soccer, tennis, track and field, swimming, and diving. Varsity intercollegiate teams for women are fielded in basketball, cross country, golf, soccer, softball, swimming and diving, tennis, track and field, and volleyball.

Tryouts for UNCW's athletic teams and spirit groups (cheerleading and dance team) are open to all students. Tryouts for athletic teams are scheduled by the coaches at the beginning of each season. Tryouts for spirit groups are held in the spring and fall each year. Student-athletes will be certified eligible according to NCAA, conference, and university regulations. All student-athletes have access to the same academic resources that are available to students in general (i.e., tutorial assistance, supplementary instruction, the Writing Services, and the Math Lab). Each student-athlete is assigned an academic advisor to assist in course selection, to provide academic counseling, and to monitor satisfactory progress toward a degree. Additional monitoring of a student-athlete's compliance with NCAA rules and regulations for eligibility purposes is conducted in the Department of Athletics, with support from external departments as well.

Campus Recreation
Student Recreation Center
910.962.3261
www.uncw.edu/campusrecreation
campusrec@uncw.edu

The Department of Campus Recreation organizes and administers a variety of structured and self-directed recreational services that enhance the overall wellness of the university community. Our primary goal is to provide quality recreational experiences directed toward positive change in the physical, cognitive, and social domains of the university community, thus enhancing the overall educational experience. This goal is accomplished by offering a wide variety of recreational activities, conducting educational workshops, and providing professional training. The Department of Campus Recreation provides a multifaceted program that includes group exercise/fitness programs, intramural sports, Discover Outdoor programs, sport clubs, and special events. Campus Recreation at UNCW takes a "something for everyone" approach to programming.

Center for Leadership Education and Services
University Union 2013
910.962.3877
www.uncw.edu/stuaff/leadserv

Students can explore leadership and service possibilities at the Center for Leadership Education and Service (CLES). The center provides programs and resources designed to inspire the development of leadership knowledge and skills while nurturing an individual's sense of responsibility for engaged citizenship. As a dynamic, student-led center, CLES empowers students by facilitating opportunities for leadership and service in local, regional, and global communities. In concert with the UNCW Cornerstone, CLES strives to foster social justice awareness, civic responsibility, and respect for individual differences.

Campus Activities and Involvement Center
Fisher Student Center 2029
910.962.3553
www.uncw.edu/activities

The university offers a variety of student involvement opportunities. Student organizations represent many diverse interests, including academic majors, honoraries, non-varsity sports, politics/activism, religion, service, and special interests.

Becoming involved is a great way to connect with other students on campus. Students who are involved on campus earn better grades and learn valuable life skills. Students are encouraged to take advantage of what the university has to offer in the way of involvement opportunities. For a comprehensive list of active student organizations, go to http://www.uncw.edu/stuaff/activities/studentorgs/directory.htm.

CHAPTER 3

Synergy

Edited by Jennifer B. Adams

What?! *A book to read over the summer? But it's my vacation!* Yes, you received your first college assignment before even starting classes. Actually, thousands of other freshmen were also reading books over the summer in preparation for their first days on campus. Many colleges and universities across the nation have instituted freshman and/or campus reading programs, but why?

There are many reasons for having students—and faculty and staff—read a common book. As a new student, you are entering a community of other learners with a variety of life experiences. A common reading program allows incoming students to have at least one thing in common and something to talk about right from move-in day. Reading a common book provides numerous opportunities to connect with, engage in, and contribute to your new community. Common reading programs also set the tone for college academic expectations. College will be work and will demand that you challenge yourself in many ways; participating in a shared reading program is one way to start this academic journey.

According to a 2007 report from the National Endowment for the Arts (NEA), among 17-year-olds, the percentage of non-readers has doubled, from 9 percent in 1984 to 19 percent in 2004. The fact is that Americans of most age levels are reading less, which, according to the study, results in lower reading scores and civic, social, and economic implications. The NEA also found that "literary readers are more likely than non-readers to engage in positive civic and individual activities—such as volunteering, attending sports or cultural events, and exercising." Overall, reading literary fiction and non-fiction, not just the latest issue of *People* or the news on CNN.com, is an important part of being a college student and in being a thoughtful, engaged citizen of your community and your world.

■ What is "Synergy"?

UNCW's Common Reading Experience, also known as "Synergy," provides:

- An introduction to academic expectations and intellectual engagement
- A common experience with new peers and faculty
- An opportunity for self-reflection and critical thinking
- A great way to get involved in and out of the classroom
- A powerful, meaningful, and FUN learning experience

Synergy supports the university mission of integration of teaching, research, and service and the stimulation of intellectual curiosity, imagination, critical thinking, and thoughtful expression.

How Will the Book Be Used?

The Common Reading book is a requirement of Freshman Seminar courses and will also be used in various courses as determined by faculty. Throughout the fall semester, there will be numerous events related to the book, including films, lectures, discussion groups, and much more.

How Are Books Selected?

The Synergy Common Reading Committee solicits recommendations from students, faculty, and staff year-round. In selecting a book, the committee considers characteristics such as:

- Potential to engage students and spark passionate discussion
- Appeal to a wide range of students
- Possibilities for classroom use and additional programming
- Richness of themes; interdisciplinary in nature

Synergy General Questions and Activities

Discussion/Journal Questions

1. As a college student, what does "intellectual engagement" mean to you?

2. What role does reading play in your life? Do you like to read for leisure? How often do you read? What do you usually read?

3. As a student and a reader, what characteristics would you look for in a future Common Reading selection?

4. Do you think UNCW's Common Reading program is a good idea? Why or why not?

Activities

1. Write a letter to the Synergy committee to propose next year's Common Reading selection. Base your proposal on the selection criteria found online at http://www.uncw.edu/commonreading/aboutprogram-selection.htm.

Group Work

Although Common Reading programs are the norm at most colleges and universities, some schools have Common Film Programs instead, in which all freshmen view the same film at the beginning of the semester and have discussions. In groups of four or five, discuss how you feel about this type of program instead of a common book program. What are possible advantages and disadvantages? What characteristics would you look for in your film selection? As a group, choose one or two films that you believe would be good candidates for such a program based on your criteria.

Each group will present its thoughts and selections to the class. The class will discuss and agree on a list of criteria for selection and vote on the best selection for a potential Common Film program. The film that is selected will then be viewed during or outside of class time.

Campus Events

Each student will be required to attend at least one scheduled Common Reading event. Possible events include a speaker and film series, discussion groups, and/or performances. A detailed event schedule can be found online at http://www.uncw.edu/commonreading/events.htm.

Event Response

After each event, write a one-page journal response in which you respond personally and critically to the event. What did you learn from this event? How did it expand your understanding of the book? What themes were addressed? What did you like and/or dislike about the event? What personal connections can you make from the event, if any?

Want to Suggest a Future Book?

Are you reading something great? Do you want to help choose the next Common Reading book? Go to http://www.uncw.edu/commonreading/suggest.htm to make your recommendation.

Website

Visit the Synergy website for information on the program, the book and author, reading resources, events, and more: http://www.uncw.edu/commonreading/.

What Are Critical Thinking and Critical Reading? and Why Should I Care?

As a college student, you will be asked to think critically in all of your classes. You will be faced with new information, challenging issues, and difficult decisions in which critical thinking skills will be helpful. The Common Reading program offers your first opportunity to engage in critical thinking *and* critical reading.

Critical Thinking Is:

RATIONAL: Critical thinkers rely on reason over emotion (though emotional responses are valid and worthy of consideration). They also rely on facts and evidence.

SELF-AWARE: Critical thinkers are more interested in the best explanation rather than being "right." This means they are aware of what influences them, including bias, assumption, and prejudice.

OPEN-MINDED: Critical thinkers consider a variety of perspectives and remain open to alternate or conflicting interpretations.

CAREFUL: Critical thinkers avoid snap judgments. They are precise, cautious, and comprehensive in their thinking.

Overall, critical thinkers are active, not passive; they question, analyze, and investigate. They are skeptical and interested.

"To read without reflecting is like eating without digesting."

~Edmund Burke

Critical Reading Is:

ACTIVE: Critical readers question the text as they read, often writing those questions and notes in the margins. They use a dictionary if necessary and use context clues. "Speak to the text" as you read—argue, agree, respond. Discuss ideas and themes with others.

AWARE OF CONTEXT: Critical readers don't just read for facts. They know that all texts exist in contexts: cultural, historical, etc.

SOPHISTICATED: Critical readers consider *how* a text is written, not just what it says. They think about choices the author makes and how the writing choices affect the reader and meaning.

MEANINGFUL: Critical readers work on making sense of a text by synthesizing what they know about the subject, the context it was written in, and the writing style. They go beyond the surface and work towards their own critical, insightful interpretation of the text.

■ Fall 2009 UNCW Common Reading Selection

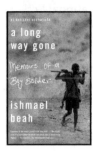

A Long Way Gone: Memoirs of a Boy Soldier
by Ishmael Beah

Book and Author Information

"In *A Long Way Gone*, Ishmael Beah, now twenty-nine years old, tells a riveting story: how at the age of twelve [in Sierra Leone, Africa], he fled attacking rebels and wandered a land rendered unrecognizable by violence. By thirteen, he had been picked up by the government army, and Beah, at heart a gentle boy, found that he was capable of truly terrible acts as a child soldier. At sixteen, he was removed from fighting by UNICEF, and through the help of the staff at his rehabilitation center, he learned how to forgive himself, to regain his humanity, and finally, to heal." —Macmillan Academic

A Long Way Gone is a powerful and meaningful personal account of war and violence and of redemption and hope. It was chosen as the Fall 2009 selection for several reasons, including its potential to spark passionate discussions and to create awareness of global issues.

Awards and Reviews

#1 National Bestseller
A *New York Times* Notable Book of the Year
A *Time* Magazine Best Book of the Year
A *Newsweek* Favorite Book of the Year
A Quill Book Award Finalist
A *Christian Science Monitor* Best Book of the Year
A YALSA Best Book for Young Adults
Winner of the Alex Award

"Everyone in the world should read this book . . . We should read it to learn about the world and about what it means to be human." —*The Washington Post*

" . . . This memoir seems destined to become a classic firsthand account of war and the ongoing plight of child soldiers in conflicts worldwide." —*Publishers Weekly*

Themes in *A Long Way Gone*

- Childhood/Loss of Innocence
- War and Violence
- Child Soldiering
- African Culture
- Family and Friendship
- Community
- Coming of Age
- Faith and Hope
- Power of Music/Hip-Hop Culture
- Post-Traumatic Stress
- Drug Abuse
- Rehabilitation and Healing
- Forgiveness
- Humanity

A Long Way Gone official website—Reviews, author info, news and multimedia
www.alongwaygone.com.

Author Information

"Ishmael Beah was born in Sierra Leone in 1980. He moved to the United States in 1998 and finished his last two years of high school at the United Nations International School in New York. In 2004 he graduated from Oberlin College with a B.A. in political science. He is a member of the Human Rights Watch Children's Rights Division Advisory Committee and has spoken before the United Nations, the Council on Foreign Relations, the Center for Emerging Threats and Opportunities (CETO) at the Marine Corps Warfighting Laboratory, and many other NGO panels on children affected by the war. His work has appeared in *VespertinePress* and *LIT* magazine. He lives in New York City." —Macmillan Academic.

Author Interviews

- Hear Ishmael Beah talk about his book and his experiences—*http:// www.alongwaygone.com/media.html.*
- Interviews on *The Daily Show* with Jon Stewart and *The Hour*— http://www.usu.edu/connections/literatureexperience/long_way/videos.cfm.
- Transcript of interview with Ishmael Beah—Powell's Bookstore, Feb. 12, 2007— http://www.powells.com/interviews/ishmaelbeah.html.

Child Soldiers: A Global Problem

Child soldiering is a unique and severe manifestation of trafficking in persons that involves the recruitment of children through force, fraud, or coercion to be exploited for their labor or to be abused as sex slaves in conflict areas. Government forces, paramilitary organizations, and rebel groups all recruit and utilize child soldiers. UNICEF estimates that more than 300,000 children under 18 are currently being exploited in over thirty armed conflicts worldwide. While the majority of child soldiers are between the ages of 15 and 18, some are as young as seven or eight years of age.

Many children are abducted to be used as combatants. Others are made to serve as porters, cooks, guards, servants, messengers, or spies. Many young girls are forced to marry or perform sexual services for male combatants. Male and female child soldiers are often sexually abused, and are at high risk of unwanted pregnancies and contracting sexually transmitted diseases.

Some children have been forced to commit atrocities against their families and communities. Child soldiers are often killed or wounded, with survivors often suffering multiple traumas and psychological scarring. Their personal development is often irreparably damaged. Returning child soldiers are often rejected by their home communities.

Child soldiers are a global phenomenon. The problem is most critical in Africa and Asia, but armed groups in the Americas, Eurasia, and the Middle East also use children. All nations must work together with international organizations and nongovernmental organizations (NGOs) to take urgent action to disarm, demobilize, and reintegrate child soldiers (US Department of State, 2004).

The Memoir: Fact or Fiction?

According to Nancy E. Zuwiyya (2006), "A memoir is a piece of autobiographical writing, usually shorter in nature than a comprehensive autobiography. The memoir, especially as it is being used in publishing today, often tries to capture certain highlights or meaningful moments in one's past, often including a contemplation of the meaning of that event at the time of the writing of the memoir. The memoir may be more emotional and concerned with capturing particular scenes, or a series of events, rather than documenting every fact of a person's life [as in an autobiography]." Whereas autobiographies are considered to be nonfiction, the memoir is often referred to as "creative nonfiction," with elements of fiction such as plot, characterization, and conflict.

The Oxford English Dictionary defines "memoir" as "a record of events or history written from the personal knowledge or experience of the writer." The word "memoir" is derived from the French *mémoire*, which comes from the Latin *memoria*, meaning "memory." The memoir is essentially the writing of a true account of an event or events in the author's life; however, if the memoirist relies on memory, can it be 100% accurate? Memories, and our stories, are built from the personal perspective, and from the ability to even remember events that happened a long time ago. People may remember events differently and certainly may be affected by events differently, even if they're telling the same story. According to Gore Vidal, American novelist and essayist, "A memoir is how one remembers one's own life."

In early 2008, *A Long Way Gone* was the subject of much controversy when reporters from *The Australian* published several articles challenging Ishmael Beah's credibility. The three reporters alleged that Beah exaggerated his story, citing his length of time as a child soldier and the shooting of his foot as examples. They also asserted that the detailed descriptions of past events would be beyond what an adult could remember about life as a 12-year-old. However, Beah heartily defends his work and denies any inaccuracies. For a review of the allegations of inaccuracy in *A Long Way Gone* and the publisher's defense of the book, read "The Fog of Memoir: The Feud over the Truthfulness of Ishmael Beah's *A Long Way Gone*," found at http://www.slate.com/id/2185928/pagenum/all/. Beah's complete statement to the press can be found at http://www.alongwaygone.com/Ishmael_Beah_statement.pdf.

Personal Response

Peter Wilson, one of the journalists who accused Beah of inaccuracy, has said, "I'm sure [Beah] went through a terrible ordeal, but the truth matters. It is plain to anyone who wants to look at this objectively that he did not experience what has been sold as the truth to hundreds of thousands of readers. The truth matters."

Do you agree or disagree with Wilson that the "truth matters"? How much does it matter? Do the potential inaccuracies in Beah's memoir affect your reading of it? How "true" do you think memoirs are meant to be?

> *"These days I live in three worlds: my dreams, and the experiences of my new life, which trigger memories from my past."*
>
> A Long Way Gone, *page 20*

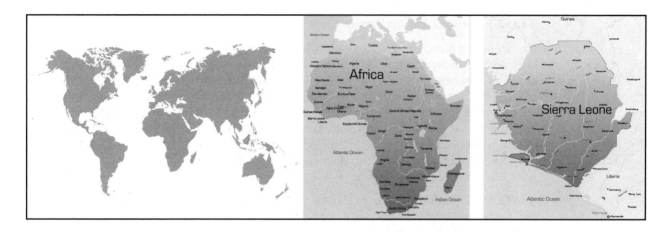

■ *A Long Way Gone* Resources

Sierra Leone Background

European contacts with Sierra Leone were among the first in West Africa. In 1652, the first slaves in North America were brought from Sierra Leone to the Sea Islands off the coast of the southern United States (Georgia and South Carolina). The capital, Freetown, was founded as a home for repatriated former slaves in 1787. In 1792, Freetown became one of Britain's first colonies in West Africa.

After 150 years of colonial rule by Great Britain, Sierra Leone achieved independence in 1961 and struggled to build a stable government. The Sierra Leone Civil War was initiated in 1991 by the Revolutionary United Front (RUF), led by Foday Sankoh, in response to poverty and corrupt government. The RUF also sought to gain control of Sierra Leone's diamond industry, using the money to finance their war efforts. The rebels pillaged the country and kidnapped young children to fight, training them to kill their own friends and family. In 1992, a group of young Sierra Leone military officers led by Valentine Strasser staged a coup, believing that the military was not doing enough to stop the rebels. They also used child soldiers in their fighting.

With an imminent rebel takeover of the capital of Freetown, British forces intervened in May 2000. Within a year of British intervention, UN forces were in full control of the country, and gradually began handing over control to the reconstituted and retrained Sierra Leone armed forces.

During the war that lasted from 1991–2002, tens of thousands of people died, including innocent Sierra Leones, and more than two million people (well/over ⅓ of the population) were displaced. A UN-backed war crimes court has been set up to try those from both sides who bear the greatest responsibility for the brutalities. The military, which took over full responsibility for security following the departure of UN peacekeepers at the end of 2005, is increasingly developing as a guarantor of the country's stability. The country is still considered a fragile state and faces the challenges of poverty, corruption, and economic mismanagement. The 70,000 former combatants who were disarmed and rehabilitated after the war have swollen the ranks of the many young people seeking employment (US Department of State, 2008).

Resources on Sierra Leone

■ US Department of State—Sierra Leone: Overview of recent history and political developments, basic facts and statistics—http://www.state.gov/r/pa/ei/bgn/5475.htm.

■ CIA World Factbook—https://www.cia.gov/library/publications/the-world-factbook/geos/sl.html.

■ Sierra Leone: A collection of links to info about the country, its history, and current affairs—http://www.africa.upenn.edu/Country_Specific/S_Leone.html.

■ BBC Timeline of Sierra Leone History (a timeline is also provided by the author in the back of *A Long Way Gone*)—http://news.bbc.co.uk/2/hi/africa/country_profiles/1065898.stm.

Fast Facts about Sierra Leone

Full Name: Republic of Sierra Leone

Capital: Freetown

Area: 71,740 sq. km. (29,925 sq. mi.); slightly smaller than South Carolina

Population: 6,144,562 (2007 est.)

Median Age: 17.5 years

Life Expectancy: 40.58 years

Literacy Rate: 36% (2002)

Ethnic Groups: Temne 30%, Mende 30%, Krio 1%, balance spread over 15 other tribal groups and a small Lebanese community

Religions: Muslim 60 percent, Christian 30 percent, Animist 10 percent

Languages: English (official, regular use limited to literate minority), Mende, Temne, Krio (English-based creole), 15 other indigenous languages

Workforce: *Agriculture* 52.5 percent; *Industry* 30.6 percent; *Services* 16.9 percent

Major Exports: Rutile, diamonds, bauxite, coffee, cocoa, fishes

Type of Government: Republic with a democratically elected president and unicameral parliament

(US Department of State, 2008)

Terms to Define and Discuss

crapes (p. 7)	Temne (p. 55)	wahlee (p. 98)	groundnut (p. 188)
kamor (p. 8)	Mende (p. 55)	brown brown (p. 121)	CAW (p. 188)
lorry (p. 10)	soukous (p. 59)	tafe (p. 137)	United Nations First
cassava (p. 17)	jerry cans (p. 59)	kalo kalo (p. 150)	International Children's
RUF (p. 21)	Sherbro (p. 63)	repatriate (p. 171)	Parliament (p. 195)
palampo (p. 23)	carseloi (p. 71)	kule (p. 177)	NGOs (p. 196)
RPGs (p. 24)	spirogyra (p. 73)	sackie thomboi (p. 181)	UN ECOSOC (p. 199)
sleepers (p. 27)	pestles (p. 76)	ablution (p. 182)	"Sobels" (p. 203)
imam (p. 44)	lappei (p. 76)	raggamorphy (p. 183)	G3 (p. 207)
sura (p. 44)	leweh (p. 76)	upline (p. 184)	Conakry (p. 209)
waleh (p. 51)	Ngor (p. 91)	poda podas (p. 185)	
Nessie (p. 51)	gari (p. 91)	SLPP (p. 188)	

"One of the unsettling things about my journey, mentally, physically, and emotionally,
was that I wasn't sure when or where it was going to end. I didn't know what
I was going to do with my life."

A Long Way Gone, *page 69*

■ *A Long Way Gone* Questions and Activities

Discussion/Journal Questions

General Response

1. What was your initial response to *A Long Way Gone*? Did you like or dislike it, and why?

2. Why do you think this book was chosen for the Common Reading Experience? Do you think it is a good choice? Why or why not?

3. What lessons are we to learn from Ishmael Beah's memoir?

4. What is the significance of the book's title?

5. Why do you think *A Long Way Gone* has been a bestselling, award-winning book?

Writing and the Memoir

1. How does this memoir style affect the story?

2. Ishmael tells his story through the past, the present, and dreams. Why do you think he chose to write the book in this manner as opposed to chronologically?

3. Ishmael began working on his memoir in a college creative writing class. In what ways can writing be helpful in understanding problems and working through them? In what ways has writing been beneficial for you?

Child Soldiering and War

1. Discuss the techniques used by the soldiers and commanders to turn the young children into child soldiers. Consider how these manipulative strategies could affect young children, perhaps putting yourself in this situation. What would you have done?

2. The volunteers at the rehabilitation center often tell the children that "none of these things are your fault." How do you feel about this? Did young Ishmael and the other children have any choice? Who do you feel is really to blame, if anyone, and why?

3. Towards the end of the book, we learn that many of Beah's friends returned to child soldiering. Why do you think this is? Do you think Beah would have returned to child soldiering if he had not fled to America? Why or why not?

4. *A Long Way Gone* describes the human toll of war, the suffering of innocents, and man's inhumanity to man. How do you feel about war, especially the current war, and why?

5. What is the role of a citizen during war? If you think war is unjust, should you say so, or is that unpatriotic? Describe the various forms patriotism can take during wartime.

Culture and Cultural Influences

1. Discuss how African culture and traditions play a role in Ishmael's life. What aspects of this culture seem to be valued most? What cultural aspects of Africa intrigued you the most? What role does your own culture play in your life? What aspects do you value the most?

2. Give examples of how American culture is portrayed throughout the book and in the author's life. What positive and negative influence does American culture have on Beah and his world?

3. Storytelling is a powerful cultural force in Ishmael's life. Provide some examples of this storytelling and consider the importance of storytelling and the oral tradition of Africa. Why is telling stories important—for Ishmael, for families, for communities, for nations?

4. What stories are important to your personal or cultural identity? What stories are important to your family history?

"I lay in my bed night after night staring at the ceiling and thinking, Why have I survived the war? Why was I the last person in my immediate family to be alive? I didn't know."

A Long Way Gone, *page 179*

Family and Friendship

1. Discuss Beah's relationship with his mother, father, and brothers. What general life lessons were his parents able to teach him that sustained him throughout his journey? What life lessons have your parents passed on to you that you think will help you through your freshman year?

2. Discuss the ways in which the idea of "family" is configured, reconfigured, challenged, and reaffirmed throughout the book. How do you define "family"?

3. How do you think Ishmael defines friendship? Why do you think this? How do you think he would characterize a "good" friend versus a "bad" friend? How do you define these?

Social Responsibility and Change for the Future

1. As a result of his experience, Beah is dedicated to relief efforts, even starting his own foundation. Are you inspired to help end child soldiering? How can each of us join in his cause?

2. Currently, what is your most important "cause"? What issue are you committed to?

3. How much are you willing to sacrifice for a greater good—culturally, environmentally, politically, and economically? What changes, if any, do you want to see in these areas?

4. Beah once commented, "I think that every human being should be aware of the possibility of change . . . Everyone can make a difference . . . If one person can change the way they interact with other people, no matter who they are or where they are from, that makes a big difference." Do you agree with Beah? Why or why not?

5. Beah was rescued because of people who have dedicated their lives to helping those in need. Give examples of times when you have helped others in need. Identify ways that you may get involved in helping others on campus and in your other communities. Think about ways others have helped you through difficult times.

College Transition and Personal Connections

1. Throughout Ishmael's journey, he relied on hope, perseverance, and his spirit. What character traits do you think will be important to a successful journey through college? Through your life?

2. How does reading a story like Beah's make the challenges you face more manageable? What actions or personality traits do you find in his story that you would attribute to his ability to overcome the challenges he faced? How might you develop similar traits or skills to help you through difficult times you face?

3. In the short "New York City, 1998" prologue that begins the memoir, Ishmael's friends find some things about his past to be "cool." If they had read this book, would they still feel that way? Why? How much does what has happened in our pasts affect the present? What are you bringing with you to college? What will you leave behind?

4. Based on Ishmael's experience, what is our capacity to make changes in who we are and what direction we will take? How much control do we have over our lives?

5. What is it about music (and rap music in particular) that matters to Ishmael, or that moves him so? Why is it so important to him, especially during his rehabilitation at Benin Home? What music do you rely on during times of difficulty? Why is it meaningful to you?

6. Villagers often run fearfully from Ishmael and his friends, believing that the boys are rebels. How do they overcome these negative assumptions? What does this mistrust say to the importance of judging others individually rather than as stereotypes? What are some stereotypes you may have to overcome while starting college?

7. How are the issues raised in *A Long Way Gone* relevant to a college student living in North Carolina? Sierra Leone is ~4,000 miles from North Carolina, across the Atlantic Ocean, with unique political, social, and economic problems. How do wars in Africa or other places in the world affect you? What have you learned from reading *A Long Way Gone* that will make a difference in the way you view the world?

Activities and Assignments

1. Imagine that you are a literary consultant on the set of a future film adaptation of *A Long Way Gone*. Filmmakers who try to adapt books have a tough job because they must select which elements of the literary source material to keep and which elements to discard. Most books are just too long to film word-for-word. Write an essay advising the director. Name two of the most important scenes to keep, and explain your choices. Try not to choose two scenes that are alike. In other words, strive to have a variety of violent/peaceful, etc.

2. Go to http://www.wagingpeace.org/articles/2000/08/00_beah_good-bad.htm to read an article written by Beah during his senior year at the United Nations High School, "When Good Comes from Bad." Write an essay in which you respond to the thesis "Sometimes good comes from bad." Use examples from your personal life and/or examples from local/global issues.

3. Use writing, poetry, song, dance, film, photography, art, collage, theatre, and/or another medium of creative expression to answer the question, "What does *A Long Way Gone* mean to me?" Volunteers will be able to share their work with the class.

4. Music plays an important role in Ishmael's life and in *A Long Way Gone*. Bring a recording of your favorite song to class on an MP3 player, CD, or other file. You will play the song for the class and explain why this song is so powerful in your life. How does it make you feel and why?

5. Practice writing your own memoir. Choose an experience or event in your life of significance. Write a two- to three-page narrative telling the details of this event and its impact on you then and now. It can be humorous, serious, insightful, etc. Let your personality shine through.

6. Beah's story spans his first 18 years or so. Make a timeline showing key moments in your life leading up to now. Include milestones, important events, and moments that show your "coming of age" from a child to a young adult.

Group Presentations

Groups of four or five students will choose one of the following topics (or a smaller topic within the larger heading) to prepare and present a presentation to the class. The presentations should be five to 10 minutes long, well researched, and well organized, and include visuals (PowerPoint, multimedia, images, etc.). Each member of the group must contribute to the planning and presentation itself.

- ■ Child Soldiering in Countries Other Than Sierra Leone
- ■ Sierra Leone (culture, history, politics, etc.)
- ■ African Culture
- ■ World Music and Social Culture
- ■ Current Events in Africa
- ■ Where Do We Go from Here? Relief Efforts and Related Organizations

For numerous links and multimedia resources, visit http://www.uncw.edu/commonreading/reading.htm.
Book and Author Resources
Information on Child Soldiers
Sierra Leone Resources
Related Organizations and Relief Efforts
Related Reading and Films
Much More

References

National Endowment for the Arts, News Room. (2007, November 19). *National Endowment for the Arts announces new reading study*. Retrieved November 27, 2007, from http://www.nea.gov/news/news07/TRNR.html.

US Department of State, Diplomacy in Action. (2008, October). *Background note: Sierra Leone*. Retrieved February 16, 2009, from http://www.state.gov/r/pa/ei/bgn/5475.htm.

US Department of State, Diplomacy in Action. (2004, June 14). *Trafficking in persons report*. Retrieved March 30, 2009, from http://www.state.gov/g/tip/rls/tiprpt/2004/34021.htm .

Zuwiyya, N.E. (2006). Memoir. *Inkspell*. Retrieved March 30, 2009, from http://inkspell.homestead.com/memoir.html.

CHAPTER 4
Motivation and Goal Setting
Paving Your Way to Success

What Is Motivation?

Motivation is the inner drive for success. Motivation is much easier to sustain if you have clear dreams and goals. Without clear goals, you are like a ping-pong ball bouncing back and forth between other people's ideas of what you should do with your life.

Ask yourself the following questions. What are your dreams for the future? What do you want to be? What are you really good at? Why are you attending college? To make your vision a reality and live a rich and fulfilling life, you need to realize that you are in control of your life. We have all heard the saying, "I will believe it when I see it." In order to realize your goals and dreams you must "believe it to see it."

■ What Are Intrinsic and Extrinsic Motivation?

Intrinsic motivation is the drive within you to accomplish a goal or task. You complete an activity or task because it has personal meaning to you or gives you pleasure and satisfaction. For example, at the beginning of the semester you have a strong desire to learn about the history of North Carolina. You read the book, complete the assignments and study for the tests because you have an intense interest in the subject area. At the end of the semester, you will feel a sense of accomplishment because you learned a great deal about the history of North Carolina.

No one forced you to study or read the chapters; you wanted to succeed in the class and most likely earned a good grade. You need to develop intrinsic motivation to maximize your college experience. If you are intensely interested in new ideas and concepts, it will be much easier for you to be successful at UNCW. What is your motivation for coming to college? Is it your personal goal, or that of another person such as a parent, sibling, grandparent or a friend? It will be much easier for you to accomplish your goals and be happy and successful in the process if the motivation comes from within you.

Extrinsic motivation is the drive that comes from someone else or an external stimulus. For example, what a parent, sibling, grandparent or a friend may do or say can motivate you to make certain choices. However, if you are only motivated by someone else's desire for you to earn a grade of A in ENG 101 this semester, it may be difficult for you to study and accomplish that goal. After a while, you may lose interest in the subject matter and your grade may suffer. If your only motivation is external, in this case the grading system, your motivation will be harder to maintain. You may also be motivated towards a goal due to an extrinsic reward such as money, a certificate, honor, praise, recognition or even friendship. Extrinsic rewards can be a positive motivation for coming to college. Think about the benefits of a college degree: more money, a successful career, or the ability to purchase a new car. It's okay to be motivated by extrinsic rewards. At some point, however, these rewards need to be a part of your intrinsic motivation to produce satisfaction and pride in your accomplishments.

■ Locus of Control: Who Is Responsible?

Motivation is often influenced by locus of control. Your locus of control is where you place the responsibility for events that happen in your life. If you have an **internal locus of control**, you place responsibility on yourself and feel that you have control over events in your life. If you have an **external locus of control**, you place responsibility on others and feel that events beyond your control influence your life. When things go wrong you may blame others instead of taking responsibility for your actions. It is better to have an internal locus of control. If you have an internal locus of control, you believe that you create and control events in your life and can change your life for the better. In fact, research indicates that students with an internal locus of control may perform better in college than students with an external locus of control.

Here are some examples of internal and external locus of control.

Students with an internal locus of control:

- ■ Believe that academic success depends on how hard they work
- ■ Try to make the best of a situation
- ■ Believe they create their own destiny
- ■ Think positively about life and school work
- ■ Rely on internal motivation

Students with an external locus of control:

- ■ Believe that events are due to fate, chance or luck
- ■ Look for someone to blame when things go wrong
- ■ Believe teachers give grades, instead of students earning them
- ■ Think negatively about life and school work
- ■ Rely on external motivation

Take a few minutes to see if you can recognize an internal and external locus of control.

Complete Exercise 1 at the back of the chapter.

■ What Is Victim and Creator Language?

Creators are people who take full responsibility for their behaviors and beliefs and have an internal locus of control. Creators believe they create their lives and have choices. **Victims**, however, do not take full responsibility for their behaviors and beliefs, and see themselves as victims of life. Victims have an external locus of control. Every day you choose to respond to situations as a creator or a victim.

For example, let's say you got a test back yesterday that you did very poorly on. You have two choices as to how you can respond. You can respond as a creator admitting you did not study as much as you could have. Or, you can respond as a victim and blame

the professor for not explaining the material thoroughly. Every day, you decide consciously or subconsciously to use either victim or creator language. To take full responsibility for your life and your college career, try to see yourself as a creator and reflect this image in the language you use.

Here are some examples of victim and creator language.

Victims:

- ■ Make excuses
- ■ Blame others
- ■ Complain
- ■ Believe they "have to" do things
- ■ Pretend their problems belong to others
- ■ Give up

Creators:

- ■ Seek solutions
- ■ Accept responsibility
- ■ Take action
- ■ "Choose to" do things
- ■ "Own" their problems
- ■ Take control of their choices

Try Exercise 2 at the back of the chapter to practice changing victim language into creator language.

■ How Are Goals and Motivation Related?

Many people talk about goals, but very few actually write them down. You may see goals as wishes and dreams, but they can be more. Goals require a detailed plan of action. Motivation is essential in goal setting. Setting clear and concrete goals will allow you to remain motivated when times are tough. We have all pushed through tough times in the past because we knew what the payoff would be.

The remainder of this chapter will focus on the skills you need to set and accomplish goals for the future.

■ Long-term and Short-term Goals

Long-term goals provide you with the "big picture" and vision for your life. Long-term goals should represent where you want to be and what you want to accomplish in a year or longer. These goals take a while to accomplish and should be set for attaining within three to five years. Long-term goals should include major life decisions. Long-term goals require a deep commitment and real life vision. One long-term goal may be to graduate from UNCW in four years.

Short-term goals should be the stepping-stones toward accomplishing your long-term goals. Short-term goals are like mini-goals, or step-by-step plans, toward accomplishing your ultimate goals. For one long-term goal, several short-term goals should be set in order to keep you on track and maintain your motivation. For example, if your long-term goal is to graduate from UNCW in four years, you will need to pass your courses this semester. Each semester you'll need to set short-term goals with your long-term goal in mind.

Here are some examples of long-term and short-term goals.

Long-term Goals:

- Graduate from UNCW with a 3.0 GPA
- Graduate from UNCW in four years
- Get a job in your chosen field two months after graduation

Short-term Goals:

- Pass each class this semester with a "B" average
- Attend each class period this semester
- Turn in all assignments on time this semester
- Get to know all of your UNI classmates this semester
- Declare a major at the end of my first year

■ How Do You Set Goals?

Now that you know why goals are important, you can learn how to set goals using the SMART principles. SMART is a handy acronym for the five characteristics of well-designed goals. Goals are more likely to be attained if you use the SMART principles.

Specific: Goals should be clear and to the point. When goals are specific, they explain what, when and how much is expected. If your goal is too vague, you won't get the sense of accomplishment once it is complete. You may also feel as though you have accomplished a goal, when you have not. For example, setting a goal such as "I will achieve a 3.0 GPA this semester" is more specific than "I will do well in my classes this semester." When setting a more specific goal, you know exactly what you have to do to accomplish the goal and gain more satisfaction from doing so.

Measurable: What good is a goal if you can't measure it? If your goals are not measurable, how can you be sure that you are making progress toward your ultimate goal? A measurable goal provides a time frame and a foreseeable outcome. For example, if you set a goal such as "I want to make a lot of money when I graduate from college," how will you know if you have accomplished this goal? What does "a lot" mean? Make sure your goals can be measured.

Achievable: Goals must be achievable and realistic for you to accomplish them. Goals should be within reach and not below your standards. If your goals are too high, you will not be able to achieve them, and your self-esteem may suffer. If your goals are too low, you may not gain satisfaction from accomplishing them. You want to have an optimistic attitude when setting your goals, but you should be honest with yourself about how realistic and achievable your goals are.

Relevant: Goals must be relevant and important to you. Effective goals are your goals, not someone else's. If your goals are unimportant to you, you will most likely lose the motivation and focus you need to reach them. Your goals need to be important for your future, and no one else's. For example, you may set a goal that is important to your parents, but it may not be important to you.

Timely: Goals should include specific deadlines. A short-term goal usually has a deadline of a month or two. A long-term goal usually has a deadline from one to five years. Without deadlines, a goal has no ending point. If no deadline is in place, you may work your whole life toward the goal. For example, if you set a goal such as "I want to get a job," you may be working all of your life to get a job. Redesign the goal to read, "I want to get a job two months after graduation."

Here are a few examples of SMART goals:

- Earn a Bachelor of Arts degree in English from UNCW in four years.
- Earn a B in ENG 101 by the end of the semester.
- Acquire at least five successful student behaviors in UNI by the end of the semester.
- Join at least one campus organization or club by the end of the semester.

Complete Exercise 3 at the back of the chapter to set your own personal goals using the SMART principles.

■ What Are Some Practical Tips for Effective Goal Setting?

Write your goals down. In order for you to remember your goals, you need to write them down. It may be difficult for you to follow the SMART principles if you don't maintain a list of short- and long-term goals. If you write your goals down, it will be easier for you to evaluate them. Your goals may also change depending on your life circumstances. Try writing your goals in a journal. Once a week, you can look through your journal and see if you are still on track toward accomplishing your goals.

Post your goals where you can see them. Placing your goals on your refrigerator, your mirror, or some other place you can see them often is very important. By seeing them every day, you will remain focused on your objective. Every time you see them, you will refresh your motivation.

Reward yourself for accomplishing your goals. Most students don't think of rewarding themselves once a goal is accomplished. However, rewards are very important for maintaining motivation. When you set goals, you should also set rewards that go along

with accomplishing each goal. Rewards should be special, relatively inexpensive, and preferably unrelated to food or alcohol. For example, you may go on a weekend trip, to a movie, or call an old friend—anything that is special or important to you. Plan to reward yourself when you reach important goals or milestones in your life.

■ Barriers: What Could Keep You from Reaching Your Goals?

For every goal you set, you are likely to encounter at least one barrier that could keep you from reaching that goal. These barriers can be conquered, but you must identify them in order to develop a plan of action. Can you think of barriers you have experienced in the past? Are these obstacles internal or external barriers?

Internal barriers are roadblocks you create for yourself. As discussed earlier in this chapter, you are in total control of your behavior. Therefore, you have control over the internal barriers you place on yourself. Internal barriers include bad habits, lack of self-confidence, poor time management skills, and using "victim language." Many of these internal barriers can be addressed by taking a new attitude. Change is not easy, but many of the internal barriers you face can be changed if you are determined to change them. You have complete control of your behavior and your life.

One example of an internal barrier is the common procrastination technique of using too many "shoulds" in your language. How many times have you said, "I should do that today?" "I should get all A's," or "I should do my homework assignment"? Using "should" in your language indicates that you know what needs to be done, but you don't do it. "Should" is an internal barrier that can be easily changed. Next time you think or say "I should," stop and replace "I should" with "I will."

External barriers are roadblocks that come from an outside source. At some point, you may encounter external barriers that prevent you from reaching your goals. Maybe you have had a teacher who didn't believe in your performance, or a parent who didn't think you could succeed at a certain subject. Both of these examples are based on the opinions of others. Can you think of a time that another person's opinions prevented you from reaching a goal?

You may work diligently at accomplishing your goal, but circumstances beyond your control may cause you to fall short. Perhaps when you graduate, there are few jobs available in your field. Or, maybe you become sick and need to sit out a semester from UNCW. When circumstances are beyond your control, there is nothing wrong with reevaluating your goals. It's better to reevaluate your goals than to let your motivation or self-esteem suffer.

Problems often arise when you change external barriers into internal barriers. For example, maybe your father does not believe that you will make a good accountant. If you allow this external barrier to affect your ability to pursue accounting, you are changing an external barrier into an internal barrier.

Here are some examples of internal and external barriers.

Internal barriers:

- ■ Lack of self-confidence
- ■ "Victim" language
- ■ "Should" in your language
- ■ Fear of failure
- ■ Procrastination

- Lack of motivation
- Negative thinking
- Poor time management skills

External barriers:

- Stereotypes
- Family expectations and responsibilities
- Lack of financial means
- Serious illness
- Poor economy

■ What Do You Do If You Do Not Achieve Your Goals?

Most people see failure as a negative word, but it doesn't have to be viewed as negative. Failure can be a valuable learning experience. Begin to see failure as a detour or a fork in the road rather than a dead end. If you did not reach a goal in the past, think for a minute about what you learned from the experience. Once you have reflected on what you learned, reevaluate the goal. It's a good idea to evaluate your goals frequently. Maybe you didn't use the SMART principles when you set your goals. Maybe your goals are not as realistic as you once thought. Make reevaluating your goals a frequent habit to ensure you stay on track.

Here are more helpful hints for overcoming failure:

1. Take a closer look at the goal you set. Is the goal specific, measurable, achievable, relevant, and timely?

2. Work out a routine to help accomplish your goal.

3. Ask for help from family or friends.

4. Evaluate your strengths and weaknesses. How can you focus on your strengths?

5. Try to predict the barriers that may get in your way, and develop a plan for overcoming these barriers.

6. Make a personal commitment to yourself.

7. Ask a friend or a mentor to help hold you accountable to the goals you have established.

■ Summary

Having an internal locus of control, using "creator" language, and setting goals effectively are essential for your success as a college student. On average, students who set long-term and short-term goals are more successful in college and in life. Implement the SMART goal setting principles into your goal setting process to make sure they are specific, measurable, achievable, relevant and timely. If you fall short in accomplishing your goals, remember to view it as a growth experience and as an opportunity to reevaluate your goals. Setting and achieving short-term and long-term goals is essential to your success as a UNCW student and for making your personal vision a reality.

■ References

Aguilar, L. S., Hopper, S. J. & Kuzlik, T. M. (1998). *The Community College: A New Beginning.* Dubuque, IA: Kendall Hunt.

Downing, S. (2002). *On Course: Strategies for Creating Success in College and in Life.* Boston, MA: Houghton Mifflin.

Fralick, M. (2000). *College and Career Success.* Boston, MA: Houghton Mifflin.

Kanar, C. C. (2001). *The Confident Student.* Boston, MA: Houghton Mifflin.

O'Neill, J. (2000). SMART Goals, SMART Schools, *Educational Leadership, 57.* 46–50.

Richmond, A. "SMART Goals: A Better Way to Track Your Progress," *Career-Intelligence.com* [internet]. 2002.

Name: _____ Date: _____

■ Exercise 1: Internal or External Locus of Control

Read each statement below. Decide if the statement represents an internal or external locus of control. Place a checkmark in the corresponding column marked "internal" or "external."

	Internal	**External**
1. Professors should provide students with study guides for exams.	_____	_____
2. The grades I receive in my classes are based on my hard work.	_____	_____
3. Events that happen in life are based on fate and luck.	_____	_____
4. I believe I create my own destiny.	_____	_____
5. I am at UNCW because my parents think I should be a nurse.	_____	_____
6. I try to make the best of every situation.	_____	_____
7. My roommate is unreasonable and hard to get along with.	_____	_____
8. I view every class as an opportunity for me to learn about myself.	_____	_____
9. It is the professor's responsibility to remind me when exams are and when assignments are due.	_____	_____
10. When I fail to reach my goals, I re-evaluate them.	_____	_____
11. Being late for class is not my fault.	_____	_____
12. I enjoy being at UNCW and am thankful I was admitted.	_____	_____
13. My professor is a lousy teacher. There is no way I can pass her exams.	_____	_____
14. I got an F on my first exam because I didn't read the assignments.	_____	_____

Answer key: The odd-numbered items represent an external locus of control and the even-numbered items represent an internal locus.

■ Exercise 2: How to Change Victim Language into Creator Language

Below are statements victim's may use. Rephrase each statement using the space provided to reflect creator language.

1. Finding a parking space is so frustrating.

2. I can't help the fact that I always oversleep and arrive late to class.

3. My professor doesn't know anything about teaching.

4. My textbooks are so boring. There is no way I can read them!

5. My roommate is so hard to get along with.

6. I can't believe I have to take so many classes for my major.

7. My parents drive me crazy every time I go home.

8. The food in the cafeteria stinks!

9. The grading scale in my Math class is unfair.

10. I have always been weak in math.

■ Exercise 3: Practice Setting Goals in Your Life Using the SMART Principles

Below is an example of Ali's life plan. Complete the other life plan for yourself. Remember to use the **SMART principles (specific, measurable, achievable, relevant and timely)** when setting your goals.

Ali's Life Plan

MY LIFE PLAN: College student
MY DREAM IN THAT ROLE: Earn a Master's degree in Sociology in 8 years.

MY LONG-TERM GOALS:

1. Graduate with a Bachelor's of Arts in Sociology from UNCW within 5 years.

2. Complete any additional courses with at least a B grade that will allow me to get into graduate school.

MY SHORT-TERM GOALS:

1. Earn a B in ENG 101 this semester.

2. Get involved in at least two campus organizations by May.

3. Apply and learn five new strategies for successful students in UNI by the end of the semester.

What Is Your Life Plan?

MY LIFE PLAN:

MY DREAM IN THIS ROLE:

MY LONG-TERM GOALS:

1.

2.

3.

4.

MY SHORT-TERM GOALS:

1.

2.

3.

4.

■ Journal Assignment

Describe an academic goal or specific achievement that you have accomplished. What steps did you take to achieve the goal? What barriers did you overcome and how did you conquer them? Who helped you achieve the goal? Describe how it felt to realize this accomplishment.

CHAPTER 5
Time Management

Have you ever met someone who seems to accomplish twice as much as you do, or someone who accomplishes only half as much as most people? These individuals are on opposite ends of the time management spectrum. One person has learned how to schedule time effectively, and the other never sets a schedule and may feel unbalanced or unsuccessful. For many people, successful time management is based on accomplishing as many tasks as possible within a given amount of time by creating and executing "to do" lists day after day, but does this method of quality vs. quantity help them accomplish their short- and long-term goals? Instead of asking "How many tasks am I accomplishing?" we should begin asking "What am I accomplishing?" and "Are these the important things for me?"

As a new UNCW student, you are already facing numerous demands on your time. Besides attending class and studying, you may be involved with clubs, organizations, athletics, work and family. Learning to manage your time appropriately will help you succeed in college and achieve your short- and long-term goals. This chapter is designed to help you organize tasks and time around your personal responsibilities and purpose by developing and using a scheduling system based on the goals you identified previously. Once you have a clear understanding of your goals and what you want to accomplish, it is much easier to prioritize tasks and schedule them appropriately.

Time Management Assessment

Before we learn the necessary strategies to improve our time management, let's take a moment to assess our current skills. Respond to each of the following statements:

1. I find calendars and daily planners a waste of time.   Yes   No

2. On average, I use my free time to accomplish important tasks.   Yes   No

3. When I have a paper or project due, I wait until the last minute to begin because I feel I work better under pressure.   Yes   No

4. Each day, I set aside time for myself.   Yes   No

5. I frequently drop whatever I'm doing to hang out with friends.   Yes   No

6. I frequently set goals for myself and examine my priorities.   Yes   No

7. At the end of a weekend, I often wish I had accomplished more.   Yes   No

8. I take time to review my notes after each class.   Yes   No

9. I often find myself surfing the Internet or napping for longer than I planned.   Yes   No

10. When it comes to managing time, there is always room for improvement.   Yes   No

Scoring:

Odd numbered statements, 1 point for each YES.

Even numbered statements, 1 point for each NO.

If your score is:
0–2   Good Job! You are well on your way to successful time management.
3–4   Not bad but there is always room for improvement.
5–7   You've got some work to do.
8–10   Time management is not in your vocabulary. Keep reading!

Getting Started

Stephen Covey, an expert on time management and author of *The 7 Habits of Highly Effective People,* describes time management as a system by which we begin "organizing and executing tasks around our priorities." However, most of us have never closely examined our priorities. Sure, we could identify the things that are most important to us right now, but could we rank every item in our life by importance? Covey suggests identifying and prioritizing tasks by using a time management matrix. The matrix consists of four quadrants that outline how we spend our time. These four quadrants, labeled

■ Covey's Four Quadrants

	URGENT	NOT URGENT
I M P O R T A N T	**I** Studying for a test the day before the test.	**II** Studying for a test three weeks before the test.
N O T I M P O R T A N T	**III** Going to a concert by a group your friend likes even though it's not your kind of music.	**IV** Spending four hours on Facebook at one sitting.

Source: Stephen Covey. *Seven Habits of Highly Effective People*

urgent, not urgent, important and *not important*, allow you to take a closer look at the urgency and importance of activities in our lives.

Urgent

Quadrant I

Example: Staying up late working on a paper that is due at 8:00 am.

Quadrant III

Example: Going to a party with friends during time you scheduled for writing a paper.

Not Urgent

Quadrant II

Example: Creating a study group early in the semester for one of your courses.

Quadrant IV

Example: Watching television mindlessly when you have school work to complete.

Unimportant—Important

How do you determine what is urgent and what is important? Urgent items are things that must be acted on immediately and are usually obvious. These items require quick response. Items of importance should be directly linked to your personal goals and responsibilities. Important items typically have long-lasting positive results and are future oriented.

Take a look at the time management matrix below:

Quadrant I activities are both urgent and important. These activities are important to our success and have approaching deadlines. This is where procrastinators like to live. People who consistently find themselves in Quadrant I are frequently stressed about deadlines. Cramming for finals is a common Quadrant I activity for college students.

Quadrant II activities are important but not urgent. This quadrant is where the most successful individuals find themselves. Tasks can be accomplished without looming deadlines, creating better experiences and greater success. Quadrant II activities include working on assignments well before they are due or studying for final exams throughout the semester.

Quadrant III activities are not important but are urgent in nature. These are activities that steal time from our day because they appear urgent. Since you have determined that these activities are not important, you do not want them to distract you from those that are aligned with your responsibilities and goals. You are often compelled to spend time on Quadrant III activities because you feel obligated to others. Activities in this quadrant could include going to a soccer game with friends the evening before an exam.

Quadrant IV activities are not important and not urgent. You waste the most time when living in this quadrant. This is not to say that these activities are bad things that you should never do; they are just not relative to your goals and purpose. The time spent in Quadrant IV could be better used in Quadrant II. Activities in Quadrant IV would include spending too much time talking on the phone, surfing the web, or watching TV.

How do you organize and prioritize your life so that you spend the majority of your time in Quadrant II? First, clearly establish your goals and understand your values. Once you have identified your goals and values, you will determine which activities and tasks are essential for accomplishing them. These activities and tasks then become short-term goals that are directly linked to long-term goals. At times, this may require you to decline activities and tasks that do not reflect the goals and responsibilities you have established. For example, your roommate invites you to a basketball game, which is of little interest to you, during a time you had scheduled to study. Attending the game would be fun but will force you to move your study time to your next available free time preventing you from using your free time on an activity you truly enjoy. By declining the opportunity you are able to stay on course and utilize your free time productively. If you consistently strive to live in Quadrant II, you will find that your activities add value to your life enabling you to accomplish goals that may have once seemed impossible.

Remember, you are in control of the time you have each day. Choose to use your time wisely and accomplish the goals you set.

■ Scheduling Your Time

Once you have defined your goals and determined which activities have a high priority in your life, you are ready to develop a scheduling system that works for you. As a college student, you will probably want something portable that is easy to access and maintain. There are a variety of paper calendars and handheld electronic devices available to help you get started. Since you will want the ability to plan your week and semester, select an option that provides daily and monthly scheduling.

Preprinted inside are the dates for important university events and deadlines. It is important to find a scheduling system that fits your lifestyle. You may want to experiment with several types to find out what works best for you. Once you have chosen your scheduling system, create a master calendar to act as a guide for your daily and monthly time management. Your master calendar should be updated each time you have a major change in your schedule. Be realistic about the time it takes to perform each activity so that you do not overbook yourself.

■ Setting Up a Master Schedule

Use the blank schedule sheet at the end of this chapter to develop your master schedule.

1. Begin by inserting your class and lab times into the master schedule. As a college student, attending class should be your first scheduling priority, so insert those times first.

2. In order of importance, insert activities such as work, meetings, commuting, eating, exercising and sleeping. Be sure to allow adequate time for each activity.

3. Note all of the free spaces in your schedule. Within these, identify your study time and recreational activities, in order of importance. In your study time, indicate the subject(s) that you will cover during each period. Remember, for each hour of class you should plan to study one to two hours outside of class. Once you have identified your study time, fill in recreational activities.

One note to commuter students . . .

Commuter students often plan their class schedules so that they are on campus only two or three days a week with back-to-back classes with no significant breaks. This may seem like a good idea, but it can be dangerous. For example, if all of your classes are on Tuesday and Thursday from 8:00 am to 3:00 pm without any breaks, you leave little time to review the material from each class. In addition, you risk becoming fatigued by the end of each day. Missing one day can put you behind in all classes instead of a few. It is likely that many of your exams, papers and projects will be due on the same day. You should weigh all of your options and determine what schedule will work best for you and allow you to give maximum attention to each of your courses.

4. Leave the remaining hours blank to allow for flexibility. Life is unpredictable and there will be times when you need to adjust your schedule. Regularly evaluate how you are using your time and make changes if necessary. Keep your master schedule in a convenient location. Not only will it guide your monthly and daily calendars, it will serve as a reference if you get off course or need to find additional time for activities.

■ Developing Your Monthly Calendar

Your monthly calendar will help you keep track of assignments, deadlines, test dates and other items of importance. Keep your monthly calendar with you at all times so that you may update it regularly. At the beginning of each semester, you will receive a course syllabus for each class. The course syllabus will identify assignment and test dates along with paper and project deadlines. Put these dates in your monthly calendar immediately. This will allow you to plan for times when assignments or due dates overlap. For example, in reviewing your course syllabi, you realize you have both an English 101 paper and a Sociology 105 paper due on October 1st. You now have the opportunity to plan ahead and give adequate time to each activity. In addition to class requirements, you will want to list university deadlines that apply to you on your monthly schedule. Include holidays, breaks and exam dates. You will want to add other activities of importance such as athletic events, birth dates, appointments and club or organization meetings. You may want to develop a system that indicates the priority of appointments or items listed on your monthly schedule.

■ Daily Calendar

Now that you have completed your master schedule and monthly calendar, you are ready to utilize a daily calendar. The daily calendar will help you keep track of the short term activities and tasks that you have to accomplish day to day and those from your master schedule and monthly calendar. Your daily calendar should begin with the hour in which you wake and can be broken down into half hour or full hour segments. You will want to review and update your daily calendar each night so that you wake with a plan of action. You may want to add a "to do" list to your daily calendar to inform you of items to accomplish in your free time. It is helpful to list these items and keep them on hand to maximize any unscheduled free time you find. However, do not feel the need to plan an activity for each hour of your day. Allow for the unexpected. Remember to include time to relax on your daily schedule.

■ Putting It into Practice

Now that you understand how to schedule your tasks and activities around your goals and responsibilities, how can you make sure you use and maintain this new system? Make a decision now to be aware and disciplined about how you use your time. You need to be self motivated when it comes to time management. Taking time to regularly evaluate and clarify your goals and responsibilities should help you find the motivation you need. If you know you are having trouble being consistent in this area, ask a friend to hold you accountable.

■ Where Does My Time Go?

This exercise will help you examine how you spend your time for one week (7 days). It is helpful to do this exercise on a regular basis since it will help you identify time wasters in your schedule. There are 11 categories listed below that represent how most college students spend their time. For one week, track the number of hours you spend on each activity. Use the "Estimated" column to indicate the number of hours you have scheduled for each activity and the "Actual" column to record the amount of time you actually spent on each activity. It is helpful to calculate each day individually and tabulate at the end of one week.

Activity	Estimated	Actual
Class Time		
Studying		
Employment		
Leisure		
Social		
Travel		
Eating		
Grooming		
Resting		
Recreation		
Exercise		
Other: _____		
Total Hours		

Note: The total should not exceed 168 hours.

Once you have completed this exercise, note the estimated time in comparison to the actual time spent on each activity. Are there times where you have wasted more hours than you expected? Are you maintaining balance between your academic, personal and social lives? If you find that the majority of your time is not spent in Quadrant II activities (important, not urgent) or that you are wasting too much of your free time, consider revising your time management system.

Balance

One of the most difficult tasks that college students face is creating and maintaining a balanced lifestyle. It is critical to your success that you find a balance between your academic, social, and personal lives. Having a time management system that you use on a daily basis will allow you to control your life and use your time productively. Since it is

your schedule, you commit to the structure and revise it as you see fit. If you find that your life is out of balance in one area, you have the ability to adjust your plan.

Time Wasters

Wasting time is a chronic problem for many people. As a busy college student, it is vital that you learn how to stay in control of your schedule. Keep in mind that time wasters are only unproductive when they are unplanned and prevent you from accomplishing the things that are important to you.

Identifying ways in which we waste time is an important part of the time management process. Let's look at the ways in which time wasters affect your daily life and keep you from accomplishing your goals. For example, during your scheduled study time you have the television on and are distracted by a basketball game. You decide to watch the game and miss your hour of study time. You then have to find additional time in your schedule to study, leaving less time for the activities you intended to accomplish. One solution would be to turn the television off during your study time.

Listed below are some common time wasters for college students. In the action plan column, list ways to avoid these time wasters.

Common Time Wasters	Action Plan
Unexpected Visitors	
Television	
Unnecessary Naps	
Phone Calls	
Surfing the Internet	
E-mail	
Video/Computer Games	
Other: _____	

Maximizing Your Time

In order to get the most out of your time each day, consider finding productive tasks that you can do in short periods of time between scheduled tasks and activities. These time-saving strategies will help you accomplish more in less time.

If you have:

Five minutes: Review for a test. Update your calendar. Revise your "to do" list. Make a phone call. Send an e-mail or mail a letter.

Fifteen minutes: Review notes from that day's classes. Revise your monthly calendar. Write a letter, pay bills, wash dishes, or start your laundry.

Thirty minutes: Review a chapter in a textbook. Exercise, clean your room, run errands, eat a meal, or plan for the upcoming week.

Think about the time you have between classes or activities. How could you use that time more productively?

■ Summary

As a student, there are numerous demands made on your time. Utilizing the time management skills presented in this chapter will help you create and maintain a balanced lifestyle. On a regular basis, review the time management matrix to determine the urgency and importance of activities in your life. Update your master calendar each semester, and let it guide your monthly and daily calendars. Practice your time management skills daily to ensure you get the most out of your college experience.

■ Time Management Tips

1. Begin with a plan of action for each day including weekends. Taking time to plan your day will save you endless hours of frustration and help you avoid the procrastination trap!

2. Identify your top "time wasters" and plan a strategy to handle each one.

3. Frequently review your goals and examine your priorities. Confirm that the majority of your activities are found in Quadrant II.

4. When an unexpected situation interrupts your daily schedule, don't panic. Take a few moments to review the remainder of your day and make the necessary adjustments.

5. Realistically set your schedule. Do not try to accomplish six hours of studying in a two hour time block. You will only set yourself up for failure.

6. Practice saying no!

7. Make a prioritized list of all the items that you need to accomplish in a given time period. Post the list in a visible area, or carry it with you.

8. Get organized! One sure way to waste time is to spend it looking for misplaced items. Organization = Efficiency!

9. Attend time management workshops offered by Student Success Center at UNCW! Practice makes perfect!

10. Plan time for yourself! A schedule without leisure time is doomed to fail!

■ Reference

Covey, S. (1989). *The 7 Habits of Highly Effective People.* New York, NY: Fireside.

Name: _____ Date: _____

_____

■ Master Schedule Blank

	Monday	Tuesday	Wednesday	Thursday	Friday	Saturday	Sunday
6:00 A.M.							
7:00 A.M.							
8:00 A.M.							
9:00 A.M.							
10:00 A.M.							
11:00 A.M.							
12:00 P.M.							
1:00 P.M.							
2:00 P.M.							
3:00 P.M.							
4:00 P.M.							
5:00 P.M.							
6:00 P.M.							
7:00 P.M.							
8:00 P.M.							
9:00 P.M.							
10:00 P.M.							
11:00 P.M.							
12:00 A.M.							

Name: _____   Date: _____

■ Sample Master Schedule

	Monday	Tuesday	Wednesday	Thursday	Friday	Saturday	Sunday
6:00 A.M.							
7:00 A.M.	Breakfast	Breakfast	Breakfast	Breakfast	Breakfast		
8:00 A.M.	Biology	Biology	Biology	Work			
9:00 A.M.	History	History					
10:00 A.M.	UNI	UNI					
11:00 A.M.	Sociology	Sociology	Sociology				
12:00 P.M.	Lunch	Lunch	Lunch	Lunch	Lunch		
1:00 P.M.	English 101	English 101					
2:00 P.M.	Biology	Lab	Study Time	Study Time	Exercise		
3:00 P.M.	Study Time						
4:00 P.M.	Exercise	Exercise					
5:00 P.M.	Dinner	Dinner	UA Meeting	Dinner			
6:00 P.M.	Dinner	Study Time					
7:00 P.M.	Study Time	Study Time	Study Time				
8:00 P.M.							
9:00 P.M.							
10:00 P.M.							
11:00 P.M.							
12:00 A.M.							

■ Journal Assignment #1

List the activities you completed yesterday in the quadrants provided.

Covey's Four Quadrants

	URGENT	NOT URGENT
I M P O R T A N T	I	II
N O T I M P O R T A N T	III	IV

Source: Stephen Covey. *Seven Habits of Highly Effective People*

■ Journal Assignment #2:

Over the next week, track your daily activities. Begin with the hour you wake and conclude at bedtime. You will want to note your activities each and every hour throughout the day. It is important to keep an accurate account of your days, including interruptions and unscheduled activities.

At the end of the week, review your schedule and answer the following questions:

1. When did you find yourself managing time successfully?

2. In what ways did you waste time?

3. What activities/events took the greatest amount of time? Would these be considered Quadrant II items?

4. Did you plan time for yourself each day?

5. Do you see room for improvement in your schedule? If so, how?

CHAPTER 6

Strategic Learning
Applying Research on Human Learning and the Human Brain to Acquire Knowledge Effectively and Comprehend It Deeply

Learning Goals

The goal of this chapter is to supply you with a well-designed set of learning strategies that are supported by solid research on how humans learn and how the human brain works.

■ Activate Your Thinking

Do you think there is a difference between learning and memorizing?

If yes, what do you think the difference is?

You are likely to experience greater academic challenges in college than you did in high school. Studies show that the percentage of students earning "As" and "Bs" drops from about 50 percent in high school to about 33 percent in college (Astin, 1993; Sax et al., 2004). Learning strategies that enabled you to earn "As" and "Bs" in the past may not earn you those grades now. Thus, to maintain or exceed your level of academic performance in high school, you will need to elevate your performance to a higher level in college. Attaining this higher level of academic performance will probably not involve just working "harder"; it will involve working "smarter" and learning to use effective strategies that are supported by research on how humans learn and how the human brain works.

■ Brain-Based Learning Principles

Learning becomes more effective and efficient when it is "brain-based" or "brain-compatible" (Hart, 1983) and capitalizes on the brain's natural learning tendencies (Caine & Caine, 1994). Despite the fact that there are differences among us in terms of our intellectual talents and learning styles, we are all members of the human species and we all possess a human brain. Just as all humans have bodily organs that perform specific functions, such as our heart and liver, we also have a brain that functions as the "learning organ" of the body (Zull, 1998). By understanding how the human brain learns, we can capitalize on this knowledge to identify general principles or common themes of learning that work effectively for all humans. You can then convert these general principles into specific strategies that may be used to learn effectively in all subject areas to promote your success across the curriculum (Weinstein, 1982).

The Brain Is Biologically Wired to Seek Meaning

Perhaps the most distinctive and most powerful feature of the human brain is that it is biologically wired to seek meaning (Caine & Caine, 1994). The human brain naturally

You perceive a white triangle in the middle of this figure. However, if you use three fingers to cover up the three corners of the white triangle that fall outside the other (background) triangle, the white triangle suddenly disappears. What your brain does is take these corners as starting points and fills in the rest of the information on its own to create a complete or whole pattern that has meaning to you. (Notice also how you perceive the background triangle as a complete triangle, even though parts of its left and right sides are missing.)

Figure 1 ■ Triangle Illusion

looks for meaning by trying to connect what it is trying to learn and understand to what it already knows. For instance, when the brain perceives the external world, it looks for meaningful patterns and connections rather than isolated bits and pieces of information (Nummela & Rosengren, 1986). In Figure 1, notice how your brain naturally ties together and fills in the missing information to perceive a meaningful whole pattern.

The brain's natural tendency to seek whole patterns with meaning applies to words as well as images. The following passage once appeared (anonymously) on the Internet. See if you can read it and grasp its meaning.

> *"Aoccdrnig to rscheearch at Cmabridge Uinverstisy, it deosn't mattaer in what order the ltteers in a word are, the only iprmoetnt thing is that the frist and lsat ltteer be at the rghit pclae. The rset can be a total mses and you can still raed it wouthit a porbelm. This is bcusae the human mind deos not raed ervey lteter by istlef, but the word as a wlohe. Amzanig huh?"*

Notice how your brain found the meaning of the misspelled words by naturally transforming them into correctly spelled words that it already knew or understood. We tend to see whole patterns because the knowledge we have in our brain is stored in the form of a connected network of brain cells (Coward, 1990). Thus, whenever we learn something, we do so by connecting what we're trying to understand to what we previously know and what we have already stored in our brain.

When we learn by making meaningful connections, this is referred to as *deep learning* (Entwistle & Ramsden, 1983). To "deeply" learn the challenging concepts you'll encounter in college will require active mental involvement and personal reflection on the information you receive. You will need to move beyond shallow memorization to deeper levels of comprehension. When you learn deeply, you don't just take in information; you take the additional step of actively reflecting on it. This also involves a shift away from the old view that learning occurs by passively absorbing information like a sponge, whereby you receive it from the teacher or text and study it in exactly the same, pre-packaged form you received it. Instead, you want to adopt a different approach to learning that involves active transformation of information you receive into a form that is meaningful to you (Entwistle & Marton, 1984; Feldman & Paulsen, 1994).

Pause for Reflection

When you try to acquire knowledge or learn new information, do you tend to memorize it in the form in which it's presented to you, or do you usually try to transform it into your own words?

Personal Story

When my son was about 3 years old, we were riding in the car together and listening to a song by the Beatles titled, "Sergeant Pepper's Lonely Heart Club Band." You may be familiar with this tune, but in case you're not, there is a part in it where the following lyrics are sung over and over: "Sergeant Pepper's Lonely, Sergeant Pepper's Lonely, Sergeant Pepper's Lonely . . . ."

When this part of the song was being played, I noticed that my 3-year-old son was singing along. I thought that it was pretty amazing for a boy his age to be able to understand and repeat those lyrics. However, when that part of the song came on again, I noticed that he wasn't singing "Sergeant Pepper's Lonely, Sergeant Pepper's Lonely . . ." etc. Instead, he was singing: "Sausage Pepperoni, Sausage Pepperoni . . ." (which were his two favorite pizza toppings).

So, I guess my son's brain was doing what it tends to do naturally. It took unfamiliar information (song lyrics) that didn't make any sense to him and transformed it into a form that was very meaningful to him!

—Joe Cuseo

New Knowledge Is Built on Knowledge Already Possessed

Acquiring knowledge isn't a matter of pouring information into the brain, as if it were an empty jar; it's a matter of building new knowledge onto knowledge you already possess (Piaget, 1978; Vygotsky, 1978), or attaching it to information that is already stored in the brain.

When people understand a concept, a physical or biological connection is made between brain cells, whereby the new information gets connected into a network of connections that have already been made in the brain (Alnon, 1992). Thus, deep learning is learning that actually changes the brain. The following figure (Figure 2) shows a microscopic section of the human brain that specializes in the learning of language. Notice that the number of brain cells (black spots) in a newborn baby and a 6-year-old child are about the same. However, the 6-year-old's brain almost looks like a forest because there are many more connections between brain cells; these connections represent all the language (e.g., vocabulary words) the child has learned in six years of life.

Shallow, Surface-Oriented versus Deep, Meaning-Oriented Approaches to Learning

It has been found that students have different methods of processing or handling information they are trying to learn (Schmeck, 1981; Entwistle & Marton, 1984). Some stu-

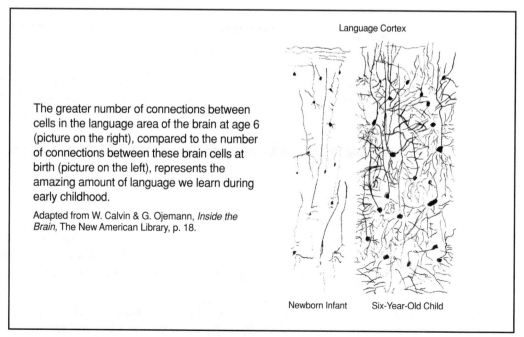

Language Cortex

The greater number of connections between cells in the language area of the brain at age 6 (picture on the right), compared to the number of connections between these brain cells at birth (picture on the left), represents the amazing amount of language we learn during early childhood.

Adapted from W. Calvin & G. Ojemann, *Inside the Brain*, The New American Library, p. 18.

Newborn Infant   Six-Year-Old Child

Figure 2 ■

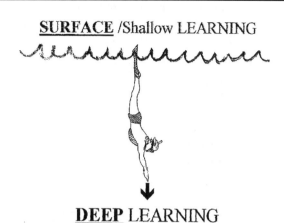

SURFACE /Shallow LEARNING

DEEP LEARNING

(Going beneath the surface to a deeper level of learning involves comprehension rather than memorization)

Studies show that academically successful students dive below the surface of shallow memorization to a deeper level of learning that involves seeking meaning and understanding.

Figure 3 ■ Memorizing Factual Information

dents take a shallow, surface-oriented approach to learning in which they spend most of their study time repeating and memorizing information in the exact form that it's presented to them. Other students use a deep, meaning-oriented style of learning in which they deal with new information by elaborating on it—changing it from the form they received it into a form of their own—by restating it in their own words and relating it to their own experiences. They spend most of their study time thinking about and trying to understand what they're learning, rather than repeating and memorizing it.

Studies of these two methods of learning reveal that the shallow, surface-oriented approach tends to result in poorer memory for studied material (Watkins, 1983) and lower college grades than the deep, meaning-oriented approach (Ramsden, 2003). For example, in a study of engineering students, those students who used a surface approach to learning earned lower grades, even though they had high class-attendance rates and spent a great amount of time studying outside of class. Despite the fact that these students attended class regularly and put in sufficient study time, their method of study was not as effective as those students who took a deeper, meaning-oriented approach to learning (Kember, Jamieson, Pomfret, & Wong, 1995).

Although there may be times in college when you simply have to remember information that is presented to you, the primary goal of your studying should be to seek deep learning and comprehension, rather than settling for shallow memorization and repetition. Seeking meaning not only results in learning that is deeper, but also results in memory that is more *durable*—it's more likely to "stick" or remain in your brain for a longer period of time (Craik & Lockhart, 1972; Craik & Tulving, 1975).

> *Remember:* Deep, long-lasting learning requires an active search for meaning via personal reflection, rather than passive memorizing via mindless repetition.

Finding meaning in what you're learning means you truly understand it, which enables you to connect it with the knowledge you already possess and apply it to new situations you'll encounter in the future (Ramsden, 2003).

Since our brains naturally seek meaning, when you learn by searching for meaning, it also makes the process of learning more stimulating and more motivating than learning by memorizing and repeating, which can quickly become very monotonous, mindless, and boring. In fact, interviews with students show that those who use a deep approach to learning are more likely to report a higher level of personal satisfaction and interest in what they're learning than students who use a surface approach (Biggs, 1987; Marton, et al., 1997; Marton & Saljo, 1984).

Pause for Reflection

Look back at your response to the question asked at the very start of this chapter about whether there is a difference between learning and memorization. Based on the information you've read thus far in this chapter, would you modify or change your answer in any way?

■ Stages in the Learning and Memory Process

Although deep learning is the ultimate goal or final stage you want to achieve, to get there requires successful completion of a series of stages in the process of learning and memory. Learning deeply, and remembering what you've learned, is a process that involves three key stages:

1. getting information into your brain (*perception*),

2. keeping it there (*storage*), and

3. finding it when you need it (*retrieval*).

You can consider these stages of human learning and memory to be similar to the way information is processed by a computer: (a) information first gets typed onto the screen, (b) the information is kept or stored by saving it in a memory file, and (c) the information is found by calling up or retrieving that file when it's needed.

We'll now take a more detailed look at each of these three key stages in the learning-memory process and relate them to learning in college.

Stage 1. Perception: Receiving Information from the Senses and Sending It to the Brain

If you are not paying attention to a sign, you could drive right by it and not perceive it.

This is the first step in the learning process because we must first attend to and receive information in order to get it into our brain—where it is then registered or perceived. All information from the outside world gets to the brain through our senses (e.g., sight and sound), but it will only reach and get registered in our brain if we pay attention to it.

Contrary to popular belief, not all information that reaches our senses is received and registered in our brain (Rose, 1993). Although information may reach our eyes and ears, if we are not paying close enough attention to it, it will not register in our brain and we will not perceive it. Have you ever had the experience of driving right past an exit that you were supposed to take? Your eyes were fully open and the exit sign was in your field of vision when you passed it, but because you weren't paying close enough attention to it, it didn't register in your brain and you never perceived it.

Only information that we pay attention to gets registered by our conscious brain because the lower, subconscious part of our brain works as an attention filter by selectively letting in or keeping sensory information from reaching the upper parts of the brain—where it is consciously perceived (Figure 4).

Pause for Reflection

People often forget the name of someone immediately after being introduced. What do you think causes this memory failure?

Information reaching our senses must pass through lower, subconscious parts of the brain that act as an attention filter or gatekeeper, determining whether sensory information will be sent to upper parts of the brain where it is consciously received (perceived).

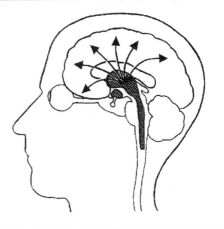

Figure 4 ■ The Brain's Human Attention System

LASSIC QUOTE

The true art of memory is the art of attention.

—*Dr. Samuel Johnson, English author*

In fact, one of the major causes of forgetting is our failure to pay enough attention to what we want to remember; as a result, this information never registers in our brain in the first place. For example, forgetting where we put our keys or where we parked our car are classic examples of inattention or "absentmindedness." We forget these sorts of things because our brain never received the information in the first place. Our mind was not consciously present

As these examples illustrate, attention is a critical prerequisite for learning and memory to take place.

> **Remember:** *If there is no attention, there can be no retention.*

In college, there are two key sensory channels or routes through which you will receive information:

1. Hearing—listening to lectures, and

2. Seeing—reading information from textbooks.

For learning to occur through either of these routes, the critical first step is to attend to and make note of the information you receive. Simply stated, you cannot learn and retain information that you've never attended to and acquired in the first place.

Personal Story

My son Michael is notorious for wanting to do everything that we ask his younger sister to do, and very little of what we ask him to do. A classic example is when we send him to any room to retrieve any object. My wife and I now measure how long it will take him to bring the wanted item back to us. (However, if we're in a hurry, we usually get it ourselves.) This is how it usually goes. "Michael, please go into the master bathroom and get the nail clippers." Michael, who will be seven at the time of this publication, walks slowly toward the bathroom. In a few minutes, he'll walk back into the room where we are, carrying some object he has started to construct (perhaps he'll grow up to be an engineer). When we ask him for the clippers, he'll say: "Oh, I forgot." In reality, he was not paying attention to our request, and it never registered in his brain. However, if we asked Maya (our daughter) to retrieve the item, Michael bowls her over to retrieve it. He listens well when Maya's name is called. The plan in our household now is to ask Maya for everything and let her actually get it when Michael is not around.

LASSIC QUOTE

We remember what we understand; we understand what we pay attention to; we pay attention to what we want.
—*Edmund Bolles,*
Remembering & Forgetting: An Inquiry into the Nature of Memory

—*Aaron Thompson, Professor of Sociology*

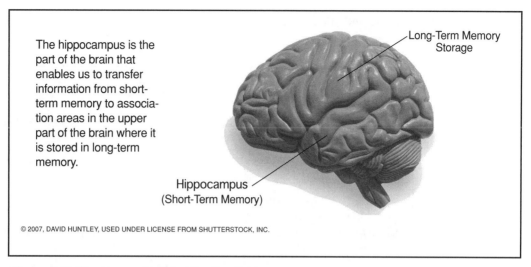

The hippocampus is the part of the brain that enables us to transfer information from short-term memory to association areas in the upper part of the brain where it is stored in long-term memory.

Long-Term Memory Storage

Hippocampus (Short-Term Memory)

Figure 5 ■ The Human Brain's Attention System

Stage 2. Storage: Keeping Information in the Brain

If information passes through our attention filter and is consciously perceived by our brain, it enters into one of the following memory systems:

- ■ short-term memory—where it lasts for only a few seconds; or
- ■ working memory—where you can consciously hold it in your mind and "work on it" for an extended period of time.

Have you ever walked into a room to do or get something, but once you got there, you had no idea why you were there? This experience illustrates the difference between short-term and working memory. What happened is that you had an idea in your short-term memory about something you were going to do or get in that room, but you then began thinking about something else after you had this thought, and by the time you got to the room, the thought had faded from your working memory. If you had kept that thought in your working memory, you would have been able to hold onto it and would have remembered why you went into the room after you got there.

To get information to stay in the brain for more than a short period of time, it has to be transferred from working memory, which is a temporary memory system, and moved into a different memory system known as *long-term memory*. Similar to a computer, we can get information onto the screen (short-term memory) and work on it (working memory), but if we want our computer to save the information we've worked on, we have to store it in the computer's long-term memory system.

The part of the brain that enables you to transfer memories from short-term to longer-term memory is known as the hippocampus (Squire, 1992) (Figure 5).

If the hippocampus is permanently damaged, an individual cannot store long-term memories. Or, if the hippocampus is temporarily slowed down by alcohol or marijuana, it can interfere with memory storage (for example, memory "blackouts" experienced by someone for events that occurred during a night of excessive drinking).

The process of storing information in long-term memory is referred to as *coding*, and the information that's stored is referred to as a *memory trace*—a physical or biological trace of the memory in the brain. (Note: The term memory "trace" is consistent with the word "learning"—which derives from the root word meaning "footprint" or "track.") Relating this to college learning, when you're studying, you are trying to register a memory trace by transferring information from working memory to encode it in long-term storage so that you can recall it at test time. How well the information you have studied will stick in your brain depends on how effectively or deeply you learned it—the deeper the learning, the stronger its memory trace.

Memory Tips

The following strategies will help you better retain and more deeply learn new information while you are studying:

- *connect or relate the information to something you already know;*
- *organize it into some classification system;*
- *take it in through multiple sensory modalities—e.g., see it, hear it, draw it, and feel it; and*
- *practice it at different times. (These strategies are discussed more fully later in the chapter.)*

Pause for Reflection

It's common to hear students say, "I knew it when I studied it, but I forgot it on the test."

What do you think causes this common occurrence?

How might students study differently to prevent this from happening?

Stage 3. Retrieval: Finding Information That's Been Stored in the Brain and Bringing It Back to Consciousness

Getting information into the brain and getting it to stay there are the first two critical stages in the learning-memory process. The final stage is finding the stored memory and bringing it back to mind. To use the computer analogy, when your computer retrieves a file, it searches through the stored files, finds the particular file you need, and then brings it back to the screen in front of you. Relating this to college learning, the retrieval stage of memory corresponds to test taking. You first attend to and receive information from lectures and readings; you later study that information; and, finally, you attempt to retrieve that information at test time.

Evidence supporting the importance of the retrieval stage of memory comes from what researchers call the "tip of the tongue" phenomenon (Brown & McNeill, 1966). You've probably said to yourself: "Oh, I've got it (the memory) on the tip of my tongue." For example, you're taking an exam, you studied the material well, and you know the information that's being asked for in the test question, but you just can't quite get it to come back to you. However, after the test is over, it suddenly comes back to you when it's too late to use it! This demonstrates the memory trace was in your brain the entire time; you just weren't able to access and retrieve it.

Thus, retrieval represents the third and final stage of the memory process. All of the key stages in the processes of learning memory that we have discussed so far are summarized visually in Figure 6.

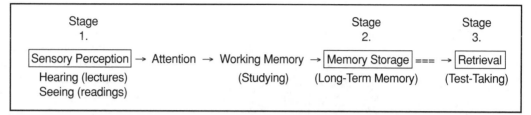

Figure 6 ■ Key Stages in the Learning and Memory Process

Pause for Reflection

For each of the three stages that make up the learning and memory process, how would you rate yourself in terms of your ability or past performance?

1. Attention to information presented in class and in reading assignments (strong, average, or weak?)

2. Studying—preparing for exams and getting information to "store" in your brain (strong, average, or weak?)

3. Test-taking—retrieving information that you've studied at test time and getting it down on paper (strong, average, or weak?)

This information about the key stages in the learning-memory process can be applied to generate a series of practical strategies that you can use to improve your performance on each of the following academic tasks:

■ listening to lectures and note-taking,
■ textbook reading, and
■ studying.

■ Lecture Listening and Note-Taking Strategies

Information from class lectures represents one of the major sources of information that your brain must first take in for successful learning to eventually take place. Described are strategies for effective lecture listening and note-taking.

The Importance of Taking Notes

Studies show that information found in professors' lectures is the number-one source of test questions (and answers) on college exams (Brown, 1988; Kuhn, 1988). When lecture information appears on a test and has not been recorded in students' notes, it has only a 5 percent chance of being recalled (Kiewra, et al., 2000). This means that you

Students who take notes during lectures have been found to achieve higher class grades than those who just listen.

should view each lecture like it is a test-review session during which your instructor is giving out test answers.

The importance of effective listening and note-taking for college success is highlighted by a study conducted with an entire freshman class of over 400 students who were given a listening test at the start of their first term in college. At the end of their first year, 49% of those students who scored low on the listening test were on academic probation at the end of their freshman year, compared to only 4.4% of students who scored high on the listening test. On the other hand, 68.5% of students who scored high on the listening test were eligible for the Honors program at the end of their first year, compared to only 4.17% of those students who had low listening-test scores (Conaway, 1982).

Contrary to popular belief that writing interferes with listening, students themselves report that taking notes actually increases their attention and concentration in class (Hartley & Marshall, 1974; Hartley, 1998). Studies also show that when students write down information that is presented to them rather than just listening to it, they are more likely to remember the most important aspects of that information when they are later given a memory test. Students who write notes during lectures have been found to achieve higher course grades than students who just listen to lectures (Kiewra, 1985), and students with a more complete set of notes tend to demonstrate higher levels of academic achievement (Kiewra & Fletcher, 1984). For instance, one study discovered that successful students (GPAs of 2.53 or higher) record more information in their notes and retain a larger percentage of the most important information than students with GPAs less than 2.53 (Einstein, Morris, & Smith, 1985). These findings are not surprising when you consider that *hearing* lecture information, *writing* it, and *seeing* it while writing, provide three different memory traces in the brain that can combine to improve your memory for that information. Furthermore, students with a good set of notes have a written record of that information, which can be re-read, reflected on, and studied later.

C **LASSIC QUOTE**

All genuine learning is active, not passive. It is a process in which the student is the main agent, not the teacher.
—*Mortimer Adler, American professor of philosophy and educational theorist*

Remember: *Come to class with the attitude that your instructors are throwing out answers to test questions as they speak; your purpose for being there is to pick-out and pick-up these answers. Take on the role of an active, investigative reporter who has an inquiring mind and an intense interest in acquiring important information.*

TUDENT PERSPECTIVE

I never had a class before when the teacher just stands up and talks to you. He says something and you're writing it down, but then he says something else."
—*First-year student quoted in Erickson & Strommer (1991) p. 8.*

■

Focus Your Attention

Attention is the critical first step to successful learning and memory. However, our attention span is limited, so it's impossible to attend to and make note of every piece of information that an instructor delivers in class. Thus, you need to use *selective attention* to attend to and select the most relevant or important information to record in your notes. Listed below are some key strategies for doing so.

■ Pay special attention to any **information your instructors put in writing**—on the board, on an overhead, on a slide, or in a handout. If your instructor has taken the time and energy to write it out, that's usually a good clue that it is important information and you're likely to see it again—on an exam.

Take Action Now!   **Box 1**

How to Detect When Instructors Are Delivering Important Information During Class Lectures

1. *Verbal cues:*

   ■ *Phrases that signal important information, such as: "The key point here is . . ." "What's most significant about this is . . ."*

   ■ *Repeating information or rephrasing it in a different way (such as saying: "In other words, . . .").*

   ■ *Following stated information with a question to check students' understanding (e.g., "Is that clear?" "Do you follow that?" "Does that make sense?" "Are you with me?").*

2. *Vocal (tone of voice) cues:*

   ■ *Information that is delivered louder or at a higher pitch than usual, which may indicate excitement or emphasis.*

   ■ *Information delivered at a slower rate or with more pauses than usual, which may be your instructor's way of giving you more time to write down these especially important ideas.*

3. *Nonverbal cues:*

   ■ *Information delivered by the instructor with more than usual:*
     a. facial expressiveness—e.g., raised or furrowed eyebrows;
     b. body movement—e.g., more gesturing and animation;
     c. eye contact—e.g., looking at the faces of students to see if they are following or understanding what is being said.

   ■ *Information delivered with the instructor's body oriented directly toward the class—i.e., delivering information with both shoulders directly (squarely) facing the class.*

   ■ *Moving closer to the students—e.g., instructor moving away from the podium or blackboard to move closer to the class.*

- Pay close attention to **information presented during the first few minutes and last few minutes of class**. Instructors are more likely to provide valuable reminders, reviews, and previews at the very start and very end of class.
- **Use your instructor's verbal and nonverbal cues** to detect important information. What the instructor writes out is not the only information that is important. It has been found that students record almost 90 percent of information that is written on the board, but they only record about 50 percent of important ideas that instructors state but don't write on the board (Locke, 1977). So, don't fall into the reflex-like routine of just writing something in your notes when you see your instructor writing something on the board. You also have to listen actively to record important ideas in your notes that you hear your instructor saying. In Box 1 are some specific strategies for detecting important information being delivered orally by your instructors during lectures.

© 2007 JUPITERIMAGES CORPORATION

Studies show that students who sit in the front and center of a classroom tend to earn higher test scores.

Taking Notes

Adopt a seating location that will maximize your focus of attention and minimize possible sources of distraction. Studies show that students who sit in the front and center of the classroom tend to attain higher exam scores (Rennels & Chaudhair, 1988). One study discovered a direct relationship between test scores and seating distance from the front of class: Students in the front scored 80 percent; those seated in the middle scored 71.6 percent; and those seated in the back rows of class scored 68.1 percent on course exams (Giles, 1982). Such results are found even when students are assigned seats by their instructor, so they are not simply due to the fact that more motivated students tend to sit in the front and center of the room. Instead, the higher academic performance of students sitting front and center is likely to have something to do with a learning advantage provided by these seating positions. Front-and-center seating probably improves academic performance by allowing students better vision of the blackboard, better hearing of what is being said by the instructor, and greater eye contact with the instructor—which may increase their sense of personal responsibility to listen and take notes on what their instructor is saying.

When you enter the classroom, step up to the front of class and sit down. In large-sized classes, it is particularly important that you sit in front and "get up close and personal" with your instructors. This will not only improve your attention and note-taking; it should also improve your instructor's ability to remember who you are and how well you per-

 TUDENT PERSPECTIVES

"I tend to sit at the very front of my classrooms. It helps me focus and take notes better. It also eliminates distractions."

—First-year student

"I like to sit up front so I am not distracted by others and I don't have to look around people's heads to see the chalk board."

—First-year student

The evolution of student attention from the back to the front of class.

formed in class, which will work to your benefit if you ever need a letter of recommendation from that instructor.

Be aware of how your social seating position affects your behavior in the classroom. Intentionally sit near classmates who will not distract you or interfere with the quality of your note-taking. Attention comes in degrees or amounts; you can give all of it or part of it to whatever task you're performing. When you are in class trying to grasp complex information, this task demands your undivided attention.

> **Remember:** *When you enter a classroom, you have a choice about where you are going to sit. Choose wisely by selecting a location that will maximize your focus of attention and the quality of your note-taking.*

Adopt a seating posture that screams attention. Sitting upright and leaning forward is more likely to maximize your attention because these signals from your body will reach and influence your mind. If your body is in an alert and ready position, your mind tends to pick up these bodily cues and follow your body's lead by becoming more alert and ready to learn. Just as baseball players assume their "ready position" in the field before a pitch is delivered so that they are in a better postural position to catch batted balls, learners who assume a ready position in the classroom put themselves in a better position to mentally "catch" spoken ideas. Studies show that when humans are ready and expecting to capture an idea, greater amounts of the brain chemical C-kinase is released at the connection points between different brain cells, which increases the likelihood that a branched learning connection is formed between them (Howard, 2000).

Also, be aware that we may sometimes give others and ourselves the impression that we're actively listening because it is the polite thing to do; however, we may just be listening passively, partially, or not at all. For instance, when we're being introduced to someone for the first time, we may appear to be politely listening and paying attention to the person's name; however, we may not be listening carefully at all because we're thinking about what to say next or worrying about the type of impression we're making. When we run into that same person again five minutes later, we're embarrassed to learn that we've forgotten the person's name—which indicates that we weren't really listening and paying attention when we first heard it.

So, one aspect of effective listening in the classroom is to pay attention to whether you're really paying attention. Often the best way to do so is to check your own body language. Listed in Box 2 are some key nonverbal signals that often provide a good indication of

Take Action Now!   **Box 2**

Nonverbal Signals Indicating That You're Paying Close Attention During Lectures

1. Your body is oriented directly toward the instructor, so that your shoulders line up squarely with the instructor's shoulders (as opposed to one shoulder facing the instructor and your other shoulder facing away—which is known as giving someone "the cold shoulder").

2. Your body is upright or tilting slightly forward (rather than leaning back—which may mean you are "kicking back" and "zoning out").

3. You make occasional eye contact with the instructor—rather than making no eye contact at all (e.g., looking out the window) or continually staring/gazing at the instructor like you're in a mesmerized trance. Studies show that when a person makes periodic eye contact and then looks away for a moment to the left or right (referred to as "lateral eye movements" or "LEMS"), this indicates that the person is really listening to and thinking about what is being said (Glenberg, Schroeder, & Robertson, 1998).

4. Your head nods periodically and slowly—not continuously and rapidly—which usually means that you want the speaker to hurry up and finish so you don't have to listen anymore.

whether or not you're listening actively and attending closely to what your instructor is saying in class.

Making a conscious effort to focus your attention in the classroom is particularly important during the first year of college because class sizes for introductory courses are often larger than other college courses or courses you had in high school. When class size gets larger, individuals tend to feel more anonymous, which may reduce their feelings of personal responsibility and their sense of active involvement. In large-class settings, it becomes especially important to fight off both distractions and the tendency to slip into "attention drift."

Lastly, there is another major advantage of maintaining your focus of attention in class: You send a clear message to your instructor that you're a motivated, conscientious, and courteous student. This can influence your instructor's perception and evaluation of your academic performance, either consciously or subconsciously. If you're on the border between two grades at the end of the term, you may get the benefit of the doubt. In contrast, inattentive or discourteous behavior in the classroom is likely to have the opposite effect on your instructors' perception and evaluation of you, which may lower your grade.

One survey revealed that college professors found the following student behaviors in the classroom to be especially irritating, so be sure to avoid them (Box 3).

Using cell phones and eating in class are both considered to be rude or uncivil behaviors (especially if both are done in the same class period!).

"The student question that drove Professor Jenkins over the edge!"

Question Frequently Asked by Students After Missing a Class

Responses from Tom Wayman, Professor of Creative Writing, University of Calgary

Nothing. When we realized you weren't here we sat with our hands folded on our desks in silence, for the full two hours.

Everything. I gave an exam worth 40 percent of the grade for this term and assigned some reading due today on which I'm about to hand out a quiz worth 50 percent.

Nothing. None of the content of this course has value or meaning. Take as many days off as you like: Any activities we undertake as a class I assure you will not matter either to you or me and are without purpose.

Everything. A few minutes after we began last time, a shaft of light descended and an angel or other heavenly being appeared and revealed to us what each woman or man must do to attain divine wisdom in this life and the hereafter. This is the last time the class will meet before we disperse to bring this good news to all people on earth . . .

And you weren't there.

Take organized notes. Keep taking notes in the same paragraph if the instructor is continuing on the same point or idea; for each new concept the instructor introduces, skip a few lines and shift to a new paragraph. Be alert to phrases that your instructor may state to indicate a shift to a new or different idea (e.g., "Let's turn to . . ."), and use these phrases as cues for taking notes in paragraph form. This will strengthen the organization of your notes, which, in turn, will improve your comprehension and retention of them. Also, leaving extra space between paragraphs will give you some room to add information that you may have missed and to add your own thoughts or to paraphrase lecture notes into your own words.

Snapshot Summary   Box 3

Pet Peeves of College Professors

Surveys show that professors really hate it when students:

1. *Carry on personal conversations with others during a lecture.*
2. *Miss class and ask, "Did I miss anything important?"*
3. *Place their head on the desk or fall asleep during class.*
4. *Are excessively tardy.*
5. *Fail to bring required materials to class.*
6. *Are excessively absent.*
7. *Miss a lecture and then expect the professor to provide them with a personal encore.*

Source: Larry Ludewig, college professor, cited in Vogt (1994).

Take your own notes in class. Do not rely on someone else to take notes for you. Taking your own notes in your own words will ensure that they have meaning to you. You can rely on classmates for the purpose of comparing notes for completeness and accuracy, or to get notes if you are forced to miss class. However, do not routinely rely on others to take notes for you. Studies show that students who record and review their own notes earn higher scores on memory tests for that information than students who review the notes of others (Fisher & Harris, 1973). These findings point to the importance of taking and studying your own notes because they have personal meaning to you.

If you do not immediately understand what your instructor is saying, don't stop taking notes. Keep taking notes, even if you are temporarily confused, because this will at least leave you with a record of the information that you can reflect on later, when you will have more time to think about it and grasp it. If you still don't understand it after taking more time to reflect on it, then you can check with your textbook, your instructor, or a classmate.

> **Remember:** Your primary goal during lectures is to get important information into your brain long enough to note it mentally and then physically—by recording it in your notes. Fully comprehending and deeply understanding that information may have to come later, when you have time to reflect on the ideas you've written.

Before individual class sessions, check your syllabus to see where you are in the course and determine how the upcoming class fits into the total course picture. This strategy will strengthen your learning by allowing you to see how the parts relate to the whole.

If possible, get to class ahead of time, so you can look over your notes from the previous class session and your notes from any reading assignment relating to the day's lecture topic. Research indicates that when students review information relating to a lecture topic before hearing the lecture, it improves their ability to take more accurate and complete notes during the lecture (Ladas, 1980). This research supports the strategy of reading textbook information relating to the lecture topic *before* hearing the lecture, because this will help you better understand the lecture and take better notes. A brief review of previously learned information serves to activate your previous knowledge, getting it into your working memory so you'll be in a better position to build a mental bridge from one class to the next. This will help you relate new information to what you've already experienced, which is essential for deep learning.

> ### Pause for Reflection
>
> *What do you tend to do immediately after a class session ends?*
> *Why?*

As soon as class ends, quickly check your notes for missing information or incomplete thoughts. You can do this by yourself, or better yet, with a motivated classmate. If you both have gaps, check them out with your instructor before s/he leaves the classroom. Even though it may be weeks before you will be tested on this material, the quicker you address missed points and misunderstood ideas, the better, because you'll be able to avoid the last-minute, mad rush of students seeking help from the instructor just before test time. You want to reserve the critical time period just before exams to review a whole set of complete and accurate notes—rather than rushing around, trying to find missing information and trying to understand concepts that were presented weeks ago.

As soon as possible after the end of a class session, reflect on your notes and make them meaningful to you. In college, your professors will often be lecturing on information that you may have little prior knowledge about, so it is unrealistic to expect that you will understand everything that's being said the first time you hear it. Instead, you'll need to take time to reflect on and review your notes to make sense of them. During this review and reflection process, we recommend that you take notes on your notes by:

- translating technical information into your own words to make them more meaningful to you, and
- reorganizing your notes to get ideas relating to the same points in the same place or category.

Studies show that when students are instructed to organize lecture information into meaningful categories, they show greater recall on a delayed memory test for that information than students who were simply told to review their notes (Howe, 1970). We recommend that you do this review and reorganization of your notes as soon as possible after class because the information may still be fresh in your mind and will become more easily locked into memory storage before forgetting takes place.

> **Remember:** Look at note-taking as a two-stage process; stage one is aggressively taking notes in class (active involvement), and stage two occurs at a later point in time—when you think about those notes more deeply (personal reflection).

Pause for Reflection

Honestly rate yourself in terms of how frequently you use the following note-taking strategies, using the following scale: 4 = always, 3 = sometimes, 2 = rarely, 1 = never.

1. I take notes aggressively in class.	4	3	2	1
2. I sit near the front of the room in my classes.	4	3	2	1
3. I sit upright and lean forward while in class.	4	3	2	1
4. I take notes on what my instructors say, not just what they write on the board.	4	3	2	1
5. I pay special attention to information presented at the very start and very end of class.	4	3	2	1
6. I take notes in paragraph form.	4	3	2	1
7. I review my notes immediately after class to check if they are complete and accurate.	4	3	2	1

■ Strategies for Improving Textbook-Reading Comprehension and Retention

© STOCKBYTE

Although keeping up with class reading is important, you should also utilize effective learning strategies to get the most from the material you read.

Following lecture notes, information from reading assignments is the second most frequent source of test questions on college exams (Brown, 1988). You will encounter test questions based on information found in your assigned readings that your professors may not have explicitly talked about in class. College professors often expect you to relate or connect what they are lecturing about in class with the reading they have assigned. Furthermore, professors often deliver class lectures with the assumption that you have done the assigned reading, so if you haven't done it, you may have great difficulty following what your instructor is saying in class. Unfortunately, studies show that only about 25 percent of students in class complete the course reading that their professor has assigned them to read before coming to class on any particular day (Hobson, 2004).

The bottom line is this: Do the assigned reading and do it according to the schedule that your instructors have assigned. This will help you comprehend lectures and improve the quality of your participation in class. Better yet, when you complete your reading assignments, use reading strategies that capitalize on the most effective principles of human learning and memory, such as those listed below.

Before Beginning to Read

Before beginning to read, first see how the assigned reading fits into the overall organizational structure of the book and the course. You can do this efficiently by just taking a look at the book's table of contents to see where the chapter you're about to read is placed in the sequence of chapters in the book, particularly the chapters that immediately precede and follow it. This will give you a sense of how the particular part you're focusing on relates to the whole. Research shows that if learners have advance knowledge of how information is organized, and if they "see the whole" (how all the information is connected) before examining its parts, their ability to understand and remember that information is improved (Ausubel, 1978; Kintsch, 1994).

Before you begin to read a chapter, preview it by reading its boldface headings and any chapter outline, objectives, summary, or end-of-chapter questions that may be provided. Sometimes when you dive into details too quickly, you lose sight of how the details relate to the big picture. As we've previously discussed, the brain's natural tendency is to perceive and comprehend whole patterns rather than isolated bits of information. Start by seeing how the different parts of the text are integrated into the whole. In so doing, you're essentially seeing the total picture of a completed jigsaw puzzle. By seeing how its separate pieces will fit together, you can more effectively comprehend the content of the chapter.

So, get in the habit of previewing what is in a chapter to get an overall sense of its organization before jumping right into the content.

After previewing the chapter, take a moment to think about what ideas or knowledge you may already have that relates to the chapter's topic. By taking a minute to think about what you may already know about the topic you're about to read, you can activate the areas of your brain where that knowledge is stored, thereby preparing it to make meaningful connections with the information you are about to read.

While Reading

Read selectively by noting or highlighting the most important information for later review. Here are three key strategies that will help you decide what to note or highlight in your reading as important information.

1. Use boldface or dark-print headings and subheadings as cues for identifying important information.

    These headings serve to organize the chapter's content, and you can use them as "traffic signs" to direct you to the chapter's most important concepts. These headings are the key clues to finding the important information in the chapter.

    Better yet, turn the headings into questions, and then read the information beneath them to find their answers. This will send you on an answer-finding mission that can keep you mentally active and allow you to read with a purpose—to find answers to the questions you've created out of the headings.

    Memory Tips: To help you remember to use this strategy, we recommend that you place a question mark after each heading while you're previewing or surveying the chapter.

    Creating and answering questions while you are reading is also motivating because you feel rewarded when you find answers to the questions you've created (Walter, Knudsbig, & Smith, 2003). Furthermore, answering questions while you are reading is an ideal way to prepare for tests because you're practicing exactly what you'll be doing on tests, which will be to answer questions. Also, you can conveniently use the heading questions as "flash cards" to review for exams by trying to remember the key information you've highlighted under each heading.

2. Pay special attention to the first and last sentences in each paragraph.

    These sentences often contain an important introduction and conclusion to the ideas covered in that passage of the text. In fact, when reading sequential or cumulative material that requires you to understand what was previously covered in order to understand what's covered next, it is a good idea to quickly reread the first and last sentences of each paragraph you've just finished reading before moving on to read the next paragraph.

3. Re-read the chapter after you've heard your instructor lecture on the chapter's topic.

    You can use your lecture notes as a guide to help you focus on what particular information in the chapter your instructor feels is most important. If you adopt this strategy, you will be able to read before lectures to help you better understand the lecture and take better class notes, and you can use your reading after lectures to help you better identify and understand the most important information contained in your textbook.

Remember: *Your goal when reading is not merely to "cover" the assigned pages, but to "uncover" the most important information and ideas contained in those pages.*

Adjust your reading speed to the type of subject matter that you're reading. Academic reading is more technical and mentally challenging than popular reading, such as reading magazines or newspapers, so do not attempt to read college texts all at the same speed. Furthermore, certain academic subjects place greater demands on your working memory than others, so you cannot expect to read all types of academic material at the same rate. For instance, material in the natural and social sciences is likely to have more technical terminology and will need to be read at a slower rate than a novel or short story. For more technical subjects, you may not understand the material when you first read it, so you may need to reread what you have just read to get a better understanding of it.

Remain aware of your reading rate. If you find yourself reading different subjects at the same speed, you may need to better regulate and accommodate your reading speed to the type of material you are reading.

Find the meaning of unfamiliar words that you encounter while reading. Knowing the meaning of specific terms is important in any college course, but it is absolutely critical in courses whose subject matter builds on knowledge of previously covered information, such as math and science. If you do not learn the meaning of key terms as you read them, you cannot build upon this knowledge to understand information that is covered later.

> **CLASSIC QUOTE**
>
> The art of reading is the art of adopting the pace the author has set. Some books are fast and some are slow, but no book can be understood if it is taken at the wrong speed.
>
> —*Mark Van Doren, Pulitzer Prize winning poet, and former professor of English, Columbia University*

Have a dictionary available, and if the textbook has a glossary, make regular use of it. In fact, you may want to make a photocopy of the textbook's glossary (typically located at the end of the text) because this will save you the hassle of having to repeatedly hold your place in the chapter with one hand while using the other to find the meaning of unfamiliar terms at the back of the textbook. The more effort it takes to look up words you don't know, the less likely you are to do it, so make your access to a glossary and dictionary as convenient as possible.

Take written notes on what you're reading. Just as you take notes in response to your instructor's spoken words in class, take notes in response to the author's written words in your text. For example, write short answers to the boldface heading questions in a reading notebook or in the text itself, using its side, top, and bottom margins. Writing requires more active thinking than highlighting because you are generating words on your own, which are words that have personal meaning to you (rather than passively highlighting words written by someone else). Try not to get into the habit of using your textbook as a coloring book, where you get so into the artwork of highlighting in metallic, kaleidoscopic colors that the artistic process becomes more important than the process of thinking actively and deeply about what you are reading.

> **CLASSIC QUOTE**
>
> I would advise you to read with a pen in your hand, and enter in a little book of short hints of what you find that is curious, or that might be useful; for this will be the best method of imprinting such particulars in your memory, where they will be ready.
>
> —*Benjamin Franklin, eighteenth-century inventor, politician, and co-signer of the* Declaration of Independence

Remember that you can write in your textbook because you own it. Even if you intend to sell it at the end of the term, you can still write in it by using a pencil and you can even highlight it in pencil—by simply bracketing or underlining key sentences. If you eventually decide to sell your book back, then you can erase the pencil markings and

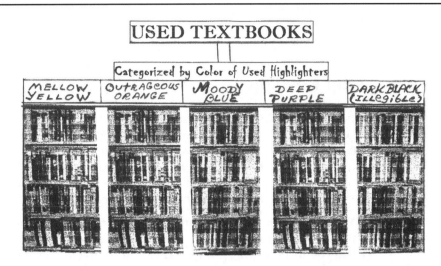

Highlighting textbooks in spectacular colors is a very popular reading strategy among college students, but it's a less effective strategy for producing deep learning than taking written notes on what you read.

probably end up with a book that will have higher resale value than one covered with hallucinogenic-like highlighting. In fact, pencils are more versatile reading tools than highlighters because they can be used more easily to do a variety of things, such as recording written notes, drawing figures or symbols, and making changes to your notes by erasing and rewriting.

Pause for Reflection

When reading a textbook, which of the following items do you usually have on hand?

Highlighter: Yes No

Pen or pencil: Yes No

Notebook: Yes No

Class notes: Yes No

Dictionary: Yes No

Make use of the visual aids that are provided in your textbooks. Don't fall into the trap of thinking that visual aids can or should be skipped because they merely supplement the written words of the text. Visual aids, such as charts, graphs, diagrams, and concept maps are powerful learning and memory tools for a couple of reasons:

1. They enable you to visualize information as a picture or image, and

2. They can organize many separate pieces of information into one meaningful whole.

Furthermore, viewing them gives you a periodic break from continually reading written words, allowing you to experience a different form of mental stimulation, which should increase your attention to what you're reading, as well as your motivation to read.

After Reading

Finish your reading session with a short review of the information that you've noted or highlighted. Forgetting information that your brain has just processed tends to occur most rapidly immediately after you stop focusing on it (Underwood, 1983). Taking a few minutes at the end of your reading time to review the most important information that you've noted or highlighted serves to lock in your memory of it before you turn your attention to something else and forget what you have just read.

Collaborate with peers to improve the effectiveness of your reading. The same benefits of participating in small-group discussions and study groups can be experienced when you form reading groups. After you complete your reading assignments, you can team-up with classmates to compare your highlighting and margin notes. You can consult with each other to identify major points in the reading, and help each other identify what information is most important to study for upcoming exams.

If you find that a certain concept explained in your text is difficult to understand, take a look at how another textbook explains that concept. Not all textbooks are created equally; some do a better job of explaining certain concepts than others. Another text may be able to explain a hard-to-understand concept much better than the textbook you purchased for the course. So, keep this option open by checking to see if your library has other texts in the same subject as your course, or check your campus bookstore for other textbooks in the same subject area as the course you're taking.

Pause for Reflection

Honestly rate yourself in terms of how frequently you use the following reading strategies according to the following scale:

4 = always, 3 = sometimes, 2 = rarely, 1 = never.

1. *I read the chapter outlines and summaries before I start reading a chapter.* 4 3 2 1
2. *I preview a chapter's boldface headings and subheadings before I begin to read the chapter.* 4 3 2 1
3. *I adjust my reading speed to the type of subject I am reading.* 4 3 2 1
4. *I look up the meaning of unfamiliar words and unknown terms that I come across before I read any further.* 4 3 2 1
5. *I take written notes on information I read.* 4 3 2 1
6. *I use the visual aids included in my textbooks.* 4 3 2 1
7. *I finish my reading sessions with a review of the important information that I noted or highlighted.* 4 3 2 1

■ Study Strategies

© COMSTOCK

When studying complex material, you need to give your complete and undivided attention to this task. Listening to music is a distraction that will shift your focus away from the information you are trying to learn.

Effective note-taking and reading ensures that you receive and gain access to the information that will show up on exams. The next step is to get that information stored in your brain so that you can later retrieve it at test time. Described below is a series of strategies for effectively storing information in your brain while studying.

Minimize Distractions

Maximize your attention while studying by blocking out all distracting sources of outside stimulation. As mentioned earlier, attention comes in a fixed quantity or amount; you can give all of it or part of it to whatever task you're working on. When you're involved with the task of studying complex material, this requires your complete and undivided attention. You don't want to divide your attention among multiple tasks by trying to study and process other information at the same time, such as listening to music, watching television, or exchanging instant messages with a friend.

Research on such multi-tasking consistently shows that trying to do more than one task at the same time interferes with the performance of the primary task you're working on—especially if that primary task involves complex thinking (Crawford & Strapp, 1994). In fact, when people multi-task, studies show that they don't pay equal and maximum attention to different tasks at the same time; instead, what they do is alternate or shift their attention back and forth from one task to another (Howard, 2000). The result is that they lose attention to one of the tasks for a while before returning to it. Probably the most common example of the dangers of trying

Studies show that doing challenging academic work while multi-tasking divides up attention and drives down comprehension and retention.

to focus on more than one task at the same time is driving a car while talking on a cell phone. Studies have repeatedly shown that a person's driving attention and performance are reduced when they try to drive and use a cell phone simultaneously (Redelmeier & Tibshirani, 1997).

Sights and sounds unrelated to what we're trying to learn tend to compete for and interfere with our attention during the learning process. When people say that they learn just as well or better while they listen to music or watch TV, this doesn't turn out to be true when they are actually tested (Crawford & Strapp, 1994). Even all the hype about how listening to classical music while studying can accelerate learning is not supported by research (Wagner & Tilney, 1983). The bottom line is that when you are learning challenging concepts or performing mental tasks that you cannot do automatically, competing external stimulation interferes with the quiet, internal reflection time needed to form deep, long-lasting connections between brain cells (Jensen, 1998).

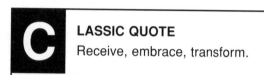

CLASSIC QUOTE
Receive, embrace, transform.

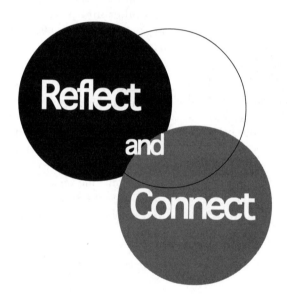

Find Meaning in Terms

Each academic field has its own specialized vocabulary that can almost sound like a foreign language to someone who has no experience in the subject area. Before you start to brutally beat these terms into your brain through sheer repetition, try to find some meaning in them, or in some part of them. You can make a meaningless term more meaningful to you by looking up its word root in the dictionary or by identifying its prefix or suffix that may give away the term's meaning. For instance, if you were studying the autonomic nervous system in biology, which is the part of the nervous system that operates without our conscious or voluntary control (e.g., our heart beating and lungs breathing), its meaning is given away by its prefix "auto"—which means self-controlling, as in the word "automatic."

If the term's root, prefix, or suffix does not give away its meaning, then see if you can make it more meaningful to you in some other way. For instance, suppose you looked up the root of the term "artery," and nothing about the origins of this term reveals its meaning or purpose. You could then create your own meaning for this term by taking its first letter ("a"), and have it stand for "<u>a</u>way"—to help you remember that arteries carry blood *away* from the heart. Thus, you've taken a meaningless biological term and made it more personally meaningful (and memorable).

Compare and Contrast

When you're studying something new, get in the habit of asking yourself the following questions:

Is this similar or comparable to something I've already learned?

How does this differ from, or contrast with, what I already know?

Research indicates that this simple strategy is one of the most powerful ways to promote learning of academic information (Marzano, Pickering, & Pollock, 2001). The power of the compare-and-contrast strategy probably stems from the fact that asking yourself, "How is this similar to and different than something that I already know?" makes learning more personally meaningful by encouraging you to relate what you're trying to learn to what you already know.

Integrate Information

Pull together information from your class notes and your assigned reading that relate to the same major concept or category; for example, get them in the same place by recording them on the same index card under the same category heading. The category heading can function like the hub of a wheel, around which individual pieces of information are attached like spokes. This will improve your learning and memory by strengthening its organization, plus it will enable you to study all course material relating to the same topic at the same time.

In contrast, when information relating to different concepts is separated in physical space, it helps you to separate them mentally, and prevents all that information from running together in your mind and confusing you.

Spreading out your studying into shorter sessions improves your memory by reducing loss of attention due to fatigue.

Divide and Conquer

Effective learning depends not only on your study method, it also depends on when you learn—your timing. Although cramming just prior to exams is better than not studying at all, it is far less effective than studying that is spread out across time. Rather than cramming all your studying into one long session, use the *distributed practice* method, which spreads out study time into several shorter sessions. Research consistently shows that short, periodic practice sessions are more effective than a single marathon session. For instance, in one study of students who were learning Spanish, half of them studied many Spanish words in a single day, while another group studied the same number of words for the same amount of time, but their study time was broken up into a number of shorter sessions held at different times. Eight years later, the students were tested for their memory of these Spanish words. Those students who learned the words in the one-day cram session recalled an average of 6 percent of the words, while students who studied the words in several shorter sessions remembered 25 percent of the words—more than four times the amount remembered by the cramming group (Bahrick & Phelps, 1987).

Spreading out your studying into shorter sessions serves to improve your memory because it:

- reduces loss of attention due to fatigue or boredom, and
- reduces mental interference by giving the brain some "cool down" time to process and lock-in information that it has received without being interrupted by the need to take in additional information (Murname & Shiffrin, 1991).

If this downtime is interfered with by the need to process additional information, the brain gets overloaded and its memory for new information becomes impaired. This is exactly what cramming does—it interferes with the brain's need for downtime by overloading it with lots of information in a limited period of time. In contrast, distributed study does just the opposite—it spreads out learning into shorter sessions with downtime in-between sessions, which allows the brain to store information that has been previously studied. To illustrate this point, consider how difficult it would be to recall the names of ten new people you meet in one evening, compared with recalling the names of ten people you meet on ten separate evenings.

Another major advantage of distributed study is that it is less stressful and more motivating than cramming. You should feel more motivated to study because you know that you're not going to have to do it for a long stretch of time and lose any sleep over it. Furthermore, you should feel more relaxed because if you discover something that you don't understand, you know that you still have time to get help with it before you'll be tested and graded on it.

Distributing study time throughout the term is particularly crucial in college courses because tests are often given less frequently than in high school. In some college courses, you may take only two to three tests per term, and those tests will cover large amounts of material. So, resist the temptation to procrastinate and cram all information into your brain on the day (or night) before the exam; and don't buy into the belief that "I work better under pressure" (which often really means, "I *only* work under pressure because I procrastinate and have no other choice").

Use a "Part-to-Whole" Method of Studying

Divide your studying into small parts or units, and then learn these parts in several short, separate study sessions in advance of exams.

TUDENT PERSPECTIVE

"Do not cram. If you start to prepare for a test about 3–5 days before, then you will only need to do a quick review the night before."

—*Advice to freshmen from an experienced student, Walsh (2005)*

The part-to-whole method of studying is consistent with and flows naturally from the distributed practice method of studying that we just discussed. With the part-to-whole method, your last study session prior to the exam is one in which you re-study what you previously studied in short sessions altogether at one time. Thus, your last study session is a review session, not a session during which you're trying to learn information for the first time.

Do not underestimate the power of studying small pieces of course material in short, separate study sessions in advance of exams. The part-to-whole study method is often resisted because of the following common (and dangerous) belief: Studying done in advance of an exam is a total "waste of time" because you'll "forget it all by the time you take the test." This is a flat-out fallacy because memory for information that you study in advance of an exam is still in your brain when you later review the day or night before the exam. Even if you cannot recall the previously studied information when you first start reviewing it, you will re-learn it much faster than you did the first time you studied it, thus proving that some memory of it was still retained in your brain (Kintsch, 1994).

The time you save when you review and re-learn something a second time is referred to by memory researchers as "relearning savings time" (Gordon, 1989) in other words, it is the amount of time saved when re-learning and remembering something a second time compared to the time it took to learn and remember it the first time. For example, suppose a student took French in high school and knew the French words for chair, table, floor, and ceiling, but two years later, this person can no longer recall the French translations of these words. So, it appears as if these French words learned in high school were completely forgotten. However, if you were to calculate the time this person would need to re-learn these French words and compare it to the amount of time it took to first learn them two years ago, much less time would be needed to re-learn these words the second time. The amount of time saved when re-learning the words the second time indicates that those French words learned in high school have not been totally forgotten; instead, traces of their memory are still in the student's brain, which enables them to be relearned much faster the next time around.

So, the old expression, "If you don't use it, you'll lose it," is not quite accurate when it comes to material that has been studied during the course of a term. Traces of these previous memories are not totally lost or erased from your brain; they are just weakened or lightened (Alnon, 1992). Often, all it takes is a mental "tune up" to get them up and working again. Thus, distributing studying into smaller parts in advance of a test is not a waste of time because it allows for re-learning savings time—plus reduced memory interference, reduced stress, and improved sleep that occur with distributed study compared to last-minute, late-night cramming.

Begin with a Review

For sequential or cumulative subjects that build on understanding of previously covered information to learn new information (e.g., math), begin each study session with a quick review of what you learned in your previous study session.

Consuming large doses of caffeine or other stimulants to stay awake for all-night cram sessions is likely to maximize anxiety and minimize memory.

Research shows that students of all ability levels learn course material more effectively when it's studied in small units, and when progression to the next unit takes place only after the previous unit has been mastered or understood (Pascarella & Terenzini, 1991, 2005). This strategy ensures that students build on their previous knowledge to understand what's coming next, and it enables *over-learning* to take place—that is, reviewing information that has already been learned further reinforces and strengthens its memory. This is particularly important in cumulative subjects that require memory for problem-solving procedures or steps, such as math and science. Continued practice of these procedures serves to make them become more automatic so you're able to retrieve them quicker (e.g., on a timed test) and use them without devoting all your mental energy to them (Newell & Rosenbloom, 1981). This frees up your working memory to focus on higher-level thinking and creative problem-solving (Schneider & Chein, 2003).

Change Things Up

Periodically change the type of academic tasks you're performing while studying. Change in work routine and in the type of mental task performed serves to increase your level of alertness and concentration by reducing "habituation"—attention loss that tends to occur after repeated exposure to the same learning task (McGuiness & Pribram, 1980). So, look to vary the type of task or work you're doing while studying. For instance, shift periodically across tasks that involve reading, writing, studying (e.g., rehearsing or reciting) and practicing skills (e.g., solving problems).

Study different subjects in different places. Different study locations provide different environmental contexts for learning, which tends to reduce the amount of interference that would normally build up if all the information was studied in the same place (Anderson & Bower, 1974). Memory research shows when lists of information are learned in different environments, memory interference is reduced. In one study, students who learned a group of 40 words in two separate study sessions held in the same room recalled an average of 15.9 words on a later memory test. In contrast, students who studied the words for the same amount of time, but whose study sessions took place in two distinctively different rooms, recalled an average of 24.4 words (Smith, Glenberg, & Bjork, 1978).

Thus, it may not only be a good idea to spread out your studying at different times, it may also be a good idea to spread out your studying in different places. In fact, ancient Greek and Roman speakers used this method of changing places to remember long speeches by walking through different rooms, mentally associating different parts of their speech with different rooms (Higbee, 1998).

The brain's attention system has a particular area that is specialized for attention to location (Ackerman, 1992), so changes in the place or space where learning occurs can stimulate greater attention (Schacter, 1992), in part because the change and novelty of the new environment provides greater sensory stimulation to the brain (La Berge, 1995). Even the act of standing up and moving to a new location can have positive effects on mental performance and brain functioning (Jensen, 1998) because it increases circulation of oxygen-carrying blood to the brain and stimulates areas of the brain that play a key role in learning (Middleton & Strick, 1994).

This research suggests that changes in the nature of the learning task and the learning environment provide changes of pace that infuse some variety into the learning process, which can improve your attention to and concentration on what you're studying. Although it may be useful to have a set schedule of study times during the week to get you into a regular, habit-forming work routine, this doesn't mean that learning occurs best by habitually performing the same learning tasks while sitting in the same seat at the same place. Instead, you should make periodic changes in the learning tasks you're performing and the environments in which you perform them to maximize attention and minimize interference (Druckman & Bjork, 1991).

> **Remember:** *Studying will be more effective if:*
>
> - *there is separation of your study material into smaller parts and separation of your study time into shorter sessions; and*
>
> - *there is variation in the type of study tasks you perform and in the study places where you perform them.*

Use All of Your Senses

When studying course material, try to use as many different sensory channels as possible because research clearly indicates that information stored through more than one sensory modality is better remembered (Bjork, 1994; Schacter, 1992). When a memory is stored in the brain, different sensory aspects of it are stored in different areas. For example, the visual, auditory, and motor sensations associated with what you're learning are all stored in different parts of the brain. Thus, when you use all of these sensory channels while learning, multiple "memory traces" of what you're studying are recorded in your brain, which leads to stronger memory (Education Commission of the States, 1996). Listed below are some of the major channels through which learning occurs and memories are stored, accompanied by specific strategies for using each of these channels while studying.

1. **Visual Learning**

   The human brain consists of two halves or hemispheres: the left hemisphere and the right hemisphere (Figure 7). Each of these hemispheres specializes in a different type of learning. In most people, the left hemisphere specializes in verbal learning, dealing primarily with words. In contrast, the right hemisphere specializes in visual-spatial learning, dealing primarily with images. Thus, if you use both words and images to learn the information you're studying, two memory traces are recorded in different halves of your brain: One memory trace is recorded in the left hemisphere—where words are encoded—and one in the right hemisphere—where images are encoded. This process of laying down a double memory trace (verbal and visual) is referred to as *dual coding* (Paivio, 1990). When this happens, memory for what you're learning is substantially strengthened, primarily because two memory traces are better than one.

   To capitalize on the advantage of dual coding, make use of any visual aids that are available to you. Use the visual aids provided in your textbook and by your instructor, and create your own by drawing pictures, symbols, or concept maps—such as flow charts or branching tree diagrams. Drawing is not just an artistic exercise; it can be used as a learning tool as well—you can draw to learn. By taking words and ideas and representing them in visual form, the resulting drawing enables you to dual code the information you're studying, doubling the number of memory traces recorded in your brain.

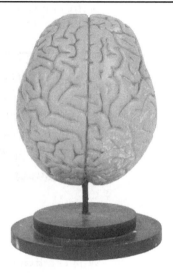

The human brain consists of two halves, known as the left hemisphere and the right hemisphere.

© 2007 JUPITERIMAGES CORPORATION

Figure 7 ■

Pause for Reflection

People remember faces better than they do names. Why do you think this is?

2. **Motor Learning (also known as Muscle Memory)**
   In addition to hearing and seeing, movement is another sensory channel that provides the brain with kinesthetic stimulation—the sensations we get from our body's muscles as a result of physical movement. Memory traces for movement are commonly stored in the cerebellum—an area in the lower back of the brain. Brain research indicates that this part of the brain plays a major role in all types of learning (Middleton & Strick, 1994). Thus, associating movement with what you're learning can improve your ability to retain it because you record an additional "muscle memory trace" of it to another area of your brain.

Personal Story

I was talking about memory in class one day and mentioned that if I forget how to spell a word, when I start to write it out, I often remember its correct spelling. One of my students then raised her hand and said the same thing happens to her when she forgets a phone number—it comes back to her when she starts dialing it. Both cases of memories coming back when movement began (writing and dialing) are classic cases of how a muscle memory trace can trigger recall of verbal or factual information that is associated with movement.

—*Joe Cuseo*

You can use movement to help you learn and retain academic information by using your body to act out what you're studying or to symbolize it with your hands (Kagan & Kagan, 1998). For example, if you're

STUDENT PERSPECTIVE
"I have to *hear* it, *see* it, *write* it, and *talk* about it."
—*First-year student, responding to the question: "How do you learn best?"*

Adjusting Your Academic Work to Your Biological Rhythms

■ *When planning your daily work schedule, be aware of your natural "biological rhythms"—your* peak periods *and* down times. *Studies show that humans vary in terms of when they naturally prefer to fall asleep and wake up; some are "early birds" who prefer to go to sleep early and wake up early, and others are "night owls" who prefer to stay up late at night and get up late in the morning (Natale & Ciogna, 1996). (Teenagers more often fall into the category of "night owls.") As a result of these differences in sleeping patterns, individuals will vary with respect to the times of day when they experience their highest and lowest levels of physical energy. Naturally, "early birds" are more likely to be "morning" people whose peak energy period occurs before noon; and "night owls" are likely to be more productive in the late afternoon and evening. Also, most people experience a "post-lunch" dip in energy in the early afternoon (Monk, 2005).*

■ *Be aware of your most productive hours of the day and schedule your highest priority work and most challenging tasks at times when you tend to work at peak effectiveness. For example, schedule your out-of-class work so that you're tackling academic tasks that require intense thinking (e.g., technical writing or complex problem-solving) at times of the day when you tend to be most productive, and schedule lighter work (e.g., light reading or routine tasks) at times when your energy level tends to be lower. Also, keep your natural peak and down times in mind when you schedule your courses. Attempt to arrange your class schedule in such a way that you experience your most challenging courses at times of the day when your body and mind are most ready to accept that challenge.*

trying to remember five points about something (e.g., five key consequences of the Civil War), when you're studying these points, count them out on your fingers as you try to recall each of them. Also, remember that talking itself involves muscle movement of your lips and tongue. Thus, by speaking aloud when you're studying, either to a friend or to yourself, your memory of what you're studying should be improved by adding kinesthetic stimulation to your brain (along with the auditory or sound stimulation your brain receives from hearing what you're saying).

Emotional Learning and Memory

Just as information reaches the brain through the senses and is stored in the brain as a memory trace, the same is true of emotions. There are numerous connections between brain cells in the emotional and memory centers of the human brain (Zull, 1998). For instance, when we're experiencing emotional excitement and energy about what we are learning, adrenaline is released and is carried through the blood stream to our brain. Once adrenaline reaches the brain, it increases blood flow and glucose production, which can stimulate learning and strengthen memory (LeDoux, 1998; Rosenfield, 1988). In fact, if an experience is very emotionally intense, the amount of adrenaline that is released can immediately and permanently store the memory in the brain for the remainder of a person's life. For instance, most people can remember exactly what they were doing at the time they experienced such emotionally intense events as the

LASSIC QUOTE
Education is not the filling of a pail, but the lighting of a fire.
—*William Butler Yeats,
Irish poet and playwright*

September 11th terrorist attack on the United States, or their first kiss, or when their favorite team won a world championship.

What does this emotion-memory link have to do with helping you remember academic information that you're studying? Research on human emotions suggests that emotional intensity, excitement, and enthusiasm do make a real difference for learning and memory. If you get "psyched up" about what you're learning, you have a much better chance of learning and remembering it. Even telling yourself that you want to learn and that you intend to remember what you're learning can increase your memory of it (Minninger, 1984; Howard, 2000).

Form Study Groups

Group learning is a natural, "brain compatible" form of learning. The human brain is biologically wired for interpersonal communication because social interaction and collaboration are critical to survival of the human species (Jensen, 1998). In fact, brain-imaging studies reveal that more activity occurs in thinking parts of the brain when people learn through social interaction than when they are learning alone or in isolation (Carter, 1998).

Research has shown that college students learn as much, or more, from peers than they do from instructors and textbooks (Astin, 1993; Pascarella, 2005). When seniors at Harvard University were interviewed, nearly every one of them who had been part of a study group considered this experience to be crucial to their academic progress and success (Light, 1990, 1992).

> **STUDENT PERSPECTIVE**
>
> "I learn best through teaching. When I learn something and teach it to someone else, I find that it really sticks with me a lot better."
>
> —College sophomore's response to the question: "How do you learn best?"

To fully capitalize and maximize the power of study groups, each member should study individually *before* studying in a group. Research on study groups indicates that they are effective only if each member has done required course work in advance of the group meeting—for example, if each group member has done the required readings and other course assignments (Light, 2001). All members should come prepared with specific information or answers to share with teammates as well as specific questions or points of

© 2007 JUPITERIMAGES CORPORATION

Forming a study group is an excellent learning strategy.

TUDENT PERSPECTIVE

"I would suggest students get to know [each] other and get together in groups to study or at least review class material. I find it is easier to ask your friends or classmates with whom you are comfortable with 'dumb' questions."
—*Advice to first-year students from college sophomore (Walsh, 2005)*

confusion about which they hope to receive help from the team. This ensures that all group members are individually accountable or personally responsible for their own learning and for contributing to the learning of their teammates.

Personal Story

When I was in my senior year of college, I had to take a theory course by independent study because the course would not be offered again until after I planned to graduate. There was another senior who found himself in the same situation. Thus, the theory instructor allowed both of us to take this course together and agreed to meet with us every two weeks. My fellow student and I studied independently for the first two weeks. I prepared for the bi-weekly meeting by reading thoroughly, yet I had little understanding of what I had read. After our first meeting, I left with a strong desire to drop the course; however, I stayed with it. Over the next two weeks, I spent many sleepless nights trying to prepare for our next meeting and had feelings of angst about not being the brightest theory student in my class of two. During the next meeting with the instructor, I found out that the other student was also having difficulty. Not only did I notice this, but the instructor also noticed. After that meeting, the instructor gave us study questions and asked us to read separately and then get together to discuss the questions. During the next two weeks, my classmate and I met several times for some stimulating discussions on theory. By being able to communicate with each other about the issues we were studying, we both ended up gaining greater understanding. Our instructor was delighted to see that he was able to suggest a learning strategy that worked for both of us.

—Aaron Thompson

Pause for Reflection

Honestly rate yourself in terms of how frequently you use the following study strategies, according to the following scale:

4 = always, 3 = sometimes, 2 = rarely, 1 = never.

1. *I block out all distracting sources of outside stimulation when I study.*   4 3 2 1

2. *I look for meaning in technical terms by looking at their prefix or suffix, or by looking up their word root in the dictionary.*   4 3 2 1

3. *I compare and contrast what I'm currently studying to what I've already learned.*   4 3 2 1

4. *I organize the information I'm studying into categories or classes.*   4 3 2 1

5. *I integrate or pull together information from my class notes and readings that relate to the same concept or general category.*   4 3 2 1

6. *I distribute or "spread out" my study time into several short sessions in advance of the exam and use my last study session before the test to review the information I previously studied.*   4 3 2 1

7. *I participate in study groups with my classmates.*   4 3 2 1

■ Self-Reflection and Self-Monitoring

Rather than mindlessly going through the motions of learning, *deep* learning requires self-reflection. Effective learners reflect and check on themselves to see if they're really understanding what they're attempting to learn, monitoring their comprehension as they go along by asking themselves questions such as, "Am I following this?" "Do I really understand it?"

CLASSIC QUOTE

We are born for cooperation, as are the feet, the hands, the eyelids, and the upper and lower jaws.
—*Marcus Aurelius,*
Roman Emperor, 161–180, A.D.

How do you know if you really know it? Probably the best answer to this question is: you know if you really know it and truly comprehend it when you find meaning in it—that is, when you can relate to it personally or can understand it in terms that make sense to you (Ramsden, 2003). When you comprehend a concept, you've learned it at a deeper level than mere memorization; and when you comprehend it, you're more likely to remember it because learning that is deep is also more durable—it stays in long-term memory for a greater length of time (Kintsch, 1970).

Discussed below are some specific strategies for checking to see if you truly understand what you're learning. These can be used as indicators or checkpoints for determining whether you've moved beyond memorization to deeper understanding of what you're studying.

Comprehension Self-Monitoring Strategies

- Can you paraphrase what you're learning? Can you restate or translate it into your own words? When you can paraphrase what you're learning, you're able to describe it by completing the sentence that begins with the phrase, "In other words, ..." This is a good indication that you've moved beyond memorization to comprehension because you have transformed what you're learning into words that are meaningful to you. Even better than saying it in your own words is writing it in your own words, because this will reinforce your memory of it and give you a record of it for later review.
- Can you explain what you're learning to someone else who is unfamiliar with it? If you can explain to a friend what you've learned, this is a good sign that you've moved beyond memorization to comprehension because you are able to translate it into less technical language that someone hearing it for the first time can understand. Studies show that students gain deeper levels of understanding for what they're learning when they are asked to explain it to someone else (Chi, et al., 1994). Often, we don't realize how well we know or don't know something until we have to explain it to someone else who's never heard of it before (just ask any teacher). If you cannot find anyone to explain it to, then explain it aloud as if you were talking to an "imaginary friend."
- Can you think of an example of what you've learned? If you can provide an example or instance that is your own—not one that has already been given by your teacher or text—this is a good sign that you truly comprehend it because you're taking a general and abstract concept or principle and applying it to a specific and concrete experience. In fact, research indicates that when humans recall technical terms they have learned, they don't retrieve the definition first; instead, they retrieve an example or concrete instance of the term and use that example or instance to reconstruct the term's meaning (Norman, 1982; Tulving, 1985). This illustrates how important concrete examples are to understanding

and retaining abstract concepts. (Have you ever noticed that when students are having trouble understanding something abstract or theoretical, they often ask their instructor: "Can you give me an example?")

■ Can you represent or describe what you've learned in terms of an analogy or metaphor, which compares it to something else that has similar meaning or works in a similar way? Analogies and metaphors are basically ways of learning something new by understanding it in terms of something else that is similar and that we already understand. For instance, in this chapter we used the computer as a metaphor for the human brain to better understand learning and memory as a three-stage process. If you can use an analogy or metaphor to represent what you're learning, this is a good sign that you understand it at a deep level because you've built a mental bridge to connect what you're trying to understand to something that you already understand.

■ Can you apply what you're learning to solve a particular problem that you've never encountered before? Perhaps the strongest sign of deep learning and comprehension is the ability to transfer something you've learned in one situation and apply it in a different context. Learning specialists sometimes refer to this mental process as "de-contextualization"—taking what has been learned in one context or situation and applying it to another (Bransford, Brown, & Cocking, 1999).

For instance, you know that you've really understood a mathematical concept when you can use that concept to solve math problems that are different than those which were used by your instructor or textbook to help you learn it in the first place. This is why it's unlikely that your math instructors will include on exams the exact same problems they solved in class or were solved in your textbook. They're not trying to trick you at test time; they're just trying to test your comprehension to determine if you've deeply learned the concept or principle, rather than simply memorized it. Similarly, if you took a course in human relations and learned the principles of conflict management, and you were later able to use those principles to settle a dispute between yourself and your roommate, this suggests you have deeply learned and understood those principles.

In fact, one of the key differences between deep learning and surface memorization is that when you've learned something deeply, you're able to continually put that learning to use in future situations that you have never encountered before (Anderson & Krathwohl, 2001). When you have simply memorized something, its future use is restricted to the same, exact situation in which you originally learned it.

CLASSIC QUOTE

The habit of active utilization of well-understood principles is the final possession of wisdom.

—*Paul Ramsden,*
Chancellor of Teaching and Learning,
University of Sydney (Australia)

Knowledge Awareness Strategies

Remain aware of the type of knowledge that you're trying to acquire and adjust your study strategy accordingly. Knowledge comes in different forms and involves different learning and memory systems. The key types of knowledge you will acquire in college usually fall into one of the following major categories.

Declarative (Semantic) Knowledge: knowing what is accurate or true and that you can "declare" or state it in words (e.g., factual information). Acquiring this type of knowledge requires studying that involves effective use of recitation or memory-improvement strategies, such as meaningful association, acrostics, or rhythm and rhyme.

Procedural (Skill) Knowledge: knowing how to do something, which usually involves procedures or skills that have multiple steps (e.g., solving math problems, conducting science experiments). Acquiring this type of knowledge requires repeated practice or rehearsal, such as practicing delivery of a speech or lines in a play. However, this repeated practice should be reflective practice, not mindless repetition. Although repetition is needed to develop certain skills, they are often developed more deeply and more rapidly if you reflect on and remain aware of the learning and thinking *process* that you are using while practicing.

CLASSIC QUOTE

We learn to do neither by thinking nor by doing; we learn to do by thinking about what we are doing.
—*George Stoddard, former professor of psychology and education, University of Iowa*

Studies show that students who consciously attend to their own thought processes when solving math and science problems become more effective problem solvers than those who just go through the motions (Resnick, 1986). For instance, expert problem-solvers ask themselves such questions as, "How did I go about solving this problem correctly?" "What were the key steps I took to arrive at the correct solution?" These are important questions to ask yourself while practicing any problem-solving skill, because you want to understand and recall the thought process behind the skill so you can use that successful thought process again in the future (e.g., on upcoming exams).

Episodic Knowledge: knowing where something is located—its place in space. The term episodic derives from "epi" meaning "on" or "at" and "odic" meaning "path." So, literally, it refers to knowing the specific place or space where something is located in relation to other things along the same path. For example, if you are taking a course in anatomy and you are trying to learn the location of each one of the internal organs of the body or each major part of the human brain, you are trying to acquire episodic knowledge. Acquiring this type of knowledge requires study strategies that make effective use of visual learning techniques, such as diagrams, concept maps, and visual imagery.

Pause for Reflection

Do you change or adjust your studying strategy, depending on the type of test you're going to take, or do you tend to study the same way for all tests?

CLASSIC QUOTE

Each problem that I solved became a rule which served afterwards to solve other problems.
—*René Descartes, seventeenth-century French philosopher and mathematician*

■ Summary and Conclusion

We covered a lot of territory in this chapter, moving through all stages of the learning and memory process—from the very first stage of perceiving and receiving information through lectures and readings, to studying and storing information in the brain, and finally, to the stage of retrieving and recalling information.

The major principles and strategies associated with academic success at all stages in the learning and memory process are consistent with, and strongly reinforce, the four major bases of college success that we discussed in the first chapter of this text, namely: active involvement, self-reflection, social interaction/collaboration, and utilizing campus resources. These four bases can be used to summarize the most important learning and memory strategies that were discussed in this chapter.

Active Involvement

This principle of college success suggests that college students need to be active agents in the learning process (rather than passive sponges or spectators), and that academic success depends on the amount or degree of personal time, effort, and energy invested in learning. The importance of this principle emerged at the very start of this chapter when it was noted that deep learning involves active building of knowledge, whereby you shape and mold information to be learned into a form that has personal meaning for you. This importance of active involvement was also evident throughout all three key stages of the learning and memory process that were discussed in the chapter. First, active attention is needed for information to be perceived and received by your conscious brain. Second, information is saved in the brain through the investment of mental, physical, and emotional energy. Third, information is actively retrieved from the brain and brought back to consciousness when taking exams.

> *Remember: We learn most effectively when we actively involve all our senses, and when we learn with passion and enthusiasm. In other words, learning becomes deeper and lasts longer when you put your "whole self" into it—your mind, your body, and your heart.*

Self-Reflection

Deep learning not only requires action, it also requires reflection. Both mental processes are needed for learning to be complete. Active involvement is necessary for engaging our attention—which enables us to initially get information into our brain—and quiet reflection is necessary for consolidation—keeping that information in our brain, by locking it into our long-term memory. Rather than immediately jumping in and pounding in what we're trying to learn through mindless repetition, we need to take a pause for a worthy cause—to reflect and connect it with something that's already in our brain.

Reflection also involves awareness of ourselves as learners. We need to periodically pause and reflect on what is going on in our mind during different learning tasks. For instance, you should occasionally step back and think about whether you are actively listening to what your instructor is saying in class, and whether you are deeply understanding what you're studying outside of class. Also, you should occasionally step back and reflect on whether you are using learning strategies that are effective for the type of material you're studying and the type of test you'll be taking.

Said in another way, you want to be a self-regulated learner (Pintrich, 1995) who is self-aware and is in control of your own effort and attention, and who can regulate or adjust:

- *how* you learn to what you are learning—adjusting your study strategies to the type of subject you're studying and the type of test you're taking,
- *when* you are learning—adjusting your study time and timing, and
- *where* you are learning—adjusting your study situation or environment.

Social Interaction/Collaboration

One of the four key bases of college success is interpersonal interaction and collaboration. Learning is strengthened when it takes place in a social context that involves human interaction.

Your two primary sources for social interaction relating to your classes are your faculty instructors and your classmates. Student interaction with faculty is positively associated with improved academic performance and increased likelihood of completing a college degree (Astin, 1993; Tinto, 1993), so take advantage of opportunities to discuss course material with your instructors immediately after class and during their office hours. The educational benefit of interacting and collaborating with your peers is well supported by research (Johnson, Johnson, & Smith, 1991). As we noted earlier in this chapter, you can collaborate with your classmates at any stage of the learning and memory process. You can form:

- **note-taking teams** immediately after class by taking a few minutes to team up with a classmate to compare your notes for accuracy and completeness;
- **reading teams,** teaming up with classmates to compare your highlighting and margin notes;
- **study teams** to prepare for upcoming exams, and
- **test-results review teams** by collaborating with other classmates to review your results together, compare answers, and identify the sources of your mistakes.

Utilizing Campus Resources

The professionals who work in the Learning Resource or Academic Success Center on your campus have been professionally trained to help you learn "how to learn." These professionals are experts on the process of learning and can help you adjust or regulate your learning strategies to meet the demands of different courses and teaching styles. This Center provides learning support in multiple formats, including instructional videos, self-assessment instruments for assessing your personal learning habits, strategies or styles, and peer tutors—who can be especially effective teachers because they are developmentally closer to you in terms of their stage of intellectual development and level of communication (Vygotsky, 1978; Whitman, 1988).

Take full advantage of the multiple forms of support that your Learning Resource or Academic Success Center can offer you. Utilizing its services should strengthen your learning and elevate your grades.

Before you exit this chapter, we would like to remind you that the learning and memory strategies discussed here are more than just "study" skills or "academic" success skills; they are *life success* skills or *lifelong learning* skills that you can and will use throughout the remainder of your personal and professional life. For example, the skills of focusing attention and active listening are not only useful in the classroom, but in social relationships outside of class and throughout life; and note taking itself is a skill that you will continue to use throughout your career (e.g., during professional meetings and committee work).

Furthermore, these lifelong learning skills are probably more important today than at any other time in history because we are now living in an era characterized by rapid technological change and dramatic growth of knowledge. This information and communication explosion is creating a greater need for people to learn continuously throughout life and a higher demand for working professionals who are skilled learners—who have learned how to learn (Niles & Harris-Bowlsbey, 2002; Herman, 2000).

> **Remember:** Putting into practice the learning strategies discussed in this chapter will not only help you prepare for college tests, it will also help you prepare for lifelong learning.

■ Learning More through Independent Research

Web-Based Resources for Further Information on Strategic Learning

For additional information relating to the ideas discussed in this chapter, we recommend the following Web sites:

www.Dartmouth.edu/~acskills/success/index.html

www.utexas.edu/student/utlc/lrnres/handouts.html

www.muskingum.edu/~cal/database/general/

www2.gsu.edu/~wwwrld/Resources/helpfultips.htm

C **LASSIC QUOTE**

In a world that is constantly changing, the most important skill to acquire now is learning how to learn.

—*John Naisbitt,*
futurologist and author
of Megatrends: Ten New Directions
Transforming Our Lives

■ Self-Assessment of Learning Strategies and Habits

Look back at the ratings you gave yourself for effective note-taking strategies, reading strategies and studying strategies. Add up your total score for each of these three sets of learning strategies (maximum score for each set would be 28):

Note Taking _____

Reading _____

Studying _____

Total Learning Strategy Score = _____

Self-Assessment Questions

1. In what learning strategy area did you score lowest?

2. Do you think that the strategy area in which you scored lowest has anything to do with your lowest course grade at this point in the term?

3. Of the seven specific strategies listed within the area that you scored lowest, which ones could you immediately put into practice to improve your lowest course grade?

4. What is the likelihood that you will put the above strategies into practice this term?

■ Case Study

Too Fast, Too Frustrating: A Note-Taking Nightmare

Joanna Scribe is a first-year student who is majoring in journalism, and she's currently enrolled in an introductory course that is required for her major (Introduction to Mass Media). Her instructor for this course lectures at a very rapid rate and uses vocabulary words that go right over her head. Since she cannot get all the instructor's words down on paper and can't understand half the words she does manage to write down, she has become frustrated and has now stopped taking notes altogether. She wants to do well in this course because it's the first course in her major, but she's afraid she will fail it because her class notes are so pitiful.

Reflection and Discussion Questions

1. Can you relate to this case personally, or know any students who are in the same boat as Joanna?

2. What would you recommend that Joanna do at this point?

3. Why did you make the above recommendation?

CHAPTER 7
Critical Thinking
Developing Critical Skills
for the Twenty-First Century

W hat are we to believe? What should we accept with reservations, and what should we dismiss outright? As we gather information about the world via the media (e.g., television, radio, the Internet, and newspapers and magazines), we tend to take much of the information at face value, ignoring the fact that the information has been selected and organized (shaped and edited) by the person or organization presenting it. People are often lulled into a false sense of security, believing that the sources of information they are basing their decisions on are objective and truthful (Chaffee, 1998). Discovering the answers to the six important questions that reporters are trained to answer near the beginning of every news article—who, what, where, when, why, and how—

is not enough to allow us to think critically about complex and sometimes controversial topics. To engage in thinking at this higher level, one needs to know how to ask questions and think independently.

The authors of this chapter view critical thinking developmentally as a set of complex thinking skills that can be improved through knowledge and guided practice. Thinking skills are categorized in the problem-solving/decision-making set of life-skills necessary for information seeking. These skills include information assessment and analysis; problem identification, solution, implementation, and evaluation; goal setting; systematic planning and forecasting; and conflict resolution. Presented in this chapter are developmental thinking models, critical thinking and problem-solving models, and information about the construction and evaluation of an argument.

■ Thinking as a Developmental Process

Cognitive psychologists study the development and organization of knowledge and the role it plays in various mental activities (e.g., reading, writing, decision making, and problem solving). What is knowledge? Where it is stored? How do you construct mental representations of your world? The personal answers to these and other questions are often found for the first time in college when students focus their attention on what they know and how they know it.

Models of Knowledge

Different forms of knowledge interact when you reason and construct a mental representation of the situation before you. Joanne Kurfiss (1988) wrote about the following three kinds of knowledge.

- **Declarative knowledge** is knowing facts and concepts. Kurfiss recognizes the considerable amount of declarative knowledge that students acquire through their college courses. To move students to a higher level of thinking, instructors generally ask students to write analytical essays, instead of mere summaries, to explain the knowledge they have acquired in the course.
- **Procedural knowledge,** or **strategic knowledge,** is knowing how to use declarative knowledge to do something (e.g., interpret textbooks, study, navigate the Internet, and find a major).
- **Metacognition** is knowing what knowledge to use to control one's situation (e.g., how to make plans, ask questions, analyze the effectiveness of learning strategies, initiate change). If students' metacognitive skills are not well developed, students may not be able to use the full potential of their knowledge when studying in college.

William Perry

You may have read about the developmental theorist William Perry. In his research on college-age students, Perry distinguished a series of stages that students pass through as they move from simple to complex levels of thinking. Basically, they move from *dualism*, the simplest stage, where knowledge is viewed as a factual quality dispensed by authorities (professors), to *multiplicity*, in which the student recognizes the complexity of knowledge (e.g., he or she understands that there is more than one perspective of the bombing of Hiroshima or the role of the United States in the Vietnam war) and believes knowledge to be subjective, to *relativism*, where the student reaches an understanding that some views make greater sense than other views. Relativism is reflected in situations where a student has made a commitment to the particular view they have constructed of the world, also known as *Weltanschauung*. Constructing a personal *critical epistemology* is an essential developmental task for undergraduates, according to Perry (Chaffee, 1998).

Bloom's Taxonomy of Thinking and Learning

Benjamin Bloom (1956) and his associates at the University of Chicago developed a classification system, or taxonomy, to explain how we think and learn (see Figure 1). The taxonomy consists of six levels of thinking arranged in a hierarchy, beginning with simple cognitive tasks (knowledge) and moving up to more complex thinking (evaluation). Thinking at each level is dependent on thinking skills at lower levels.

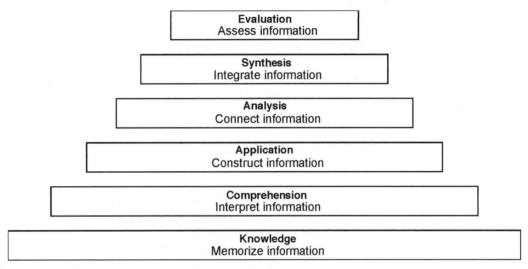

Figure 1 ■ Bloom's Hierarchy of Thinking

One of the reasons that college students often experience difficulty learning and studying during their first semester is that the learning and study strategies from high school are not necessarily effective in the new setting. In high school you are generally asked to memorize, comprehend, and interpret information. In college you are asked to do all that and more. To be successful in a college setting, you need to learn how to apply, analyze, synthesize, and evaluate information. Let's look at Bloom's six levels of learning and thinking.

Knowledge Level. If you are cramming for a test, chances are good that you are thinking at the knowledge level, the lowest level of thinking. You are basically attempting to memorize a lot of information in a short amount of time. If you are asked on the test to identify, name, select, define, or list particular bits of information, you might do okay, but you will most likely forget most of the information soon after taking the test.

Comprehension Level. When you are classifying, describing, discussing, explaining, and recognizing information, you are in the process of interpreting information. At the bottom of your lecture notes for the day, see if you can summarize your notes using your own words. In doing so, you can develop a deeper understanding of the material just covered in class.

Application Level. At this third level of thinking, you are constructing knowledge by taking previously learned information and applying it in a new and different way to solve problems. Whenever you use a formula or a theory to solve a problem, you are thinking at the application level. Some words used to describe how you process information at this level are *illustrate, demonstrate,* and *apply.* To increase thinking at the application level, develop the habit of thinking of examples to illustrate concepts presented in class or during reading. Be sure to include the examples in your notations in your books and notes.

Analysis Level. When you analyze information, you break the information down into parts and then look at the relationships among the parts. In your literature class, if you read two plays from different time periods and then compare and contrast them in terms of style and form, you are analyzing. When you analyze, you connect pieces of information. You *discriminate, correlate, classify,* and *infer.*

Synthesis Level. When you are synthesizing information, you are bringing together all the bits of information that you have analyzed to create a new pattern or whole. When you synthesize, you *hypothesize, predict, generate,* and *integrate.* Innovative ideas often emerge at the synthesis level of thinking.

Evaluation Level. This is the highest level of thinking according to Bloom's taxonomy. When you evaluate, you judge the validity of the information. You may be evaluating opinions ("Is that person really an expert?") or biases.

Answer the following questions to test your understanding of Bloom's taxonomy. According to Bloom's taxonomy of thinking, which level of thinking would you be engaging in if you were asked to

- ■ Read an article about an upcoming candidate in a local election and then summarize the candidate's characteristics?
- ■ View a video about hate and prejudice and then write an essay about how you can confront hate and prejudice on a personal level?
- ■ Determine the most effective way for you to study?
- ■ Identify and define the parts of the forebrain?
- ■ Judge a new campus parking policy created by your college's parking services?

■ Models of Critical Thinking/Problem Solving

Critical Thinking

One of the primary objectives of a college education is to develop the skills necessary to become an autonomous, independent learner. Critical thinking prepares you to be an independent thinker. To ensure that you are thinking critically, you can follow the CRITICAL model developed by the authors (Glauser & Ginter, 1995). This model identifies important steps and key ideas in critical thinking: construction, refocus, identify, think through, insight, conclusions, accuracy, and lens.

Construction. Each of us constructs a unique view of the world. Our construction, or perception, of the world is based on our thoughts and beliefs. Our cultural background influences our perceptions, and they form the basis of our assumptions. For example, you might assume that a college education can help you to get a better job. How do you know this? Maybe you know this because a parent or teacher told you so. If this is the only bit of information on which you are basing your assumption about the value of a college education, you have not engaged in critical thinking. If you had engaged in critical thinking, you would have analyzed and synthesized information that you gathered about the benefits of a college education. If you have based your decision to attend this college on good critical thinking, then you will know why you are here and will more likely be motivated to graduate.

Perceptions of information, behaviors, and situations are often based on unexamined assumptions that are inaccurate and sketchy. The first step in this model is to investigate personal underlying biases that are inherent in your assumptions about any issue before you. For example, let us say that you are with some friends and the topic of surrogate motherhood comes up. Maybe you have already formed an opinion about the issue. This opinion could be based on strong critical thinking, but if not, then your opinion is merely a strong, personal feeling. If you choose to look at surrogate motherhood from a critical-thinking perspective, you would begin by examining your own thoughts and beliefs about motherhood and surrogacy. No matter what issue is before you (e.g., racism, abortion, euthanasia, genetic engineering), the process is the same; begin by examining your own assumptions. As you do this, look for biases and other patterns of thinking that have become cemented over time and are influencing the way you view the issue.

Refocus. Once you have acknowledged some of your own biases, refocus your attention so you can hear alternative viewpoints. Refocus by reading additional information, talking to people with opposing viewpoints, or maybe watching a movie or a video. You are trying to see other people's perspectives. Read carefully, and listen carefully with the intent to learn. Can you think of any books that you have read or movies that have influenced the way you see a particular issue?

To illustrate the effect of refocusing, list three sources of additional information (e.g., book, movie, another person, newspaper, or experience) that changed your mind about something important to you. Explain how it changed you.

1. _____

_____

_____

2. _____

_____

_____

3. _____

_____

_____

Identify. Identifying core issues and information is the third step of critical thinking. After you have gathered all your additional information representing different viewpoints, think over the information carefully. Are there any themes that emerge? What does the terminology related to the issue tell you? Look at all the facts and details. We all try to make sense out of what we hear and see by arranging information into a pattern, a story that seems reasonable. There is a tendency to arrange the information to fit our perceptions and beliefs. When we engage in critical thinking, we are trying to make sense of all the pieces, not just the ones that happen to fit our own preconceived pattern.

Think Through. The fourth step of critical thinking requires that you think through all the information gathered. The task is to distinguish between what is fact and what is fiction and what is relevant and not relevant. Examine premises and decide if they are logically valid. Look for misinformation. Maybe you have gathered inaccurate facts and figures. Check the sources for reliability. Asking questions is a large part of good critical thinking.

This step of the model is where you analyze and synthesize information. You are continually focusing your attention in and out, similar to the way you might focus a camera. This step of the critical-thinking process can be very creative. You are using both parts of the brain. The right brain is being speculative, suspending judgment, and challenging definitions. The left brain is analyzing the information received in a more traditional style, thinking logically and sequentially. While thinking critically, have you detected any overgeneralizations (e.g., women are more emotional and less rational than men are) or oversimplifications (e.g., the high dropout rate at the local high school is due to an increase in single-parent families)?

Insight. Once key issues have been identified and analyzed, it is time to develop some insight into some of the various perspectives on the issue. Sometimes some of the best insights come when you can sit back and detach yourself from all the information you have just processed. Often new meanings will emerge that provide a new awareness. You might find that you have developed some empathy for others that may not have been there before. When you hear the term "broken home," what images do you conjure up? How do you think a child who resides with a single parent or alternates between divorced parents' homes feels when hearing that term applied to his or her situation? A lot of assumptions are embedded in such concepts.

Conclusions. If you do not have sufficient evidence to support a decision, suspend judgment until you do. An important tenet of critical thinking is not to jump to conclusions. If you do, you may find that you have a fallacy in your reasoning. A fallacy is an instance of incorrect reasoning. Maybe you did not have sufficient evidence to support your decision to major in biology, or maybe your conclusions about the issue of euthanasia do not follow logically from your premise. Also look at the conclusions you have drawn, and ask yourself if they have any implications that you might need to rethink? Do you need to consider alternative interpretations of the evidence?

Accuracy. You are not through thinking! In addition to looking for fallacies in your reasoning, you also need to consider some other things.

- Know the difference between reasoning and rationalizing. Which thinking processes are your conclusions based on?
- Know the difference between what is true and what seems true based on the emotional attachment you have to your ideas and beliefs.
- Know the difference between opinion and fact. Facts can be proven; opinions cannot.

Lens. In this last step of critical thinking, you have reached the understanding that most issues can be viewed from multiple perspectives. These perspectives form a lens that offers a more encompassing view of the world around you. Remember that there are usually many solutions to a single issue.

Problem Solving

Problem solving involves critical thinking. Are problem solving and critical thinking the same? Not really. Problem solving is about having the ability and skills to apply knowledge to pragmatic problems encountered in all areas of your life. If you were trying to solve a financial problem or decide whether or not to change roommates, you probably

would not need a model of thinking as extensive as the one previously described. The following steps offer an organized approach to solving less complex problems.

1. Identify the problem. Be specific and write it down.

2. Analyze the problem.

3. Identify alternative ways to solve the problem.

4. Examine alternatives.

5. Implement a solution.

6. Evaluate.

Identify the problem. What exactly is the problem you wish to solve? Is it that your roommate is driving you crazy, or is it that you want to move into an apartment with your friend next semester? Be specific.

Analyze the problem. Remember, analysis means looking at all the parts. It is the process by which we select and interpret information. Be careful not to be too selective or simplistic in your thinking. Look at all the facts and details. For example, suppose you want to move into an apartment with your friends. Do you need permission from anyone to do so? Can you afford to do this? Can you get a release from your dorm lease? Your answer to all the questions might be yes, with the exception of being able to afford it. You want to move, so now the problem is a financial one. You need to come up with the financial resources to follow through on your decision.

Identify alternative ways to solve the problem. Use convergent and divergent thinking. You are engaging in **convergent thinking** when you are narrowing choices to come up with the correct solution (e.g., picking the best idea out of three). You are engaging in **divergent thinking** when you are thinking in terms of multiple solutions. Mihaly Csikszentmihalyi (1996) says, "Divergent thinking leads to no agreed-upon solution. It involves fluency, or the ability to generate a great quantity of ideas; flexibility, or the ability to switch from one perspective to another; and originality in picking unusual associations of ideas" (1996, p. 60). He concludes that a person whose thinking has these qualities is likely to come up with more innovative ideas.

Brainstorming is a great way to generate alternative ways to solve problems. This creative problem-solving technique requires that you use both divergent and convergent thinking. Here are some steps to use if you decide to brainstorm.

- Describe the problem.
- Decide on the amount of time you want to spend brainstorming (e.g., 10 minutes).
- Relax (remember some of the best insights come in a relaxed state).
- Write down everything that comes to your mind (divergent thinking).
- Select your best ideas (convergent thinking).
- Try one out! (If it does not work, try one of the other ideas you selected.)

Students have successfully used the process of brainstorming to decide on a major, choose activities for spring break, develop topics for papers, and come up with ideas for part-time jobs. Being creative means coming up with atypical solutions to complex problems.

Examine alternatives. Make judgments about the alternatives based on previous knowledge and the additional information you now have.

Implement a solution. Choose one solution to your problem and eliminate the others for now. (If this one fails, you may want to try another solution later.)

Evaluate. If the plan is not as effective as you had hoped, modify your plan or start the process over again. Also look at the criteria you used to judge your alternative solutions.

Think of a problem that you are currently dealing with. Complete Exercise 1 ("Creating Breakthroughs") at the end of the chapter. This is an opportunity to try to solve a problem using this six-step problem-solving model.

■ Arguments

Critical thinking involves the construction and evaluation of arguments. An argument is a form of thinking in which reasons (statements and facts) are given in support of a conclusion. The reasons of the argument are known as the **premises**. A good argument is one in which the premises are logical and support the conclusion. The validity of the argument is based on the relationship between the premises and the conclusion. If the premises are not credible or do not support the conclusion, or the conclusion does not follow from the premises, the argument is considered to be **invalid** or fallacious. Unsound arguments (based on fallacies) are often persuasive because they can appeal to our emotions and confirm what we want to believe to be true. Just look at commercials on television. Alcohol advertisements show that you can be rebellious, independent, and have lots of friends, fun, and excitement by drinking large quantities of alcohol—all without any negative consequences. Intelligence is reflected in the capacity to acquire and apply knowledge. Even sophisticated, intelligent people are influenced by fallacious advertising.

Invalid Arguments

It is human irrationality, not a lack of knowledge, that threatens human potential.
—Raymond Nickerson, in J. K. Kurfiss, Critical Thinking

In the book *How to Think About Weird Things*, Theodore Schick and Lewis Vaughn (1999) suggest that you can avoid holding irrational beliefs by understanding the ways in which an argument can fail. First, an argument is fallacious if it contains **unacceptable premises**, premises that are as incredible as the claim they are supposed to support. Second, if they contain **irrelevant premises**, or premises that are not logically related to the conclusion, they are also fallacious. Third, they are fallacious if they contain **insufficient premises**, meaning that the premises do not eliminate reasonable grounds for doubt. Schick and Vaughn recommend that whenever someone presents an argument, you check to see if the premises are acceptable, relevant, and sufficient. If not, then the argument presented is not logically compelling, or valid.

Schick and Vaughn abstracted from the work of Ludwig F. Schlecht the following examples of fallacies based on illogical premises.

Unacceptable Premises

- **False dilemma** (also known as the either/or fallacy) presumes that there are only two alternatives from which to choose when in actuality there are more than two. For example: You are either with America or against us. You are not with America, therefore you are against us.
- **Begging the question** is also referred to as arguing in a circle. A conclusion is used as one of the premises. For example: "You should major in business, because my advisor says that if you do, you will be guaranteed a job." "How do you know this?" "My advisor told me that all business majors find jobs."

Irrelevant Premises

- **Equivocation** occurs when the conclusion does not follow from the premises due to using the same word to mean two different things. For example: Senator Dobbs has always been *patriotic* and shown a deep affection and respect for his country. Now, though, he is criticizing the government's foreign policy. This lack of *patriotism* makes him unworthy of reelection.
- **Appeal to the person (*ad hominem*, or "to the man")** occurs when a person offers a rebuttal to an argument by criticizing or denigrating its presenter rather than constructing a rebuttal based on the argument presented. As Schick and Vaughn note, "Crazy people can come up with perfectly sound arguments, and sane people can talk nonsense" (1999, p. 287).
- **Appeal to authority** is when we support our views by citing experts. If the person is truly an expert in the field for which they are being cited, then the testimony is probably valid. How often do you see celebrities endorsing products? Is an argument valid just because someone cites an article from the *New York Times* or the *Wall Street Journal* for support?
- **Appeal to the masses** is a type of fallacy that occurs when support for the premise is offered in the form, "It must be right because everybody else does it." For example: It's okay to cheat. Every college student cheats sometime during their undergraduate years.

- **Appeal to tradition** is used as an unsound premise when we argue that something is true based on an established tradition. For example: It's okay to drink large quantities of alcohol and go wild during Spring Break. It's what students have always done.
- **Appeal to ignorance** relies on claims that if no proof is offered that something is true, then it must be false, or conversely, that if no proof is offered that something is false, then it must be true. Many arguments associated with religions of the world are based on irrelevant premises that appeal to ignorance.
- **Appeal to fear** is based on a threat, or "swinging the big stick." For example: If you don't start studying now, you will never make it through college. Schick and Vaughn remind us, "Threats extort; they do not help us arrive at the truth" (1999, p. 289).

Insufficient Premises

- **Hasty generalizations** are often seen when people stereotype others. Have you noticed that most stereotypes are negative? When we describe an individual as pushy, cheap, aggressive, privileged, snobbish, or clannish and then generalize that attribute to the group we believe that person belongs to, we are committing a hasty generalization.
- **Faulty analogy** is the type of fallacy committed when there is a claim that things that have similar qualities in some respects will have similarities in other respects. For example: Dr. Smith and Dr. Wilson may both teach at the same college, but their individual philosophies about teaching and learning may be very different.
- **False cause** fallacies occur when a causal relationship is assumed despite a lack of evidence to support the relationship. Do you have a special shirt or hat that you wear on game days to influence the odds that the team you are cheering for wins?

■ Closing Remarks

Belgian physicist Ilya Prigogine was awarded the Nobel Prize for his theory of dissipative structures. Part of the theory "contends that friction is a fundamental property of nature and nothing grows without it—not mountains, not pearls, not people. It is precisely the quality of fragility, he says, the capacity for being shaken up, that is paradoxically the key to growth. Any structure—whether at the molecular, chemical, physical, social, or psychological level that is insulated from disturbance is also protected from change. It becomes stagnant. Any vision—or any thing—that is true to life, to the imperatives of creation and evolution, will not be 'unshakable' (Levoy, 1997 p. 8).

Throughout this textbook you will read about how change affects you now as a student in college and throughout the rest of your life. Education is about learning how to look and how to listen to what instructors, books, television, and other sources of information are saying, and to discover whether or not what they are saying is true or false.

In reference to education and learning, the philosopher Jiddu Krishnamurti said that there should be "an intent to bring about change in the mind which means you have to be extraordinarily critical. You have to learn never to accept anything which you yourself do not see clearly" (1974, p. 18). He said that education is always more than learning from books, or memorizing some facts, or the instructor transmitting information to the student. Education is about critical thinking, and critical thinking is the foundation of all learning.

Critical thinking is thinking that moves you beyond simple observations and passive reporting of those observations. It is an active, conscious, cognitive process in which there is always intent to learn. It is the process by which we analyze and evaluate information, and it is how we make good sense out of all the information that we are continually bombarded with.

Marcia Magolda believes that critical thinking fosters qualities such as maturity, responsibility, and citizenship. "Both the evolving nature of society and the student body has led to reconceptualizations of learning outcomes and processes. In a postmodern society, higher education must prepare students to shoulder their moral and ethical responsibility to confront and wrestle with the complex problems they will encounter in today and tomorrow's world. Critical, reflective thinking skills, the ability to gather and evaluate evidence, and the ability to make one's own informed judgments are essential learning outcomes if students are to get beyond relativity to make informed judgments in a world in which multiple perspectives are increasingly interdependent and 'right action' is uncertain and often in dispute." (Magolda & Terenzini, 1999, p. 3)

■ Sources

Bloom, B. (1956). *Taxonomy of educational objectives: The classification of educational goals. Handbook I: Cognitive domain.* London: Longmans.

Chaffee, J. (1998). *The thinker's way.* Boston: Little, Brown.

Csikszentmihalyi, M. (1996). *Creativity.* New York: HarperCollins.

DiSpezio, M. (1998). *Challenging critical thinking puzzles.* New York: Sterling.

Glauser, A., & Ginter, E. J. (1995, October). *Beyond hate and intolerance.* Paper presented at the southeastern Conference of Counseling Center Personnel, Jekyll Island, GA.

Johnson, D., & Johnson, F. (2000). *Joining together.* Boston: Allyn and Bacon.

Krishnamurti, J. (1974). *Krishnamurti on education.* New York: Harper & Row.

Kurfiss, J. G. (1988). *Critical thinking: Theory, research, practice, and possibilities. Critical thinking*, 2. Washington, DC: ASHE-Eric Higher Education Reports.

Levoy, Gregg. (1997). *Callings.* New York: Three Rivers Press.

Magolda, M. B., & Terenzini, P. (1999). Learning and teaching in the twenty-first century: Trends and implications for practice. In C. S. Johnson & H. E. Cheatham (Eds.), *Higher education trends for the next century: A research agenda for student's success.* Retrieved November 30, 1999, from http://www.acpa.nche.edu/ seniorscholars/trends/ trends.htn

Perry, W. (1970). *Forms of intellectual and ethical development during the college years: A scheme.* New York: Holt, Rinehart and Winston.

Schick, T., & Vaughn, L. (1999). *How to Think About Weird Things: Critical Thinking for a New Age.* Mountain View, CA: Mayfield.

■ Exercise 1. Creating Breakthroughs

Select a problem related to being a student at your college.

1. State the problem.

2. Analyze the problem.

3. Brainstorm alternative solutions.

4. Examine your alternatives. Pick the five best options from your brainstorming and record them below.

    a. _____

    b. _____

    c. _____

    d. _____

    e. _____

When you consider your problem and the list of options that you have created, what kind of criteria do you want to use in judging your options? For example, let us say that you stated your problem as needing money to stay in school. The best five options you came up with for getting money to stay in school were to work full time and go to evening school, alternate between going to school for a year and then working for a year, take out a student loan, study hard and raise your GPA to obtain a scholarship, and beg your family for money. The criteria you choose to judge your options might be that you do not want to be really stressed out, you want your plan to be reliable, and you want to owe as little as possible upon graduation.

List three criteria you will use to evaluate your options.

    C1. _____

    C2. _____

    C3. _____

Now, using a scale from 1–5, rate each option using your criteria, with 5 being the highest rating.

Options	C1	C2	C3	Total (C1 + C2 + C3)
a.				
b.				
c.				
d.				
e.				

■ Exercise 1 (continued)

What are your two best options?

_____

_____

5. Implement a solution. Which option will you choose to act on?

What kinds of resources will you need? (List four.)

_____

_____

_____

_____

List some of your planning steps.

_____

_____

_____

_____

_____

_____

_____

_____

_____

_____

_____

6. Evaluate. Look over what you have listed as resources and planning steps, and decide if you forgot something important. Indicate below if you believe the plan you have come up with is feasible, and whether you left something out that now should become part of your solution.

■ Exercise 2. Critical-Thinking Puzzle

Without lifting your pencil from the paper, draw six straight lines that connect all sixteen of the dots below. To make things more challenging, the line pattern that you create must begin at the X.

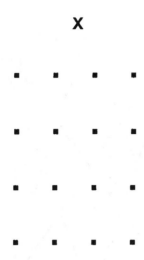

(The solution can be found at the end of this chapter.)

Source: DiSpezio, M. (1998). *Challenging critical thinking puzzles.* New York: Sterling.

Solution to Exercise 2

Critical-Thinking Puzzle

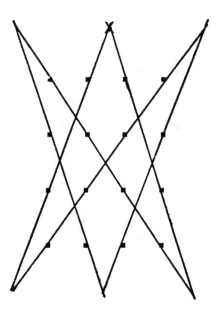

DiSpezio, M. (1998). *Challenging critical thinking puzzles.* New York: Sterling.

CHAPTER 8
Randall Library

The William Randall Library is one of the most prominent and essential features on the UNCW Campus, central to the mission of the university and vital to your undergraduate education in many ways. Randall Library's holdings include 438,933 bound volumes; 333,180 government documents; 23,797 documents in microforms; 23,484 reels of microfilm; 859 maps; 2,559 sound (phonograph and sound) records; 4,623 CDs; and over 10,000 ERIC documents. It subscribes to 4,493 serials, and the audiovisual collection totals over 20,848 items. In addition to the general collection, the Curriculum Materials Center (CMC) is an area of the library designated specifically for educators. The CMC provides resources such as state-adopted textbooks, the Standard Course of Study, audiovisual materials, and samples of instructional materials from across the country.

The mission of the Randall Library is to effectively support the university's teaching, scholarship, artistic achievement, and service functions by providing in a timely manner:

- Dynamic collections of informational resources in all formats
- Efficient links to remote informational resources
- Appropriate facilities, technologies, services, and professional support needed by students, faculty, and staff as they endeavor to fulfill their academic, professional, and individual goals

The library also provides appropriate information resources and services to all citizens and scholars outside the university community. Special efforts are made to collect, preserve, and make available information resources relating to the coastal region in which the library is located. The library faculty and staff are committed to implementing innovative and creative methods centered on the needs of its users to inspire and support intellectual curiosity, imagination, rational thinking, and thoughtful expression.

This chapter is designed to give you a quick introduction to the library and its purpose as an integral part of UNCW.

■ Research

Research Services can help you find information for papers, projects, and other research.

Walk-Up Service

Get assistance in finding information at the Reference Desk. This desk is located on the first floor of the library and is open during regular desk hours. You can also get assistance via email, telephone, and instant messaging.

Research Assistance Program (RAP)

With an emphasis on undergraduate students, Randall Library's Research Assistance Program service is provided for students, faculty, and staff at UNCW to make appointments with a librarian for one-on-one assistance in helping you find the information you need for your papers, projects, or other research. This service will help you to use the research databases, library catalog, and other resources to find articles and books for your papers, and show you how to obtain resources that are not found in the library.

Databases

Randall Library subscribes to many web-based databases, including EBSCOhost, Academic Search Premier, and WorldCat. These can be accessed from any campus computer or from other remote locations. You must log in with a PIN to access Randall Library from off-campus. To access databases from off-campus, renew materials online that you have checked out, access electronic reserve readings, and place holds on materials that are currently checked out by another patron:

1. Access the PIN Login screen.

2. Enter your first or last name.

3. Enter your University ID.

4. Enter a library PIN, up to 30 letters, numbers, or both. Do not use symbols.

5. If this is the first time you have set a PIN, the next screen will ask you to enter the PIN twice.

6. Your PIN is now set.

7. If you have any difficulty, please contact the reference desk at 910-962-3760.

■ Why Do We Have Libraries?

What purpose does a library serve for UNC Wilmington? A library is necessary for several reasons, but its most important function is providing access to information. The library does this by:

■ Collecting information and preserving it
■ Organizing information so that you can find it
■ Providing services that help you get the information you need when you need it

Don't I Get All the Information I Need in My Classes?

What happens in the classroom is only a small part of the education process. Some of the most important learning you will do at UNC Wilmington takes place outside the classroom, when you pursue topics from your class in greater depth by doing your own research. In fact, learning how to answer your own questions is just as important to your overall educational experience as passing any midterm or final. Acquiring this skill is one of the greatest challenges you will face as a student.

So, by the time you graduate, you should be able to:

■ Use various tools and resources to locate the information you need to support a thesis
■ Analyze that information to see how it can be used in your research
■ Synthesize it with other information that you have found
■ Evaluate it for accuracy, objectivity, and other biases

Mastering these skills will improve your "information literacy." You will use these skills time and again in the "real world" to make decisions, persuade others to your point of view, or simply learn something on your own.

To Find Information, Can't I Just Use Google or Wikipedia?

While it is true that the Internet contains a near infinite amount of information, there are major drawbacks to using it as a primary source of information:

- A lot of information on the Internet is inaccurate or deliberately misleading
- The Internet is not organized, which can make finding what you need very difficult
- The Internet will not lead you to the most scholarly of resources or copyrighted materials
- Often, older research articles and writings are not available online

On the other hand, Randall Library provides free and open access to high-quality scholarly information, current coverage of events both local and worldwide, and many other resources that will help you complete your assignments and further your education. It is true that some questions can be easily answered by using Google or Wikipedia, but when doing academic work you will need to gather information from the resources that only a resource like Randall Library can provide.

So What's So Special about Randall Library?

All libraries share some basic similarities, but there are several key factors that may make Randall Library different from others you have used in the past.

Size

Randall Library has over 860,000 holdings (i.e., books, government documents, AV materials), which is probably bigger that what you have experienced in the past.

Archives

The Archives consist of papers, reports, theses, photographs, and other important records of the University of North Carolina Wilmington. If you want to view the collections, come visit UNCW Archives in Room 2008, Randall Library. The material here is a unique and valuable historical collection and requires special handling and a controlled environment. While these materials are for use only in the library, we hope you will explore the many artifacts and materials available to you:

- Student publications including honors papers, theses, yearbooks, and the *Seahawk* since 1948
- Chancellors' papers, minutes of board meetings, other university papers
- Faculty Scholarship Collection—work produced by the faculty in many formats: art, video, books, journal articles
- The University Mace, University Seals, assorted awards
- Visual collections including videos, photographs, and slides

Workshops

The Randall Library workshop series provides the UNCW community with opportunities to learn about new technologies, resources, and issues affecting the changing information landscape.

Past workshops have included:

- **Library Lowdown: Randall Library Resources in a Nutshell**
- **All About Google**
- **Second Life: Living in a Virtual World**
- **Top Ten Firefox Add-ons for Research and Teaching**
- **Wikipedia 360: The Good, the Bad and the Anonymous**

Courses

Librarians from Randall Library teach several credit-bearing academic courses. This is a great way to earn credit while improving your research skills.

The courses are:

LIB 101. Basic Library & Information Research Skills (1 hour)
Concepts and methodology for locating, selecting, and evaluating information, with an emphasis on electronic resources. Overview of the structure and organization of information.

LIB 103. Introduction to Library Research and Technology (3 hours)
Exploration of concepts in library science and information technology. Emphasis on the evolving nature, trends, and issues relating to information. Development of skills in information retrieval and analysis using both print and electronic resources.

LIB 104. Library and Information Research Skills in Business (3 hours)
This course is an introduction to business information resources and research including the evolution of information, trends, and issues in using resources such as catalogs and subscription databases. Students learn to construct effective search strategies, find and retrieve information, critically evaluate resources, and use websites for research.

Laws of Library Science

1. Books are for use.

2. Every reader his book.

3. Every book its reader.

4. Save the time of the reader.

5. The library is a growing organism.

~S. R. Ranganathan, 1931

CHAPTER 9
Academic Advising

Few experiences in your academic career have as much potential for influencing your development as academic advising. Advisors help you understand your role as part of the academic community, develop sound academic and career goals, and ultimately become a successful learner. Academic advising needs to be much more than issuing an advising code or simply selecting courses. In developing a relationship with their academic advisor, students have the opportunity to get to know a faculty member with experience and expertise in their particular field of study. Faculty advisors can help you make educated choices and decisions that have the potential to impact your future. Through regular contact—whether face-to-face, by telephone, or by e-mail—an academic advisor can better understand a student's academic, social, and personal experiences and needs.

Your academic advisor will help you plan your program of study based on your career interests, strengths, and personal assets. Advisors are very knowledgeable in the areas of university requirements, general education options, departmental curriculum, and major/career choices. Plan to meet with your advisor at least two times during each semester. Get to know them and ask questions. It is very important to develop a positive relationship with your academic advisor early in your college experience.

Meeting with Your Advisor

Who Is My Advisor and How Do I Contact Him/Her?

If you are a new freshman, you can check on your student SeaNet account to learn who your academic advisor is, as well as his/her location and contact information. You are strongly encouraged to make an appointment right away to get to know your advisor. To schedule this appointment, you may call the University College at 910.962.3245, or e-mail your question to us at uc@uncw.edu with other questions.

How Will I Know When to Meet with My Advisor?

You should meet with your advisor to get acquainted, and you are encouraged to meet with him/her whenever you have concerns about your academic progress or adjustment to university life. Your advisor can help you resolve your difficulties and may refer you to additional resources on campus. You are required to meet with your advisor at least twice per year at pre-registration. If you are a freshman or an undeclared sophomore, University College will send you a reminder to sign up for pre-registration advising online. Make an appointment, and begin to build a relationship with your advisor early in the semester. Your advisor will be able to better assist you if they are familiar with your background and educational goals.

When meeting with your advisor during the pre-registration period, it is crucial that you come prepared. You will have a short amount of time and a great deal of information to cover. Review your degree requirements and write down a list of questions prior to your meeting. Use the schedule of courses in SeaNet to check course availability. Arrive with a tentative schedule and two or three alternate courses. It is your responsibility to choose your courses. Activity 2 in this chapter will help prepare you for this meeting.

Getting Registered

Is it time to register for classes again already? You are probably just getting adjusted to your current schedule. What do you do? Registering for classes was easy during orientation, but now you are on your own. Don't panic; there is still plenty of help available. This time around you will need to schedule an individual advising session with your advisor to obtain assistance in your course selection for the next term. Alternate PINs change each semester; therefore, you are required to see your advisor each term. You will receive your new Alternate PIN from your academic advisor. Remember, all first-year students are assigned to University College for academic advising.

Read the Catalogue

The Undergraduate Catalogue is a resource tool that no student should be without. Topics in the Undergraduate Catalogue include degree requirements, academic policies, and course descriptions. From admissions to graduation, it's all there. This is your guide to the rules of the game. Use the table of contents and alphabetized index online to quickly access information in the catalogue. The catalogue is available online at http://www.uncw.edu/catalogue/.

Course Selection

Informed course selection is vital to your success at UNCW. You want to maintain a balanced course load that you find manageable and scholastically challenging. Listed below are several tips regarding course selection:

- Review the required courses for your major.
- Consider taking an elective in an area of interest.
- Use your talents; take courses that play to your strengths.
- Try to limit writing-intensive courses to one per semester.
- Balance your schedule. Do not limit your classes to exclusively Mondays and Wednesdays or Tuesdays and Thursdays.
- Do you want to stay fit? Think about enrolling in a physical education activity course.
- Remember your body clock. If you are not a morning person, avoid 8:00 a.m. classes, when possible. If you struggle to get up for early classes, get more sleep the night before; it is really that simple.

Progress toward Graduation in Four Years

To graduate in four years, students must successfully complete all graduation requirements and an average annual course load of 31 semester hours. This course load requires the student to take approximately 15–16 hours per semester or earn hours through summer enrollment. Among the factors responsible for extending the time necessary to complete degree requirements beyond four years are a student's late decision to change majors, requiring additional course work; part-time employment while enrolled; family responsibilities; and unilateral decisions to take fewer than the recommended average of 15–16 hours per semester.

Suggested Academic Workload Guidelines

Be aware that academic excellence and scholastic achievement usually require a significant investment of time in study, research, and out-of-class projects. To provide guidance to students in planning their academic and work schedules, the following recommendations are offered:

- In general, students should expect to devote between two and three hours outside of class for each hour in class. Thus, students with a 15-hour course load should schedule between 30 and 45 hours weekly for completing outside-of-class reading, studying, and homework assignments.
- Students who are employed more than 5–10 hours each week should consider reducing their course load (credit hours), depending upon their study habits, learning abilities, and course work requirements.

■ Pre-Registration Information

What Is Pre-Registration and When Does It Take Place?

Pre-registration is the period of time in the semester during which currently enrolled students sign up for the next semester's courses. In the case of spring pre-registration, students may sign up for both summer sessions as well as the following fall semester. In the fall, students usually meet with their advisors soon after fall vacation and pre-register during the first or second week of November. In the spring, students usually meet with their advisors after spring vacation and pre-register in the last week of March or the first week of April.

What Is Pre-Registration Advising and Why Is It Required?

UNCW requires that all students meet with their academic advisors before they can register for courses. Your academic advisor will give you an Alternate PIN that will allow you to use SeaNet to register. It is important to meet with your advisor even if you have met with someone else who helped you plan courses already. Each semester, your assigned academic advisor will review with you your "Degree Audit," a computer print-out showing what Basic Studies requirements you still have to complete before graduating. After you declare a major, your Degree Audit will also reflect your major requirements. Your advisor will answer your questions, discuss your progress in your current courses, and check the appropriateness of your plan for the following semester.

Registration for Currently Enrolled Students

Please check for your registration times and status as well as class schedule information in SeaNet. You may register for classes by accessing SeaNet at www.uncw.edu and clicking on "Current Students," and then following the link to "SeaNet."

Your user ID for SeaNet will be a nine-digit number that begins with "85," and your PIN is initially your birthdate in format MM/DD/YY. You will be required to change your PIN to another six-digit number. You will also be required to supply a security question and answer. If you do not know your user ID, please follow the link on the user login page for assistance.

Before you access SeaNet to register, you must first meet with your academic advisor. The department of your major can tell you what you will need to bring to your advising session. Your advisor will have your Alternate PIN. You must have this number to register. You can check your time ticket on SeaNet; log on and go to "Check Registration Status." You may not register before your assigned time; however, you may register or add or drop anytime after your assigned time.

Withdrawing from a Course

You should make every effort to get help in a course before withdrawing. Talk with your professor and seek additional help from such university resources as the University Learning Center, the Math Lab, and the Writing Center.

If you withdraw before the deadline (remember to check the Academic Calendar each semester), you will receive a "W" in the course, which will not affect your grade point average. However, courses for which you receive a "W" do count as attempted hours. The number of attempted hours is important for determining financial aid eligibility. In

addition, students who withdraw need to consider when to make up the hours in order to stay on track for a timely graduation. Before withdrawing, students should consider all the implications, including whether doing so will drop them below full-time status, whether it will negatively impact any financial aid/scholarships/health insurance, and how it will impact plans for graduation. Students are urged to discuss the decision with their academic advisor and their financial aid counselor (if applicable).

Students who decide to withdraw must go in person to the Office of the Registrar (James Hall). You will need your UNCW ID card.

What If I Withdraw after the Deadline?

You will receive a "WF" for the course, which counts in your grade point average as an "F." The course will also be counted in your attempted hours (see above). A "WF" can be replaced if you repeat the course, according to UNCW's Course Repeat Policy.

■ Declaring a Major

When to Declare a Major

The minimum requirement to declare most majors at UNCW is to have earned (passed) 24 semester hours; some majors have additional admissions requirements. Consult your catalog and your advisor. In general, most students declare a major at the end of their freshman year or the beginning of their sophomore year.

The 45-Hour Rule and Declaring a Major

Undergraduate students must declare and be accepted into a major field of study before or during the semester that they complete 45 semester hours of credit. Students will not be allowed to pre-register or register for the following semester until a major or a pre-major has been declared. Additional advising may be required prior to registration for continuing students who have completed 30 hours or more and have not declared a major or a pre-major.

Transfer students are required to select a major or a pre-major at the time of admission to UNCW. Advising of transfer students is done within the chosen major field.

Schools, departments, and programs with admission requirements have a pre-major, and that academic unit provides discipline-specific advice. Students accepted into pre-major status should have a high probability of completing the admission requirements in the major within two semesters of acceptance.

■ Degree Audits for Students

How to View a Degree Audit

1. Log on to your Student SeaNet account.
2. Click on "Student Services & Financial Aid."
3. Click on "Student Records."
4. Click on "Degree Audit."
5. Click on "Submit an Audit."
6. Click on "Run Audit."
7. Click on "View Submitted Audit."
8. Click on the degree program link and view your audit.

How to View a What-If Audit

After clicking on "Submit an Audit":

1. Click on "What-If."
2. Select a college, degree, major and catalogue year from the drop-down menus.
3. Click on "Run Analysis."
4. Click on "View Submitted Audit."
5. Click on the degree program link and view your audit.

How to View an Alphabetical Listing of Undergraduate Courses

To run an alphabetical listing of undergraduate courses, go to the "What-If" option and select the *College of Arts and Sciences* as the college, *Non-degree* as the degree, *Undeclared* as the major, and *Fall 2009* as the catalogue year.

How to View a Transfer Evaluation

To run a transfer evaluation of courses, go to the "What-If" option and select the *College of Arts and Sciences* as the college, *Non-degree* as the degree, *Transfer Evaluation* as the major, and *Fall 2009* as the catalogue year.

Retention, Dismissal, and Readmission

Retention Chart

Total Quality Hours and Transfer Hours	Required Grade Point Average for Eligibility to Continue at UNCW	Warning
1–26	1.50	1.50–1.99
27–58	1.75	1.75–1.99
59–88	1.90	1.90–1.99
89 or more	2.0	

Transfer students are placed in the above retention chart based on total hours transferred from all institutions attended. Transfer students' grade point averages are computed only on quality hours attempted through the University of North Carolina Wilmington.

Academic Probation

Full-time students (at least 12 hours) who do not earn at least a 1.00 semester GPA and pass at least nine academic hours in any semester will be reviewed by the appropriate dean to determine academic eligibility. Transfer students are placed in the above retention chart based on total hours transferred from all institutions attended. Transfer students' grade point averages are computed only on quality hours attempted through the University of North Carolina Wilmington.

Students who do not meet the minimum grade point requirement for retention at the conclusion of the spring semester will be declared academically ineligible. The student will be allowed to make up deficiencies during this university's summer sessions immediately following the spring semester in which the ineligibility was declared. If such deficiencies are not removed after the completion of the summer sessions, the student will not be permitted to enroll for two consecutive regular semesters (fall and spring). Readmission is contingent upon the results of the Re-enrollment Review. Academically ineligible students may enroll in any summer session.

If a student is allowed to re-enroll, he/she must see an academic advisor before registering for classes. Students who have been declared academically ineligible for the first time may seek administrative review of mitigating circumstances for authorization to continue with their studies on a conditional basis. Students seeking a review must submit the required appeal form and a written statement outlining their circumstance to the appropriate dean. This process must be completed prior to the beginning of the semester in which such students wish to enroll. A second declaration of academic ineligibility will result in dismissal from the university. Eligibility for continued residence or for readmission is restored by completion of sufficient work only during the summer sessions at the University of North Carolina Wilmington.

■ Academic Dismissal

Students who do not meet the minimum grade point requirement for retention at the conclusion of the spring semester will be academically ineligible. The student will be allowed to make up deficiencies during this university's summer sessions immediately following the spring semester in which the ineligibility was declared.

- ■ If a student is not in good academic standing at the conclusion of the summer sessions, the student will be dismissed from the university and will not be permitted to enroll for two consecutive regular semesters (fall and spring).
- ■ Full-time (at least 12 hours) students who earn a 0.0 GPA in any semester will be dismissed from the university and will not be permitted to enroll for two consecutive regular semesters.
- ■ Readmission in both cases above is contingent upon the results of the Re-enrollment Review.
- ■ If a student is allowed to re-enroll, he/she must see an academic advisor before registering for classes.
- ■ Academically dismissed students may enroll in any summer session.

Students who have been academically dismissed for the first time may seek administrative review of mitigating circumstances for authorization to enroll in the following semester under an academic contract.

Students seeking a review must submit the required appeal form and a written statement outlining their circumstance to the appropriate dean. The appeal must be submitted to the appropriate dean within 10 days after the end of the last semester (spring or summer) in which a student is registered. Students must understand that the submission of an appeal does not guarantee the student will be allowed to enroll. The appeal process may take several days to be completed.

After a second declaration of academic dismissal, eligibility for continued residence can be restored only by completion of sufficient work during the summer sessions at the University of North Carolina Wilmington.

■ Common Questions Related to Academic Standing

What Are the Grade Point Values for Individual Grades?

Grade	=	Grade Point Value
A	=	4.00
A-	=	3.67
B+	=	3.33
B	=	3.00
B-	=	2.67
C+	=	2.33
C	=	2.00
C-	=	1.67
D+	=	1.33
D	=	1.00
D-	=	0.67 (Passing)
F	=	0.00 (Failure)
WF	=	0.00 (Failure/Late Withdrawal)

* I, IP, W, NR, Z, and P grades do not have grade point values and do not affect the GPA calculation.

What GPA Do I Need to Make the Dean's List?

To be included in the Dean's List at the close of each semester, students must meet one of the following criteria:

1. Students carrying 12–14 hours must earn a grade point average of 3.50 or better with no grade less than B (3.00).

2. Students carrying 15 hours or more must earn a grade point average of 3.20 or better with no grade less than B (3.00).

3. Students participating in the Honors Program who are carrying 12–14 total hours but are not receiving a grade for the current semester of honors work shall be eligible for the Dean's List if their grade point average on the remaining 9–11 hours otherwise meets current standards for the Dean's List. Students carrying 11 hours or fewer are not eligible for the Dean's List. Pass/fail hours will not be used in the calculation of Dean's List.

How Is a GPA Calculated?

The GPA is determined by dividing the accumulated number of quality points earned by the accumulated number of quality hours earned.

How Does My Transfer GPA Affect My UNC Wilmington GPA?

Transfer courses are NOT calculated in your UNC Wilmington GPA.

How Does Repeating a Course Affect My GPA?

Students who receive a grade lower than a "C" in a course taken at UNC Wilmington may repeat the course at UNC Wilmington. For the first five different courses repeated, the previous grade and hours of credit for the repeated course will not be used in calculating the student's GPA and hours toward graduation. All grades shall remain on the student's transcript.

What Happens after My Five Repeats Have Been Used?

A student who goes beyond the five course repeats will not have the privilege of excluding these grades from the calculation.

Can I Replace the "F" with a Course Taken at Another College?

No. Since grades do not transfer, the "F" would remain in your GPA. However, if a student retakes a course at another college and earns a "C" or better, he/she will receive credit for that course. This is not generally advisable, however, since once a student earns a "C" or better in a course at any institution, he/she may NOT retake the course at UNC Wilmington for credit. Therefore, passing the course elsewhere with a "C" creates a situation in which it is impossible for the student to replace his/her original grade of "F" at UNC Wilmington, since a student cannot receive credit for the same course twice.

What Should I Do If I Am Declared Academically Ineligible?

Contact your academic advisor. Furthermore, any student who does not meet the minimum grade requirement for retention at the conclusion of the spring semester will be allowed to make up deficiencies during the UNC Wilmington summer sessions that immediately follow the spring semester in which he/she was declared ineligible. If such deficiencies are not removed, the student will be suspended from the university.

Can I Attend a College Near My Home to Restore My Academic Eligibility?

No. Since only the hours transfer in from other institutions, and not the grades, you cannot improve your GPA by taking courses elsewhere. In fact, taking hours elsewhere may actually worsen the situation, because the minimum GPA required to be retained in good standing increases with the total number of hours the student has attempted at all colleges attended.

Where Can I Go on Campus to Receive Assistance with Questions I Might Have About My GPA?

Your first resource is always your academic advisor.

■ Summer School and Transient Study

Odds are that sometime during your academic career at UNC Wilmington, you will attend summer school. Students take classes in the summer for a number of reasons, including:

- Satisfying some additional basic studies requirements
- Accelerating your degree program
- Taking care of prerequisite courses
- Tackling challenging courses that you want to focus all of your attention on

UNCW offers a full array of summer school courses over two sessions. If you have never spent a summer in Wilmington, it is certainly something to consider. On-campus housing is available for either or both summer school sessions. Along with the great weather and the beach, there is a festival or special event almost every weekend.

UNCW's Office of International Programs also offers a wide range of summer options. Options are available for all majors, and recent summer destinations have included Jordan, Turkey, China, India, Japan, Australia, Brazil, Germany, France, and England.

The Office of International Programs is pleased to fund a number of education abroad grants awarded to students who apply to for summer education abroad programs. Selection is based on academic qualifications, including an academic reference, academic record, and a personal essay. Any full-time UNCW student earning academic credit abroad on a UNCW-sponsored summer study abroad program may apply. Grants awarded generally range from $250–$900 and are awarded annually in spring. **Grant applications are typically due by March 1**, but check the OIP website for more details (www.uncw.edu/intprogs).

You also have the option of taking summer courses at a another community college or another university. This can be an effective way to save money by living at home and/or working a part-time job while attending classes. This is known as transient study. If you are interested in exploring transient study, follow the instructions below to ensure that you take the right courses for your specific degree program from a regionally accredited institution.

Instructions for Transient Study

Before enrolling at the visiting institution:

1. The student should submit a request for Permission for Transient Study. The request form is available in SeaPort. The link for the Transient Study request is on the Student tab.

2. The Registrar's office will determine the UNCW course equivalencies.

3. The department will then determine if the course is appropriate for the student's degree program and either approve or deny the request.

■ Activity 1

Example

ENG 101	B+ (3.33) ×	3 sh attempted =	9.99 quality points
MAT 151	B– (2.67) ×	3 sh attempted =	8.01 quality points
BIO 201	B (3) ×	4 sh attempted =	12 quality points
PED 101	A– (3.67) ×	2 sh attempted =	7.34 quality points
UNI 101	A (4) ×	2 sh attempted =	8 quality points
Totals:		14 semester hours	45.34 quality points
45.34 QP / 14 sh attempted =		3.23 GPA	

If the semester ended today, what grade would you earn in each of your classes? Plug your classes and grades into the chart below. Calculate your GPA using the example above as a guide.

Totals:		semester hours	quality points
QP / sh attempted =		GPA	

Name: _____ Date: _____

◼ Activity 2: Advising Preparation Worksheet

My advisor:

My advisor is _____

The office location is _____

My advisor's phone number and e-mail are _____

My advisor's office hours are _____

My advising appointment is scheduled for (date and time) _____

Registration:

I am allowed to register beginning (date and time) _____

My Alternative PIN is _____

Proposed Schedule:

Below, list a proposed course schedule for next semester; include a minimum of three alternate class selections.

CRN	Class Title	Day	Time	Gen Ed/Major Req

Now let's take it a step further. What might your schedule look like the following semester?

Class Title	Day	Time	Gen Ed/Major Req

CHAPTER 10

Finding a Path to Your Future Profession
Career Exploration, Preparation, and Development

Learning Goals

The primary goal of this chapter is to supply you with specific strategies that you can use now and throughout your remaining years of college to promote your career exploration, preparation, and development.

■ Activate Your Thinking

Before you start digging into the meat of this chapter, take a moment to answer the following question: Have you decided on a career?

    a. If yes, why did you pick this career? (Was your decision influenced by anybody or anything?)

    b. If no, are there any careers you're considering as possibilities?

■ Why Career Planning Should Begin in the First Year of College

We know what you might be thinking: "Have I decided on a career? Give me a break; I've barely begun college!" This is probably the way most college seniors felt when they were first-year students. However, if you ask these seniors how they feel now, they would probably say something like: "I can't believe I'm about to graduate. How did time fly by so fast?" For these seniors and other students who will be graduating in this century, they are likely to continue working until age 75 (Herman, 2000). Also, consider the fact that once you begin full-time work, you will spend the majority of your waking hours at work. The fact is, the only other single activity that you will spend more time doing in your lifetime is sleeping. When you consider that such a sizable amount of our lifetime is spent working, plus the fact that work can influence our sense of self-esteem and personal identity, it is never too early to start thinking about your career choices.

> *Remember: When you are doing* career *planning, you're also doing* life *planning; you are planning how to spend your future life doing what you want to do.*

It is true that college graduation and career entry are years away, but the process of investigating, planning, and preparing for career success should begin during your first year of college. If you are undecided about a career, or have not even begun to think about what you'll be doing after college, don't be discouraged. In fact, you can join the club, because research indicates that the majority of college students are in the same boat. Three of every four beginning students are uncertain or have doubt about their career choice (Frost, 1991; Cuseo, 2005).

Even if you may have already decided on a career that you've been dreaming about since you were a preschooler, you will still need to make decisions about what specific type of specialization within that career you will pursue. For example, if you are interested in pursuing a career in law, you will eventually need to decide what branch of law you wish to practice (for example, criminal law, corporate law, or family law). You will also need to decide about what employment sector or type of industry you'd like to work in, such as: for profit, non-profit, education, or government. Each of these sectors will provide you with different options relating to the same career. For example, a student who is interested in an advertising career may work for an advertising agency (for profit) to encourage the purchase of a certain product, or may work in the non-profit sector to create a campaign for increasing public awareness of safety issues (e.g., persuade the public not to drink and drive). This student could also decide to create an effective advertisement designed to increase reading (education sector), or attempt to persuade people to enter public service positions (government). As these examples illustrate, there are still many options to consider and decisions to be made, even if you have decided on a particular career path.

Thus, no matter how certain or uncertain you are about your career path at this point in time, you will need to begin exploring different career options and start taking your first steps toward formulating a career development plan.

■ Career Exploration and Development Strategies

Reaching an effective decision about a career involves four steps:

Step 1. Awareness of yourself—such as your personal abilities, interests, and values.

Step 2. Awareness of your options—the variety of choices (career fields) available to you.

Step 3. Awareness of what particular options (careers) best fit you—that is, deciding on what are the best matches for your personal abilities, interests, and values.

Step 4. Awareness of how to prepare for and gain entry into the career of your choice.

Step 1. Self-Awareness

The more you know about yourself, the better your choices and decisions will be. Self-awareness is a particularly important step to take when making career decisions because the career you choose to pursue says a lot about who you are and what you want from life. Your personal identity and life goals should not be based on or built around your career choice; instead, it should be the other way around: **Your personal identity and life goals should be considered first and should provide the foundation on which you build your career choice.**

One way to gain greater self-awareness of your career interests, abilities, and values is by taking psychological tests or assessments. These assessments allow you to see how your interest in certain career fields compares with other students who have taken the same assessment, and how your interests compare with people working in different career fields who have experienced career satisfaction and success. These *comparative perspectives* can give you important reference points for assessing whether your level of interest in different careers is high, average, or low, relative to other students and working professionals. By seeing how your results compare with others, you may become aware of your distinctive or unique interests. Your Career Development Center is the place on campus where you can find these career-interest tests, as well as other instruments that may allow you to assess your career-related abilities and values.

In addition to career assessments, the learning styles instruments may sharpen self-awareness of your personal interests and preferences, and may provide useful information for making career choices. Also, self-assessment questions about your personal interests, abilities, and values to help you select a college major may also be used to help you select a career path.

Lastly, when making choices about a career, you may also have to consider one other important aspect of yourself: your personal needs. A personal "need" may be best understood as something stronger than an interest. When you satisfy a personal need, you are doing something that makes your life more satisfying or fulfilling. Psychologists have identified a number of important human needs that vary in strength or intensity from

Take Action Now!   Box 1

Personal Needs to Consider When Making Career Choices

As you read the needs listed in the box below, make a note after each one, indicating how strong the need is for you (high, moderate, or low).

When exploring career options, keep in mind how different careers may or may not satisfy your level of need for autonomy, affiliation, competence, and sensory stimulation, each of which is described below.

1. **Autonomy:** *Need to work independently, without close supervision or control.*

   Individuals high in this need may experience greater satisfaction working in careers that allow them to be their own boss, make their own decisions, and control their own work schedule. Individuals low in this need may be more satisfied working in careers that are more structured and involve a supervisor who provides direction, assistance, and frequent feedback.

   S TUDENT PERSPECTIVE

   "To me, an important characteristic of a career is being able to meet new, smart, interesting people."

   —*First-year student*

2. **Affiliation:** *Need for social interaction, a sense of belongingness, and the opportunity to collaborate with others.*

   Individuals high in this need may be more satisfied working in careers that involve frequent interpersonal interaction and teamwork with colleagues or co-workers. Individuals low in this need may be more satisfied working alone, or in competition with others, rather than careers that emphasize interpersonal interaction or collaboration.

3. **Achievement:** *Need to experience challenge and achieve a sense of personal accomplishment.*

   Individuals high in this need may be more satisfied working in careers that push them to solve problems, generate creative ideas, and continually learn new information or master new skills. Individuals low in this need may be more satisfied with careers that do not continually test their abilities, and do not repeatedly challenge them to stretch their skills by taking on new tasks or different responsibilities.

   S TUDENT PERSPECTIVE

   "I want to be able to enjoy my job and be challenged by it at the same time. I hope that my job will not be monotonous and that I will have the opportunity to learn new things often."

   —*First-year student*

4. **Sensory Stimulation:** *Need to experience variety, change, and risk.*

   Individuals high in this need may be more satisfied working in careers that involve frequent changes of pace and place (e.g., frequent travel), unpredictable events (e.g., work tasks that vary considerably from day to day), and moderate stress (e.g., working under pressure of competition or deadlines). Individuals with a low need for sensory stimulation may feel more comfortable working in careers that involve regular routines, predictable situations, and minimal levels of risk or stress.

one individual to another. Listed in Box 1 are personal needs that we feel are the most relevant or important ones to consider when making decisions about careers.

Pierce Howard, author of *The Owner's Manual for the Brain*, puts it this way: "It is stressful to attempt to be someone different from who we are, to try to be solitary when our nature is to be gregarious. Being true to our nature is, in some ways, the ultimate goal. Attempting to be something different is an obstacle to that goal. Don't expect a recluse to be motivated to sell, a creative thinker to be motivated to be a good proofreader day in and day out, or a sow's ear to be happy in the role of a silk purse" (2000, pp. 386–387).

Personal Story

While enrolled in my third year of college with half of my degree completed, I had an eye-opening experience. I wish this experience had happened in my first year, but better late than never (although earlier is best)! Although I had chosen a career during my first year of college, the decision-making process

> **S** TUDENT PERSPECTIVE
>
> "For me, a good career is very unpredictable and interest-fulfilling. I would love to do something that allows me to be spontaneous."
> —*First-year student*

was not a good critical thinking, systematic one. I chose a major based on what sounded best, and would pay me the most money. Although these are not necessarily bad variables, the lack of a good process to determine these variables was bad. In my junior year of college I asked one of my professors why he decided to get his Ph.D. and become a professor. He simply answered, "I wanted autonomy." This was an epiphany for me! He explained that when he looked at his life he determined that he needed a career that offered independence, so he began looking at career options that would offer that. After that explanation, autonomy became my favorite word, and this story became a guiding force in my life. After going through a critical self-awareness process, I determined that autonomy was exactly what I desired, and a professor is what I became.

—*Aaron Thompson, Professor of Sociology, and co-author of this text*

Taken altogether, there are four key aspects of yourself that should be considered when exploring careers: your personal *abilities*, *interests*, *values*, and *needs*. As illustrated in Figure 1, these are the four pillars that provide a solid foundation for effective career choices and decisions. You want to choose a career that you're good at, interested in, passionate about, and that fulfills your personal needs.

Lastly, since a career decision is a long-range decision that will involve your life beyond college, self-awareness should not only involve personal reflection about who you are now, it also involves *self-projection*—reflecting on how you see yourself in the more distant future. When you engage in the process of self-projection, you begin to see a connection between where you are now and where you want to be.

> **S** TUDENT PERSPECTIVE
>
> "I think that a good career has to be meaningful for a person. It should be enjoyable for the most part [and] it has to give a person a sense of fulfillment."
> —*First-year student*

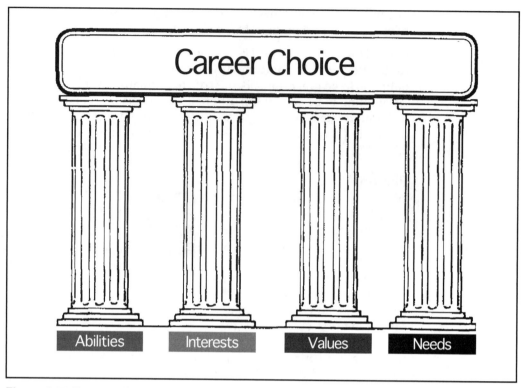

Figure 1 ■ Personal Characteristics Providing the Foundation for Effective Career Choice

Pause for Reflection

Project yourself ten years into the future and visualize your ideal career and life.

Try to answer the following questions about your ideal future-life scenario:

1. What are you spending most of your time doing during your typical workday?

2. Where and with whom are you working?

3. How many hours are you working per week?

4. Where are you living?

5. Are you married? Do you have children?

6. How does your work influence your home life?

CLASSIC QUOTE

You've got to be careful if you don't know where you're going because you might not get there.

—*Yogi Berra, former all-star baseball player*

Ideally, your choice of a career would be one that leads to a future career scenario in which your typical workday goes something like this: You wake up in the morning and hop out of bed enthusiastically—eagerly looking forward to what you'll be doing at work that day. When you're at work, time flies by, and before you know it, the day's over. When you return to bed that night and look back on your day, you feel good about what you did and how well you did it. For this ideal scenario to have any chance of really happening or even coming close to happening, you have to select a career path that is true to yourself—that closely matches your abilities (what you do well), your interests (what you like to do), your values (what you feel good about doing), and your needs (what brings you satisfaction and fulfillment in life).

Your career choice should make you look forward to going to work each day.

Step 2. Awareness of Your Options

In order to make effective decisions about your career path, you need to have accurate knowledge about the nature of different careers and the realities of the work world. The Career Development Center is the first place to go for this information, as well as for help with career exploration and planning. In addition to helping you explore your personal career interests and abilities, the Career Development Center is also your key campus resource for learning about the nature of different careers and for strategies on how to locate career-related work experiences.

The federal government lists more than 30,000 different career fields, many of which you may have never heard of, but which may represent good career options for you. You can learn about careers through nine major routes or avenues:

1. Reading about careers,

2. Becoming involved in co-curricular programs on campus relating to career development,

3. Taking career development courses,

4. Interviewing people in different career fields,

5. Observing people at work in different careers,

6. Internships,

7. Co-op programs,

8. Volunteer service, and

9. Part-time work.

"HUNTER OR GATHERER? THOSE ARE MY ONLY OPTIONS?"

There are many more career choices in today's work world than there were for our early ancestors.

Strategies for using each of these routes to acquire accurate information about careers are discussed below.

1. Reading about Careers

Your Career Development Center and your College Library are key campus resources where you can find a wealth of reading material on careers, either in print or online. Here are some of the most useful sources of written information on careers:

■ *Dictionary of Occupational Titles (DOT)* (http://www.occupationalinfo.org) This is the largest printed resource on careers; it contains concise definitions of over 17,000 jobs. It also includes such information as:

© CORBIS

- ■ specific work tasks that people in the career typically perform on a regular basis;
- ■ type of knowledge, skills, and abilities that are required for different careers;
- ■ the interests, values, and needs of individuals who find working in their careers to be personally rewarding; and
- ■ background experiences of people working in different careers that qualified them for their positions.

There are many resources for finding information on careers, many of which can be accessed on the Internet.

■ *Occupational Outlook Handbook (OOH)* (http://www.bls.gov/oco) This is one of the most widely available and frequently used resources on careers. It contains descriptions of approximately 250 positions, including information on the nature of work, work conditions, places of employment, training/education required for career entry and advancement, salaries, careers in related fields, and sources of additional information about particular careers (e.g., professional organizations and governmental agencies). A distinctive feature of this resource is that it contains information about the future employment outlook for different careers.

■ *Encyclopedia of Careers and Vocational Guidance* (Chicago: Ferguson Press) As the name suggests, this is an encyclopedia of information on qualifications, salaries, and advancement opportunities for a wide variety of careers.

■ *Occupational Information Network (O*NET) Online* (http://online.onetcenter.org) This is America's most comprehensive source of online information about careers. It contains an up-to-date set of descriptions for almost 1,000 different careers, plus lots of other information similar to that found in the *Dictionary of Occupational Titles (DOT)*.

In addition to these general sources of information, the Career Development Center or College Library should have books and other published materials relating to specific careers or occupations (e.g., careers for English majors). You can also learn a lot about careers by simply reading advertisements for position openings. You can find them in your local newspaper or at online sites, such as careerbuilder.com and monstertrak.com. When reading job descriptions, note the particular tasks, duties, or responsibilities that they involve, and ask yourself if these positions fit your profile of abilities, interests, needs, and values.

2. Becoming Involved in Co-Curricular Programs on Career Planning and Development

Periodically during the academic year, co-curricular programs devoted to career exploration and career preparation are likely to be offered on your campus. For example, your Career Development Center may sponsor career exploration or career planning workshops, which you can attend free of charge. Also, your Career Development Center may organize a "career fair" in which professionals working in different career fields are given booths on campus where you can visit with them and ask them questions about their careers. (See the end-of-chapter assignment for questions that you could ask.)

We strongly encourage your involvement in co-curricular programs that relate to career exploration and development. They have already been covered by the cost of your tuition, so get your money's worth and take advantage of them. Research suggests that such programs have positive effects on college students' career planning and decision-making (Brown & Krane, 2000; Hildenbrand & Gore, 2005).

3. Taking Career Development Courses

Many colleges offer career development courses for elective credit. These courses typically include self-assessment of your career interests, information about different careers, and strategies for career preparation. The things that students do in these courses are what they should do anyway (on their own), so why not do them as part of a career development course and receive academic credit for doing them? Studies show that students who participate in career development courses experience significant benefits in terms of their career choice and career development (Pascarella & Terenzini, 2005).

It might also be possible for you to take an *independent study* course that will allow you to investigate issues in the career area you are considering. An independent study is a project that you work out with a faculty member, which usually involves writing a paper or detailed report. It allows you to receive academic credit for an in-depth study of a topic of your choice, without having to enroll with other students in a traditional course that has regularly scheduled classroom meetings. You could use this independent-study option to choose a project that relates to a career you may be interested in pursuing. (To see if this option is available at your campus, check the college catalogue or consult with an academic advisor.) Also, if you have a free choice of a topic to write about in a writing course or to speak about in a speech course, consider researching your career interest and use this as a topic for your paper or presentation.

4. Information Interviews

One of the best and most overlooked ways to get accurate information about careers is to interview professionals who are actually working in careers that you are considering. Career development specialists refer to this strategy as "information interviewing." Although you might think that working professionals would have little interest in taking time out of their day to speak with a student, most of them do not mind being interviewed about their careers; in fact, they often enjoy it (Crosby, 2002).

Information interviews provide you inside information about what careers are really like, because you're getting that information directly "from the horse's mouth." Participating in information interviews can also help you gain experience and confidence with interview situations, which may help you prepare for future job interviews. Furthermore, if you make a good impression during the information interview, the person you interviewed may suggest that you contact him or her again after graduation in case there are any position openings. If there are, you might be the person being interviewed and possibly being hired.

Because information interviews can be a source of valuable information about careers (and provide possible contacts for future employment), we strongly recommend that you complete the information interview assignment that is included at the end of this chapter.

5. Observing People at Work in Different Careers

In addition to learning about careers from reading and interviews, you can experience careers more directly by placing yourself in workplace situations or environments that enable you to observe workers actually performing their jobs. Two college-sponsored programs that may allow you to observe working professionals are the following:

- Job Shadowing Programs: These programs allow you to follow around ("shadow") and observe a professional during a "typical" workday.
- Externship Programs: An externship is basically an extended form of job shadowing, which lasts for a longer period of time (e.g., 2–3 days).

Visit your Career Development Center to find out about what job shadowing or externship programs may be available at your college. If none are available in a career field that interests you, then consider finding one on your own, using strategies similar to those we recommend for information interviews in the end-of-chapter assignment. The only difference would be that, instead of asking the person for an interview, you would be asking if you could observe that person at work. In fact, you might ask the same people who were willing to give you an information interview if they would also be willing to let you observe them at work. Just remember that one or two days of observation will give you some first-hand information, but not a thorough understanding of that field.

Pause for Reflection

If you were to observe or interview a working professional in a career that interests you, what position would that person hold?

---

6. Internships

In contrast to job shadowing or externships, whereby you observe someone at work, an internship program involves you with the work itself; that is to say, you actually *participate* and *perform* work duties related to the career. The word "internship" implies that you are involved "internally" with the work process, and actually doing the work—as opposed to an "externship" where you are "external" to the work process, observing someone else doing the work.

Another distinguishing feature of internships is that you can receive academic credit, and, sometimes, financial compensation for the work you do. An internship usually totals 120 to 150 work hours, which may be completed at the same time you're enrolled in a full schedule of classes; or, internship hours could be completed during the summer.

A key advantage of an internship is that it enables college students to avoid the classic "catch-22" situation they often run into when interviewing for their first career position after graduation. The interview scenario often goes something like this: Employer asks the college graduate, "What work experience have you had in this field?" The recent graduate replies,

An internship is an excellent way to get experience in a career before you graduate.

"Got Experience?"—The "killer question" that college graduates can't answer after college unless they've had some career-related work experience during college (e.g., internships or volunteer service).

"I haven't had any work experience because I've been a full-time college student." This situation can be avoided if students have an internship *during* their college experience. We strongly encourage you to participate in an internship while in college; this will enable you to beat the "no experience" rap after graduation and will distinguish yourself from many other college graduates. In fact, research reveals that students who have internships while in college are more likely to experience positive gains in development of career-related skills and find employment immediately after college graduation (Pascarella & Terenzini, 2005).

Although internships are typically available to students during their junior or senior year, there may also be internships available to first- and second-year students on your campus. If your school offers internships only for juniors or seniors, or does not offer internships that relate to your particular career interests, you can pursue an internship on your own. There are published guides that describe a wide variety of career-related internships, along with information on how to apply for them (e.g., *Peterson's Internships* and the *Vault Guide to Top Internships*). You could also search for internships on the Web (e.g., www.internships.com and www.vaultreports.com). Another good resource for possible information on internships is the local Chamber of Commerce in the town or city where your college is located, or the local Chamber of Commerce in your hometown.

7. Cooperative Education (Co-op) Programs

A co-op is similar to an internship, but involves work experience that lasts longer than one academic term and often requires students to stop their course work temporarily in order to participate in the program. There are, however, some co-op programs that allow students to continue to take classes while working part time at their co-op position; these are sometimes referred to as "parallel co-ops." Students are paid for participating in co-op programs, but do not receive academic credit—just a notation on their college transcript (Smith, 2005).

Typically, co-ops are only available to juniors or seniors, but you can begin now to explore co-op programs by looking through your college catalog and visiting your Career Development Center to see if your school offers co-op programs in career areas that may interest you. If you find any, plan to get involved with one, because it can provide you with an authentic source of career information and work experience.

The value of co-ops and internships is strongly supported by research, which indicates that students who have these experiences during college:

- are more likely to report that their college education was relevant to their career,
- receive higher evaluations from employers who recruit students on campus,
- have less difficulty finding an initial position after graduation,
- are more satisfied with their first career position after college,
- obtain more prestigious positions after graduation, and
- report greater job satisfaction (Gardner, 1991; Knouse, Tanner, & Harris, 1999; Pascarella & Terenzini, 1991, 2005).

In one statewide survey, which asked employers to rank a variety of factors in terms of their importance for hiring new college graduates, internships and cooperative education programs received the highest ranking from employers (Education Commission of the States, 1995). Furthermore, employers often report that when full-time positions become available in their organization or company, they are more likely to turn first to their own interns and co-op students (NACE, 2003).

8. Volunteer Service

In addition to helping your community, volunteer service can help *you*. It can serve to promote your career exploration and preparation by allowing you to experience different work environments and to gain work experience in fields related to your areas of service. For example, volunteer service to different age groups (e.g., children, adolescents, or the elderly) and service in different environments (e.g., hospital, school, or laboratory) can provide you with first-hand work experience, while simultaneously giving you a chance to test out your interest in possibly pursuing future careers relating to these areas of service. Volunteer experiences also enable you to network with professionals outside of college who may serve as excellent references and resources for letters of recommendation. Furthermore, if these professionals are impressed with your volunteer work, they may become interested in hiring you on a part-time basis while you're still in college, or on a full-time basis after you graduate from college.

Personal Story

I am an academic advisor and was once advising two first-year students, Kim and Christopher. Kim was thinking about becoming a physical therapist, and Chris was thinking about becoming an elementary school teacher. I suggested to Kim that she visit the hospital nearby our college to see if she could do volunteer work in the physical therapy unit. The hospital did need volunteers, so she volunteered in the physical therapy unit, and she absolutely loved it. That volunteer experience confirmed for her that physical therapy is what she wanted to pursue as a career. She completed a degree in physical therapy and is now a professional physical therapist.

I suggested to Chris, the student who was thinking of becoming an elementary school teacher, that he visit some of the local schools to see if they could use a volunteer teacher's aide. One of the schools did need his services, and Chris volunteered as a teacher's aide for about 10 weeks. At the halfway point during his volunteer experience, he came into my office to tell me that the kids were just about driving him crazy and that he no longer had any interest in becoming a teacher! He ended up majoring in communications.

Kim and Chris were the first two students whom I ever advised to get involved in volunteer work for the purpose of testing their career interests. Their volunteer experiences proved so valuable for helping both of them—in different ways—to make their career decision that I now encourage all students I advise to get volunteer experience in the field they're considering as a career.

—Joe Cuseo

It might also be possible to do volunteer work on campus by serving as an informal teaching assistant or research assistant to a faculty member. Such experiences are particularly valuable for students intending to go to graduate school. If you have a good relationship with any faculty members on campus who are working in an academic field that interests you, consider asking them if they would like some assistance, either with their teaching or research responsibilities. It is possible that your volunteer work for a college professor may enable you to make a presentation with your professor at a professional conference, or may even result in your name being included as a co-author on an article published by the professor you assisted.

Pause for Reflection

Have you done volunteer work prior to college? If you have, did you learn anything from your volunteer experiences that might help you decide what types of work best match your interests or talents?

9. Part-Time Work

Jobs that you hold during the academic year or during the summer should not be overlooked as sources of career information and as resume-building experiences. Part-time work can provide you with opportunities to learn or develop skills that may be relevant to your future career (e.g., organizational skills, communication skills, and ability to work effectively with co-workers from diverse backgrounds or cultures).

Also, work in a part-time position may eventually turn into a full-time career. The following personal story illustrates how this can happen.

Personal Story

One student of mine, an English major, worked part time for an organization that provides special assistance to mentally handicapped children. After he completed his English degree, he was offered a full-time position in this organization, which he accepted. While working at his full-time position with handicapped children, he decided to go to graduate school on a part-time basis and eventually completed a Master's Degree in Special Education, which qualified him for a promotion to a more advanced position in the organization, which he also accepted.

—Joe Cuseo

It might also be possible for you to obtain part-time work experience on campus through your school's *work-study program*. A work-study job allows you to work on campus in a variety of possible work settings, such as the Business Office, college library, Office of

Public Relations, or Computer Services. On-campus work can provide you with valuable career-exploration and resume-building experiences, and the professionals for whom you work can serve as excellent references for letters of recommendation to future employers. To see if you are eligible for your school's work-study program, visit the Financial Aid Office on your campus.

Learning about careers through first-hand experience in actual work settings (e.g., shadowing, internships, volunteer services, and part-time work) is critical to successful career exploration and development. These first-hand experiences represent the ultimate "career-reality test." They allow you direct access to information about what careers are truly like—as opposed to how they are portrayed on television or in the movies, which often paint an inaccurate or unrealistic picture of careers, making them appear more exciting or glamorous than they actually are. We strongly recommend using the strategies suggested in this section to get direct, first-hand experiences in real work environments, so you can make realistic career choices, rather than unrealistic choices that are based on second-hand information that reaches you indirectly—after passing through the sanitized and fantasized filter of popular media.

In summary, first-hand experiences in actual work settings equip you with five powerful career advantages. Such experiences enable you to:

1. Learn about what work is really like in a particular field,

2. Test your interest and skills for certain types of work,

3. Strengthen your resume by adding experiential learning to your classroom learning,

4. Acquire references for letters of recommendation, and

5. Make personal contacts that allow you to network with employers who may refer or hire you for a position after graduation.

So, get actively involved in first-hand work experiences. Use your campus resources (e.g., Offices of Career Development Center and your Financial Aid Office), read items posted on campus kiosks and hallway bulletin boards, use your local resources (e.g., Chamber of Commerce), and use your personal contacts (family and friends) to locate and participate in work experiences that are related to your career interests. When you land an internship, work hard at it, learn as much as you can from it, and build relationships with as many people as possible because these are the people who can provide you with future contacts, references, and referrals.

> # C LASSIC QUOTE
> Give me a history major who has done internships and a business major who hasn't, and I'll hire the history major every time.
>
> —*William Ardery,*
> *senior vice president, investor*
> *communications company*
> *(quoted in* The New York Times*)*

If you start gaining work experience early in college through volunteerism and part-time work, and participate later in an internship or cooperative education program as junior or senior, you will be able to graduate from college with an impressive amount of work experience under your belt (and on your resume).

Step 3. Awareness of What Career Options Best Fit You

When considering your career options, do not be misinformed and mislead by popular myths about careers. The following myths can lead students to make poor career choices or decisions.

Myth #1. Once you have decided on a career, you have decided on what you'll be doing for the rest of your life.

This is simply and totally false. The term "career" derives from the same root word as "race course," and like a racecourse, a career involves movement that typically takes different turns and twists. Like any race on any course, it's not how fast you start, but where you finish that matters most. This ability to move and change direction is what distinguishes a professional career from a dead-end job. According to the United States Bureau of Labor, Americans average four different careers in a lifetime; it also predicts that today's college graduates will change jobs 12 to 15 times, and these jobs will span across 3 to 5 different career fields (United States Bureau of Labor Statistics, 2005). You might find these statistics hard to believe because one of the reasons you are going to college is to prepare for a particular career. However, don't forget that the liberal arts component of your college education provides you with general, transferable skills that can be applied to many different jobs and careers.

Remember: *It is highly unlikely that your first career choice after college is what you will be doing for the remainder of your working life. Instead, your first career choice is likely to be a temporary choice, not a permanent choice that determines how you will make a living until the day you die (or retire).*

Myth #2. I need to pick a career that's in demand, which will get me a job with a good starting salary right after graduation.

CLASSIC QUOTE
Money is a good servant but a bad master.

—*French proverb*

Looking only at careers that are "hot" now and have high starting salaries can distract students from also looking at themselves, causing them to overlook the most important question of whether or not these careers are truly compatible with their personal abilities, interests, needs, and values.

Starting salaries and available job openings are factors that are external to us that can be easily "seen" and "counted," so they may get more attention and be given more weight in the decision-making process than things that are harder to see or put a number on, such as our inner qualities and whether they are really compatible with the choices we're considering. In the case of career decision-making, this tendency can result in college students choosing careers based exclusively on external factors (salaries and openings) without giving equal consideration to internal factors such as personal abilities, interests, and values. This, in turn, can lead some college graduates to choose and enter careers that eventually leave them bored, frustrated, or dissatisfied.

> **CLASSIC QUOTE**
>
> There is perhaps nothing worse than reaching the top of the ladder and discovering that you're on the wrong wall.
>
> —*Joseph Campbell, American professor and writer*

Also, keep in mind that careers which may be in high demand now may not be in such high demand by the time you graduate, nor may they remain in high demand for many years after you graduate. On the other hand, there will always be at least some demand for employees in almost all careers, because there will always be natural attrition (loss) of workers due to retirement or death.

The number of job offers you receive immediately after graduation and the number of dollars you earn as your first (starting) salary are very short-term and short-sighted standards for judging whether you've made a good career choice. Keep in mind the distinction between career *entry* and career *advancement*. Some college graduates may not bolt out of the starting gate and begin their career path with a well-paying first position, but they will steadily work their way up and get promoted to more advanced positions. Beware of advice from others who may tell you that you need to pick a career that's in demand. All this means is that you may be able to enter the field immediately and easily after graduation; it does not necessarily mean you will advance in that field just as quickly and easily. In other words, what is good in the short run (career entry) may not necessarily be good in the long run (career advancement).

Criteria to Consider When Evaluating Career Options

Effective decision-making requires identification of important factors that should be taken into consideration when evaluating your options, plus determining how much weight each of these factors should carry. As we have emphasized throughout this chapter, the factor that should carry the greatest weight or amount of influence in career decision-making is how compatible your choice is with your personal abilities, interests, needs, and values.

> **STUDENT PERSPECTIVES**
>
> "A big paycheck is a plus but it is not necessary. I would rather be inspired."
> —*First-year student*
>
> "I would rather make little money doing something I love than be rich doing something that makes me miserable."
> —*First-year student*

Suppose you have discovered more than one career option that is compatible with these four key dimensions of yourself. What other aspects of a career should be considered to help you reach a decision or make a selection? Many people would probably say money, but as the length of the following list suggests, there are other important aspects or characteristics of careers that should be factored into the decision-making process.

1. Work Conditions

These would include such considerations as:

© 2007 JUPITERIMAGES CORPORATION

- the nature of the work environment (e.g., physical and social environment);
- geographical location of the work (e.g., urban, suburban, rural);
- work schedule (e.g., number of hours per week, flexibility of hours); and
- work-related travel (opportunities to travel, frequency of travel, locations traveled to).

When evaluating career options, be sure to take into account things like the amount of travel required.

2. Career Entry

Can you enter into the career without much difficulty, or does the supply of people pursuing the career far exceed the demand (e.g., professional acting), thus making entry into that career very competitive and difficult? If your first and ideal career choice is very difficult to enter, this doesn't mean you should automatically give up on it, but you should have a career to fall back on—in case you can't (or until you can) break into your ideal career.

3. Career Advancement (Promotion)

An ideal first job educates and prepares you to advance to an even better one. Does the career provide opportunities to be promoted to more advanced positions?

4. Career Mobility

Is it easy to move out of the career and into a different career path? This may be an important factor to consider because careers may rise or fall in demand, and because your career interests or values may change as you gain more work and life experience.

5. Financial Benefits

This includes salary—including both starting salary and expected salary increases with greater work experience or advancement to higher positions; it also includes fringe benefits—such as: health insurance, paid vacation time, paid sick-leave time, paid maternity- or paternity-leave time, paid tuition for seeking advanced education, and retirement benefits.

6. Impact of Career on Personal Life

How would the career affect your family life, your physical and mental health, or your self-concept and self-esteem? Remember that you should not build your life around a career; you should build your career around your life. Your work life and personal life have to be considered simultaneously when making career choices, because the nature of your work can affect the nature (and quality) of your personal life.

> **Remember:** A good career decision should involve consideration of how the career may affect all key dimensions of your "self" (social, emotional, physical, etc.) at all key stages of your life cycle—young adulthood, middle age, and late adulthood.

Pause for Reflection

Think about a career you are considering, and answer the following questions:

1. *Why are you considering it? (What led or caused you to become interested in this choice?)*

2. *Would you say that your interest in this career is motivated primarily by intrinsic factors—that is to say, factors "inside" of you, such as your personal abilities, interests, needs, and values? Or, would you say that your interest in the career is influenced more heavily by extrinsic factors—that is to say, factors "outside" of you, such as starting salary, pleasing parents, meeting family expectations, or meeting an expected role for your gender (male role or female role)?*

3. *If money was not an issue and you could earn a comfortable living in any career, would you choose the same career?*

LASSIC QUOTE

Students [may be] pushed into careers by their families, while others have picked one just to relieve their anxiety about not having a career choice. Still others may have picked popular or lucrative careers, knowing nothing of what they're really like or what it takes to prepare for them.

—*Lee Upcraft, Joni Finney, and Peter Garland, Student Development Specialists*

Since the cost of college can be very high, family members paying this hefty cost (or helping you pay it) may sometimes get nervous about making such a steep financial commitment if you choose a career path that they are not familiar with, do not agree with, or do not understand (Helkowski & Shehan, 2004). If you happen to choose such a path, they may strongly oppose it, or may pressure you to change your mind. It may be tempting to reduce their anxiety, or your guilt about causing their anxiety, and conform to their wishes. However, **the decision you make about what career path to follow should really be *your* choice, because it's really a decision about *your* life.** Although you should be grateful to those who have provided you with the financial support to attend college and should be open to their input, the final decision is yours to make.

Don't let gender stereotypes limit your choice of a major or career.

Step 4. Awareness of How to Prepare for and Gain Entry into the Career of Your Choice

Whether you're keeping your career options wide open, or if you think you've already decided on a particular career, you can start preparing for success in any career field right now. In this section, we will discuss specific strategies that you can begin using immediately to prepare for successful career entry and development.

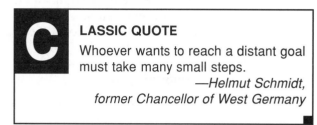

LASSIC QUOTE

Whoever wants to reach a distant goal must take many small steps.
—*Helmut Schmidt,*
former Chancellor of West Germany

Self-Monitoring: Watching and Tracking Your Personal Skills and Positive Qualities

Many students think that a college credential or diploma itself is the passport to a good job and career success (Ellin, 1993; Sullivan, 1993). However, for most employers of college graduates, what matters most is not the credential but the specific skills and personal qualities an applicant possesses and can bring to the position (Educational Commission of the States, 1995). You can start building these personal skills and qualities by *self-monitoring*—watching or observing yourself, and keeping track of the skills you are using and developing during your college experience.

Although completing assignments, getting good grades, and getting a degree are all important end products, it is equally important to reflect on and keep track of the particular skills you've used, learned, or developed in the process of completing these products. More important than memorizing facts, figures, and formulas are the new skills you are acquiring or refining, the new perspectives or vantage points from which you are viewing things, and the different dimensions or elements of the "self" that you are developing. We suggest you create a list of specific liberal arts skills, perspectives, and areas of self-development associated with a liberal arts education. Save that list and use it periodically as a checklist to keep aware of, and to keep track of, the skills and perspectives you are developing in college. It is important to make a conscious and deliberate attempt to do so, because the development of skills and perspectives can occur subtly and subconsciously, often getting embedded within or buried below all the factual material you are consciously trying to learn. Skills and perspectives are mental habits, and like other habits that are repeatedly practiced, their development can be so gradual that you may not even notice how much growth is actually taking place (like watching grass grow).

Don't overlook the fact that *learning* skills are also *earning* skills. The skills you are acquiring in college may appear to be just *academic*-performance skills, but they are also *career*-performance skills. For instance, in the process of completing such academic tasks as taking tests and writing papers, you are often using a variety of career-relevant skills, such as: analyzing, organizing, communicating, and problem-solving.

Career development specialists recommend that you track your skills and "sell" them to employers and enhance your career prospects (Lock, 2000). Be sure to make a conscious effort to track the specific skills and perspectives you are developing in college, so you will be able to showcase and sell them to future employers.

One specific strategy you can use to track your developing skills is to keep a *career-development journal* of your completed academic tasks and assignments, accompanied

by the specific skills you used to complete them. Also, be sure to record skills in your journal that you are developing in non-academic situations, such as those skills used while performing part-time jobs, personal hobbies, co-curricular activities, or volunteer services. Keep in mind that a skill is any positive or productive action that you can apply in different situations, which usually include most work situations. Since skills are actions, it is best to record them as action verbs in any career-development journal you may be keeping.

Personal Story

One day after class I had a conversation with one of my students (Max) about his personal interests. He said he was considering a career in the music industry and was now working part time as a disc jockey at a night club. I asked him what it took to be a good disc jockey, and in less than five minutes of conversation, we discovered that there were many more skills involved in doing his job than either of us had realized. He was responsible for organizing 3–4 hours of music each night he worked; he had to "read" the reactions of his audience (customers) and adapt or adjust his selections to their musical tastes; he had to arrange his selections in a sequence that periodically varied the tempo (speed) of the music he played throughout the night; and he had to continually research and update his music collection to track the latest trends in hits and popular artists. Max also said that he had to overcome his fear of public speaking in order to deliver announcements that were a required part of his job.

Although we were just having a short, friendly conversation after class about his part-time job, Max wound up reflecting on and identifying multiple skills that were involved in doing it. We both agreed that it would be a good idea to get these skills down in writing, so he could use them as selling points for future jobs in the music industry, or in any industry.

—Joe Cuseo

In addition to reflecting on your developing skills, also reflect on and keep track of your positive traits or personal qualities. While it is best to record skills as verbs because they represent actions, it may be best to record positive traits or qualities as adjectives because they are descriptions.

The key to discovering career-relevant skills and qualities is to get in the habit of stepping back from your academic work and out-of-class experiences to reflect on the skills and qualities you're developing, and then get them down in writing before they slip your mind. You are likely to find that many of the performance skills and personal qualities that you develop in college will be the very same ones that your future employers will seek from you in the workforce. Box 2 contains lists of some important career-success skills and personal qualities that you are likely to develop during your college experience.

Snapshot Summary   **Box 2**

Personal Skills Relevant to Successful Career Performance

The following behaviors represent a sample of useful skills *that are relevant to success in a wide variety of careers (Bolles, 1998). As you read these skills, underline or highlight any of them that you have performed, either inside or outside of school.*

advising	assembling	calculating	coaching	coordinating
creating	delegating	designing	evaluating	explaining
measuring	motivating	negotiating	operating	planning
researching	supervising	initiating	mediating	producing
proving	resolving	sorting	summarizing	synthesizing
translating				

The following represent a sample of personal traits *or* qualities *that are relevant to success in multiple careers. As you read these traits, underline or highlight any of them that you feel you possess.*

energetic	enthusiastic	ethical	outgoing	imaginative
industrious	loyal	precise	observant	open-minded
patient	persuasive	positive	productive	reasonable
reflective	sincere	tactful	thorough	flexible
broad-minded	cheerful	congenial	conscientious	considerate
courteous	curious	dependable	determined	prepared
punctual	persistent	productive		

Remember: *Keeping track of your developing skills and your positive qualities is as important to your career success as completing courses, earning credits, and obtaining a diploma.*

Self-Marketing: Packaging and Presenting Your Personal Strengths and Achievements

There are many more advantages and benefits associated with the college experience than "getting a better job" and "making more money." However, national surveys of new college students indicate that these are the primary reasons why they're attending college (Sax, et al., 2004). We acknowledge that this is an important goal for beginning students, so we devote this section to a discussion of strategies for packaging and presenting the skills you've developed in college to future employers. To do this most effectively, it might be useful to view *yourself* (a future college graduate), as an eventual "product" and *employers* as future "customers" who could potentially purchase you and your skills. As a first-year student, it could be said that you are in the early stages of the product-development process. You want to begin the process of developing yourself into a high-quality product, so that by the time you graduate, your "finished product" will be one that employers will be interested in purchasing.

All the career-development strategies we've discussed thus far may be viewed as strategies for developing yourself into a quality product that will be attractive to future employers (or future schools) after graduation. However, using these strategies effectively to develop yourself into a high-quality product may still not close the deal. You also have to effectively *market* yourself so that employers or schools will notice your product, be attracted to it, and be persuaded to purchase it. An effective marketing plan will allow you to give employers a clear idea of what you have to offer and will reduce the likelihood that you will accept the first job you are offered (if it does not match your capabilities).

The major routes or channels through which you can effectively "advertise" or market your personal skills, qualities, and achievements to future employers are your:

1. College transcript
2. Co-curricular experiences
3. Personal portfolio
4. Personal resume
5. Letters of application (cover letters)
6. Letters of recommendations (letters of reference)
7. Networking skills
8. Personal interviews.

These are the primary tools you will use to showcase yourself to employers and that employers will use to evaluate you. We'll now discuss how you can strategically plan, prepare, and sharpen each one of these tools in a way that maximizes its power and persuasiveness.

1. Your College Transcript

A college transcript is a listing of all the courses you enrolled in, along with the grades you received in those courses. There are two key pieces of information included on your college transcript that can influence decisions to hire you, or influence decisions to admit you to graduate or professional school: (1) the grades you earned in your courses, and (2) the types of courses you completed.

Simply stated, the better your grades are in college, the better are your employment prospects after college. Research on college graduates indicates that the higher their grades are, the higher:

■ the prestige of their first job,
■ their total earnings, and
■ their job mobility.

This relationship between college grades and career success exists for students at all types of colleges and universities, regardless of the reputation or prestige of the institution they are attending (Pascarella & Terenzini, 1991; 2005). In other words, research indicates that *how well* students do academically in college has a greater influence on their career success than does the name of the school that appears on their diploma.

The particular types of courses that are listed on your college transcript can also influence employment and acceptance decisions. Listed below are the types of courses that should be good selling points if they appear on your college transcript.

■ Honors Courses

If you achieve excellent grades during your first year of college, you may apply or be recommended for the honors program at your school, which qualifies you to take courses that are more academically challenging. If you qualify for the honors program, we recommend that you accept the challenge. Even though "A" grades may be more difficult to achieve in honors courses, the presence of these courses on your college transcript clearly shows that you were admitted to the honors program and that you were willing to accept this academic challenge.

■ Leadership Courses

Many employers hire college graduates with the hope or expectation that they will advance and eventually assume important leadership positions in their company or organization. Although a leadership course is not likely to be required for general education, or for your major, it is an elective course worth taking. It can enrich the quality of your college experience and the quality of your college transcript.

■ Interdisciplinary Courses

An interdisciplinary course is one that interrelates or integrates two or more disciplines (academic fields). Most career challenges cannot be fully addressed or understood by any one single field of study. For instance, careers that involve the challenge of effective management and leadership rely on principles drawn from multiple fields of study, including psychology (e.g., understanding human motivation), sociology (e.g., promoting harmonious group relationships), business (e.g., managing employees effectively), and philosophy (e.g., incorporating social ethics).

We recommend that you strongly consider taking at least one interdisciplinary course while in college. Even if interdisciplinary courses are not required for general education or your major, taking them will enable you to see connections across different subjects, which can be a very stimulating learning experience in its own right. Also, their appearance on your college transcript would clearly distinguish your transcript from those of most other college graduates. Furthermore, interdisciplinary courses may enhance your employment prospects because studies indicate that executives value new employees who have interdisciplinary experiences and who take an interdisciplinary approach to solving work-related problems. For instance, national surveys have shown that, "Business leaders point to the need for entry-level employees who have the practical ability to reach across artificial disciplinary boundaries to bring all relevant information to bear on concrete problems" (Daly, 1992).

■ International or Cross-Cultural Courses

International or cross-cultural courses are those that cross national and cultural boundaries. The importance of such courses is highlighted by the fact that today's world is characterized by more international travel, more interaction among citizens from different countries, and more economic interdependence among nations than at any other time in world history (Office of Research, 1994). Boundaries between countries are also breaking down as a result of more international trading (importing-exporting goods), more multinational corporations, and more international communication—resulting from rapid advances in electronic technology (Dryden & Vos, 1999; Smith, 1994). As a result, employers have begun to place higher value on employees who have international knowledge and foreign language skills (Fixman, 1990; Office of Research, 1994). Taking courses that have an international focus, or which focus on cross-cultural comparisons, can help you develop the type of global perspective that strengthens the quality of your liberal arts education and the attractiveness of your college transcript to potential employers. In addition to gaining a global perspective from courses that emphasize international knowledge and foreign language skills, you might also consider participating in a study-abroad program in a country outside of the United States, which may be available to you during the regular academic year or during the summer.

Pause for Reflection

Are you aware of what study-abroad opportunities are available at your college or university?

Are you seriously considering a study-abroad experience? If not, why not?

■ Diversity (Multicultural) Courses

America's workforce is more ethnically and racially diverse today than at any other time in history, and it will grow even more so in the years ahead (United States Bureau of Labor Statistics, 2005). Successful career performance in today's diverse workforce requires sensitivity to human differences and the ability to relate to people from different cultural backgrounds (National Association of Colleges & Employers, 2003; Smith, 1997). Your participation in college courses relating to diversity awareness and appreciation, and your involvement in courses emphasizing effective multicultural interaction and communication, represent valuable additions to your college transcript that will strengthen your career preparation.

■ Senior Seminars or Senior Capstone Courses

These courses are designed to put a "cap" or final touch on your college experience, helping you tie it all together and make a smooth transition from college to life after college. They may include such topics as resume building, portfolio preparation, job-interview strategies, job-location strategies, development of a college-to-career plan, and strategies for applying to and preparing for graduate or professional school after college. Some capstone courses may also involve a senior thesis or research project in your major field, which can provide a powerful finishing touch to your major and may be particularly valuable for helping you gain acceptance to graduate or professional school.

Participation in campus organizations can be a valuable source of experience that contributes to your career preparation and development.

2. Your Co-Curricular Experiences

Participation in student clubs, campus organizations, and other types of co-curricular activities can be a very valuable source of experiential learning that can complement classroom-based learning and contribute to your career preparation and development. When college graduates are asked to look back at their college experience and identify what aspects of it helped prepare them for their career, they frequently report that their co-curricular experiences helped them develop skills that enhanced their work performance and career advancement (Marchese, 1990; Kuh, 1993). These personal reports have been confirmed by employers' on-the-job evaluations of college graduates, which indicate that the best predictor of success in careers involving management or leadership was previous involvement in co-curricular experiences during college, particularly those involving student leadership (Howard, 1986; Pascarella & Terenzini, 1991, 2005). It has also been found that student involvement in leadership experiences during college is associated with increased self-esteem (Astin, 1993).

Because there is such a solid body of research supporting the value of co-curricular experiences, we strongly recommend your involvement in campus clubs and organizations. We especially recommend involvement with co-curricular activities that:

- allow you to develop leadership and helping skills (e.g., leadership retreats, student government, college committees, peer counseling, or peer tutoring),
- enable you to interact with others from diverse ethnic and racial groups (e.g., multicultural club, international club), and
- provide you with out-of-class experiences that relate to your academic major or career interests (e.g., student clubs relating to your college major or intended career field).

Keep in mind that co-curricular experiences are also resume-building experiences that provide evidence of involvement in your educational community and commitment to your school. So, be sure to showcase these experiences to prospective employers. Furthermore, the campus professionals with whom you may interact while participating in co-curricular activities (e.g., the Director of Student Activities or Dean of Students) can serve as valuable references for letters of recommendation to future employers, or graduate and professional schools.

Lastly, some colleges allow you to officially document your co-curricular achievements on a special transcript, often referred to as a *student development transcript* or *co-curricular transcript*. If your college offers such a transcript, we recommend that you take full advantage of it. When the idea of such a transcript was first introduced, national surveys were conducted to assess its potential usefulness. These surveys revealed that college admissions officials and employers of college students both thought the transcript would be very useful in helping them select applicants (Bryan et al., 1981). If your college does not offer such a transcript, be sure to describe your co-curricular experiences on your resume and your letters of application. Do not just cite or list the names of these activities. Provide details about the duties you performed and the specific skills that were required of you and acquired by you.

The ritual of burning completed coursework in high school is not recommended in college. (Instead, save your best work, and include it in a personal portfolio.)

3. Personal Portfolio

You may have heard the word "portfolio," and associated it with a collection of artwork that professional artists put together to showcase or advertise their artistic talents. However, a portfolio can be a collection of any materials or products that illustrates an individual's skills and talents, or demonstrates an individual's educational and personal development. For example, a portfolio could include such items as written papers, exam performances, research projects, senior thesis, audiotapes or videotapes of oral presentations, artwork, DVDs of theatrical performances, or CDs of musical performances.

You can start the process of portfolio development right now by saving your best work and performances. Store them in a traditional portfolio folder, or save them on a computer disc and create an electronic portfolio. Another option would be to create a Web site and upload them there. Eventually, you should be able to build up a well-stocked portfolio that documents your skills and demonstrates your development for possible presentation to future employers or future schools. (For useful information and assistance on how to develop an electronic portfolio, starting early in your first year and continuing through your senior year, go to www.kzoo.edu/pfolio.)

Pause for Reflection

If you were to predict what your best "work products" in college will be—those most likely to appear in your personal portfolio—what do you think they'd be?

---

4. Personal Resume

Unlike a portfolio, which contains actual products or samples of your work, a resume may be described as a listed summary of your most important accomplishments, skills, and credentials. If you have just graduated from high school, you may not have accumulated enough experiences to construct a fully developed resume. However, you can start now to build a "skeletal resume," which contains major categories or headings (the skeleton), under which you'll eventually include your specific experiences and accomplishments. See Box 3 for a sample skeleton resume. As you acquire experiences, you can then flesh-out the resume's skeleton by gradually filling in its general categories with specific skills, accomplishments, and credentials.

This process can be an excellent strength-recognition exercise that elevates your self-esteem. It essentially forces you to focus on your accomplishments by providing a visual record of them. Furthermore, developing a framework for organizing your accomplishments will also provide an outline for your personal goal setting—by serving as a visible reminder of the things you plan to do or accomplish. As you fill in and build up your resume, you can literally see how much you have achieved, which, in turn, can boost your confidence and motivation to continue achieving. Every time you look at your growing resume, you are reminded of your past accomplishments, which, in turn, can energize and motivate you to reach your future goals.

5. Letters of Application (a.k.a., Cover Letters)

A letter of application refers to the letter you write when applying for an employment position or acceptance to a school. When writing this letter, we recommend that you demonstrate your knowledge of:

- *you*—e.g., your personal interests, abilities, and values (use specific, concrete examples);
- the *organization* or *institution* to which you are applying—show them that you know something specific about its purpose, philosophy, programs, and the position you are applying for; and
- the *"match"* or *"fit"* between you and the organization (e.g., between the skills you possess and the skills that the position requires).

Focusing on these three major points should make your letter complete, and will allow the letter to flow in a natural sequence that moves from a focus on *you*, to a focus on

---

Take Action Now!   **Box 3**

Constructing a Resume

Use this "skeletal resume" as an outline or template for beginning construction of your own resume and for setting your future goals. (If you have already developed a resume, use this template to identify and add categories that may be missing from your current one.)

Name (First, Middle, Last)
e-mail address

Current Address: *Permanent Address:*
P.O. Box or Street Address   *P.O. Box or Street Address*
City, ST   *City, ST*
Phone #   *Phone #*

EDUCATION: *Name of College or University, City, State*
              Degree Name (e.g., Bachelor of Science)
              College Major (e.g., Accounting)
              Graduation Date, GPA

RELATED WORK *Position Title, City, State*   *Start and stop dates*
EXPERIENCES: *(begin list with most recent date)*

VOLUNTEER (COMMUNITY SERVICE) EXPERIENCES:

NOTABLE COURSES
(e.g., leadership, international, or interdisciplinary courses)

CO-CURRICULAR EXPERIENCES
(e.g., student government, peer leadership)

PERSONAL SKILLS and POSITIVE QUALITIES:
List as bullets, and list as many as you think relate (directly or indirectly) to the position.

HONORS/AWARDS: *In addition to those received in college, you may include those received*
                       in high school.

PERSONAL INTERESTS: *Include items that showcase any special hobbies or talents that are*
                       not directly related to school or work. (Employers may use this
                       information to see how well you may fit in with the work
                       culture or relate to current employees.)

them, to a focus on the *relationship* between you and them. Here are some suggestions for developing each of these three points in your letter of application.

- ■ **Organize information about yourself into a past-present-future sequence of personal development.**

For instance, point out:

- ■ where you have been—your past history or background experiences that qualify you to apply (academic, co-curricular, and work experiences)
- ■ where you are now (why, at the present point in time, you've elected to apply to them)
- ■ where you intend to go (what you hope to do or accomplish for them once you get there).

This past-present-future strategy should result in a smooth chronological flow of information about you. Also, by focusing on where you've been and where you're going, you demonstrate the ability to self-reflect on your past and self-project to your future.

When describing yourself, try to identify specific examples or concrete illustrations of your positive qualities and areas in which you have grown or improved in recent years. While it is important to highlight all your major strengths, this doesn't necessarily mean you must cover up any area in which you feel you still need to improve or develop. No human being is perfect; in fact, one indication of someone with a healthy self-concept is that person's ability to recognize and acknowledge both personal strengths and personal weaknesses— areas in need of further development. Including a touch of honest self-assessment in your letter of application demonstrates both sincerity and integrity. (And it may reduce the risk that your letter will be perceived or interpreted as a "snow job" that piles on mounds and pounds of self-flattery, under which even the tiniest ounce of self-honesty or personal humility is totally buried and concealed.)

- ■ **Do some advanced research about the particular organization to which you're applying.**

In your letter of application, mention some specific aspects or characteristics of the organization that you've read or learned about; for example, one of its programs that impressed you or attracted your interest to them. This sends the message that you have taken the time and initiative to learn something about their organization, which is a very positive message for them to receive about you.

Pause for Reflection

Have you met a faculty member or other professional on campus who is getting to know you well enough to write a personal letter of recommendation for you?

If yes, who is this person, and what position does he or she hold on campus?

- ■ **Make it clear why you feel there is a good fit or match between you and the organization to which you've applied.**

Point out how your specific qualities, skills, interests, or values are in line with the organization's needs or goals. By doing some research on the particular institution or organization that you're applying to, and including this information in your letter of application, you will immediately distinguish your application from the swarms of standard form letters that companies receive from applicants who mail-out multiple copies of the exact same letter to multiple companies.

6. Letters of Recommendation (a.k.a., Letters of Reference)

Your letters of recommendation can be one of your most powerful selling points. However, to maximize the power of your recommendations, you need to give careful thought to:

- *who* you want to serve as your references,
- *how* to approach them, and
- *what* to provide them.

Specific strategies for improving the quality of your letters of recommendation are suggested in Box 4.

7. Networking Skills

Would it surprise you to learn that 80 percent of jobs are never advertised? This means that the jobs you see listed in a classified section of the newspaper and posted in a career development office or employment center represent only 20 percent of available openings at any given time. Almost one-half of all job hunters find employment through people they know or have met, such as friends, family members, and casual acquaintances. When it comes to locating positions, *who* you know can be as important as *what* you know or how good your resume looks. Consequently, it's important to continually expand the circle of people who know your career interests and abilities, because they can be a powerful source of information about employment opportunities.

You can start expanding your circle of contacts by visiting the Career Development Center on your campus to find out what employers come to campus to interview graduating seniors. See if it is possible to obtain the names of representatives from those companies who have come to your college. Some of this information may also be available on your Career Center's online job listings. Also, ask if it is possible to receive the names of college alumni who may be working in fields related to your career interests. Some career centers have an online database that allow you to network with alumni who are working in careers that relate to your interests. Once you have selected a major, you may begin networking with seniors who will be graduating in your major by joining a club or organization that involves students majoring in the same field as you (e.g., philosophy club, business club). Lastly, be sure to share copies of your resume with friends and family members, just in case they may come in contact with employers who are looking for somebody with your career interests and qualifications.

8. Personal Interviews

A personal interview is your opportunity to make a positive "in-person" impression. You can make a positive first impression during any interview by showing that you've done your homework and have come prepared. In particular, you should come to the interview prepared with knowledge about yourself and your audience.

You can demonstrate knowledge about yourself by bringing a mental list of your strongest selling points to the interview and being ready to speak about them when the opportunity arises. You can demonstrate knowledge of your audience by doing some homework on the organization you are applying to, the people who are likely to be interviewing you, and the questions they are likely to ask. Try to acquire as much information as possible about the organization and its key employees that may be available to you online and in print.

Take Action Now!   Box 4

The Art and Science of Requesting Letters of Recommendation: Effective Strategies and Common Courtesies

■ *Select recommendations from people who know you well.*

Think about people with whom you've had an ongoing relationship, who know your name, and who know your strengths; for example, an instructor who you've had for more than one class, an academic advisor whom you see frequently, or an employer for whom you've worked for an extended period of time.

■ *Seek a balanced blend of letters from people who have observed you perform in different settings or situations.*

The following are key settings in which you may have performed well and key people who may have observed you perform well in these settings:

a.   the classroom—*for example, a professor for an academic reference*
b.   on campus—*for example, a student life professional for a co-curricular reference*
c.   off campus—*for example, a professional for whom you've performed volunteer service, part-time work, or an internship.*

■ *Pick the right time and place to make your request.*

Be sure to make your request well in advance of the letter's deadline date (e.g., at least two weeks). First, ask the person if s/he is willing to write the letter, then come back with forms and envelopes. Do not approach the person with these materials in hand because this may send the message that you have assumed or presumed the person will automatically say "yes." This is not the most socially sensitive message to send someone whom you're about to ask for a favor.

Lastly, pick a place where the person can give full attention to your request. For instance, make a personal visit to the person's office, rather than making the request in a busy hallway or in front of a classroom full of students.

■ *Waive your right to see the letter.*

If the organization or institution to which you are applying has a reference-letter form that asks whether or not you want to waive (give-up) your right to see the letter, waive your right—as long as you feel reasonably certain that you will be receiving a good letter of recommendation.

By waiving your right to see your letter of recommendation, you show confidence that the letter to be written about you will be positive, and you assure the person who receives and reads the letter that you didn't inspect or screen it to see if it was a good one before sending it off.

■ *Provide your references with a fact sheet about yourself, which includes your specific experiences and achievements*—both inside and outside the classroom.

This will help make your references' job a little easier by giving them points to focus on. More importantly, it will help you because your letter becomes more powerful when it contains concrete examples or specific illustrations of your positive qualities and accomplishments (rather than sweeping generalizations or glittering generalities that could be said about anybody).

On your fact sheet, be sure to include any exceptionally high grades you may have received in particular courses, as well as volunteer services, leadership experiences, special awards or forms of recognition, and special interests or talents that relate to your academic major and career choice. Your fact sheet is the place and time for you to "toot your own horn," so don't be afraid of coming across as a braggart or egotist. You're not being conceited; you're just documenting your strengths.

■ *Provide your references with a stamped, addressed envelope.*

This is a simple courtesy that makes their job a little easier and demonstrates your social sensitivity.

■ *Follow up with a thank-you note to your references about the time your letter of recommendation should be sent.*

This is simply the right thing to do because it shows your appreciation, and it is the smart thing to do because if the letter hasn't been written yet, the thank-you note serves to gently remind your reference to write the letter.

■ *Let your references know the outcome of your efforts (e.g., your successful admission into graduate school or acceptance of a job offer). This is a courteous thing to do, and your references are likely to remember your courtesy, which could strengthen the quality of any future letters they may write for you.*

Now WHAT???

This scenario can be avoided when students take a *proactive* approach to *career planning* before their senior year, and take an *active* approach to *job-hunting* during their senior year.

To prepare for interviews, visit your Career Development Center and inquire about questions that are commonly asked during personal interviews. You might also try to speak with seniors who have interviewed with recruiters and ask them if certain questions tended to be frequently asked. Once you begin to participate in actual interviews, try to recall and make note of the questions you were asked. Although you may be able to anticipate some of the general questions that are asked in almost any interview, it's likely there will be unique questions asked of you that relate specifically to your personal qualifications and experiences. If these questions are asked in one of your interviews, there is a good chance they may be asked again in a future interview. So, try to get in the habit of mentally reviewing your interview as soon as you complete it, and attempt to recall the major questions you were asked while they're still fresh in your mind. This will also make it much easier to explain why you are a good candidate in a thank-you letter you may send the person who interviewed you. Consider developing an index-card catalog of questions that you've been asked during interviews—with the question on one side and your prepared response on the reverse side. The better organized and prepared you are for personal interviews, the quality of your answers will increase and the level of your anxiety will decrease.

When you know yourself (what about yourself you're going to say), and when you know your audience (who they're likely to be and what they're likely to ask), you should then be ready to answer what probably is the most important interview question of all: "What can *you* do for *us*?"

■ Summary and Conclusion

When it comes to converting a college degree into successful career entry, studies show that students who make this conversion most successfully have two characteristics in common: a *positive attitude* and *personal initiative* (Pope, 1990). They do *not* take a passive approach that assumes a good position will just fall into their lap, nor do they feel that they are owed a good career simply because they have a college degree. Instead, they become actively involved in the job-hunting process and use multiple job-search strategies (Brown & Krane, 2000).

CLASSIC QUOTE

Know thyself, and to thine own self be true.

—*Plato, ancient Greek philosopher*

In national surveys, employers rank attitude of the job applicant as the number-one factor in making hiring decisions, rating it higher in importance than such other factors as reputation of the applicant's school, previous work experience, and recommendations of former employers (Education Commission of the States, 1995; Institute for Research on Higher Education, 1995). Graduation from college with a diploma is not a guarantee that you'll be hired immediately after graduation, nor is it an automatic passport to a high-paying job. Your college degree will open career doors, but it's your attitude, initiative, and effort that will enable you to step through those doors and into a successful career.

One study tracked a large number of college students after graduation to determine how successful they were in finding jobs. The results of this study indicated that those students who were most successful in getting outstanding career positions after graduation had two characteristics in common:

1. They engaged in career preparation and career development activities while in college, and

2. They took personal initiative during the job-hunting process.

These successful graduates were later interviewed and asked what advice they would give new college students. The advice they gave is nicely summarized in the following statement issued by a nationally known college advisor:

A big reason for their success, which shines through their answers and the advice they give, is initiative. They tell students to get involved in campus activities, but for substance, not for show; to take some career-related courses; to get internships and to have summer work experiences; and finally, to use initiative in investigating career possibilities and in looking for an actual job. Eighty-six percent of them said their own personal initiative was crucial to their being hired for their first job (Pope, 1990, p. 57).

The advice of these successful graduates reinforces the key points made in this chapter: Your career success *after* college depends on what you do *during* college. Touching all the bases that lead to *college* success will also lead to *career* success, namely:

1. **Get actively involved in the college experience**—get good grades in your classes and get work-related experiences outside of the classroom.

2. **Use your campus resources**—capitalize on all the career preparation and development opportunities that your Career Development Center has to offer.

3. **Interact and collaborate with others**—network with students in your major, college alumni, and career professionals.

4. **Take time for personal reflection**—deepen awareness of who you are, so you follow a career path that's true to you, and maintain awareness of your developing skills and personal qualities, so that you can successfully sell yourself to future employers.

> **Remember:** When you make the most of your college experience, you get the most out of your college degree, and you maximize the value of both for your future career.

■ Learning More through Independent Research

Web-Based Resources for Further Information on Careers

For additional information relating to the ideas discussed in this chapter, we recommend the following Web sites:

For career descriptions and future employment outlook:
www.bls.gov/oco

For internships:
www.internships.com and www.vaultreports.com

For information on electronic portfolios:
www.kzoo.edu/pfolio

■ Conducting an Information Interview

One of the best and most overlooked ways to get accurate information about a career is to interview professionals who are actually working in that career, which is known as "information interviewing." An information interview has multiple advantages for your career exploration and development, which include:

■ getting inside information about what a career is really like,

■ networking with professionals in the field, and

■ enabling you to gain experience and confidence with interview situations that may help you prepare for future job interviews.

Steps

1. **Select a career that you may be interested in pursuing.**

   Even if you are currently keeping your career options wide open, pick a career that might be a possibility. You can use the resources cited in this chapter to help you identify a career that may be most appealing to you.

2. **Find someone who is working in the career you selected and set up an information interview with that person.**

   To help locate possible interview candidates, consider members of your family, friends of your family members, and family members of your friends. Any of these people may be working in the career you selected and may be good interview candidates, or they may know other people who could be good candidates. The Career Development Center and the Alumni Association on your campus may also be able to provide you with graduates of your college, or professionals working in the local community near your college, who are willing to talk about their careers with students. Lastly, you might consider using the Yellow Pages or the Internet to find names and addresses of possible candidates. Send them a short letter or e-mail, asking about the possibility of scheduling a short interview. Mention that you would be willing to conduct the interview in person or by phone, whichever would be more convenient for them.

   If you do not hear back within a reasonable period of time (e.g., within a couple of weeks), send a follow-up message; if you do not receive a response to the follow-up message, then consider contacting someone else.

3. **Conduct an information interview with the professional who has agreed to speak with you.**

   Use the suggested strategies and potential questions in the following box.

Suggested Strategies for Conducting Information Interviews

■ ***Thank the person for taking the time to speak with you.***

This should be the first thing you do after meeting the person, before you officially begin the interview.

■ ***Take notes during the interview.***

This not only benefits you—by helping you remember what was said; it also sends a positive message to the person you're interviewing—by showing the person that his or her ideas are important and worth writing down.

■ ***Prepare your interview questions in advance.*** *Here are some questions that you might consider asking:*

1. *How did you decide on your career?*

2. *What qualifications or prior experiences did you have that enabled you to enter your career?*

3. *How does someone find out about openings in your field?*

4. *What specific steps did you take to find your current position?*

5. *What advice would you give to beginning college students about things they could start doing now to help them prepare to enter your career?*

6. *During a typical day's work, what do you spend most of your time doing?*

7. *What do you like most about your career?*

8. *What are the most difficult or frustrating aspects of your career?*

9. *What personal skills or qualities do you see as being critical for success in your career?*

10. *How does someone advance in your career?*

11. *Are there any moral issues or ethical challenges that tend to arise in your career?*

12. *Are members of diverse racial and ethnic groups likely to be found in your career field?*

    This is an especially important question to ask if you are a member of an ethnic or racial minority group.

13. *What impact does your career have on your home life or personal life outside of work?*

14. *If you had to do it all over again, would you choose the same career?*

15. *Would you recommend that I speak with anyone else to obtain additional information or a different perspective on this career field? (If the answer is "yes," you may follow-up by asking: "May I mention that you referred me?") This question is recommended because it's always a good idea to obtain more than one person's perspective before making an important choice or decision, especially one that can have a major influence on your life—such as a career choice.*

If the interview goes well, consider asking if it might be possible to observe or "shadow" your interviewee during a day at work.

Personal Reflection Questions

After completing your interview, take a moment to reflect on it and answer the following questions:

1. What information did you receive that impressed you about this career (if any)?

2. What information did you receive that distressed or depressed you about this career (if any)?

3. What was the most useful thing you learned from conducting this interview?

4. Knowing what you know now, would you still be interested in pursuing this career? (If "yes," why?) (If "no," why not?)

■ Case Study

Career Choice: Conflict and Confusion

Josh is a first-year student whose family has made a great financial sacrifice to send him to college. He deeply appreciates the tremendous sacrifice his family has made for him and wants to pay them back as soon as possible. Consequently, he has been looking into careers that offer the highest starting salaries to college students immediately after graduation. Unfortunately, none of these careers seem to match Josh's natural abilities and personal interests, so he's confused and starting to get stressed out. He knows he'll have to make a decision soon because the careers with high starting salaries involve majors that have a large number of course requirements, and if he expects to graduate from college in four years, he'll have to start taking some of these courses during his first year.

Reflection and Discussion Questions

1. If you were Josh, what would you do?

2. Do you see any way that Josh might balance his desire to pay back his parents as soon as possible with his desire to pursue a career that's compatible with his interests and talents?

3. What other questions or factors do you think Josh should consider before making his decision?

CHAPTER 11

Maintaining a Healthy Lifestyle

Most people think of wellness as the absence of disease. Actually, wellness is more than just "not being sick." Wellness is a continuum of healthy choices and behaviors that emphasize the importance of balance in your life. Wellness is a way of life that includes the decisions you make daily. Do you exercise? Do you eat well? Do you get enough sleep? Do you engage in safe sex? Do you feel extremely stressed before an exam? Do you share your thoughts and feelings with a friend or family member? Do you get regular medical checkups with your doctor? All of these questions examine your wellness continuum. True wellness requires assessment of your health-related choices and behaviors. As you read this chapter, consider the aspects of wellness that your life may be lacking. What important strategies should you implement for complete wellness in your life?

■ The Wellness Continuum

Your wellness continuum should include a balance between the following six components:

Physical

Optimal physical health includes eating well, exercising regularly, maintaining a healthy weight, making responsible decisions about sex, learning about and recognizing diseases, and preventing injuries. Good physical health allows you to perform daily tasks in life.

Emotional

The ability to monitor and explore your thoughts and feelings is an essential component of emotional wellness. Other important aspects of emotional wellness include optimism, self-confidence, self-control, trust, the ability to share your feelings, and managing stress. Monitoring your stress is the key to balanced emotional wellness.

Spiritual

To maintain spiritual wellness, you must have guiding values, beliefs, and principles that give purpose and meaning to your life. Spiritual wellness includes managing emotions such as compassion, forgiveness, joy, love, anger, fear, and anxiety. Many times organized religion can assist you in developing your spiritual wellness. However, there are also other ways to develop meaning and purpose in your life, such as meditation, art, or nature.

Interpersonal or Social

It is essential for you to develop successful and satisfying relationships with people in your life. Developing interpersonal wellness includes caring for your family or friends, sharing intimacy with others, and developing good interpersonal skills. You can also develop interpersonal wellness by getting involved in campus and community activities.

Intellectual

Being open to new ideas, thinking critically, mastering new skills, and maintaining a sense of creativity and curiosity are all aspects of intellectual wellness. The ability to acquire and use knowledge is essential to your overall wellness. Savoring new experiences and opportunities to learn is also a part of intellectual wellness.

Environmental or Planetary

Your personal health also depends on the health of the planet. Therefore, it is important that you take care of your surroundings. Environmental wellness includes being concerned about ultraviolet radiation, air and water pollution, household hazards, secondhand smoke, and personal safety.

Each dimension of wellness is directly related to the choices you make in other dimensions. For example, regular exercise (physical dimension) can increase your self-esteem (emotional dimension), which can in turn affect your confidence at work or school (interpersonal dimension). It is essential that you develop wellness in each of these areas to enjoy overall wellness in your life. Take a few minutes to assess each of the six dimensions of wellness in your life by completing Exercise 1 at the end of this chapter.

■ The Importance of Sleep

You will spend approximately one-third of your life sleeping. Sleep reenergizes your body for the next day's activities. Lack of sleep can cause physical, psychological, social, and academic problems. It is an essential component of wellness. Most college students find that six to eight hours of sleep each night is sufficient to feel refreshed. Some students, however, need more or less sleep. It is important that you find the amount of sleep that is required to refresh and regenerate your body.

Seven Tips for a Good Night's Sleep

- Consume less or no caffeine and avoid alcohol.
- Drink fewer fluids before going to sleep.
- Avoid heavy meals near bedtime.
- Avoid nicotine.
- Exercise regularly.
- Try a relaxing routine, like a hot bath or shower, before bedtime.
- Establish a regular bedtime and a time to wake in the morning.

■ The Benefits of Exercise

Exercise is an important component of wellness that affects your body's overall ability to function. Benefits of exercise include reduced risk of chronic disease, improved immune system, and improved psychological and emotional well-being. Twenty to thirty minutes of cardiovascular exercise three to five days a week, including activities such as walking, jogging, biking, and swimming, would be ideal. The Student Recreation Center is an excellent campus resource where you can participate in a variety of exercise and wellness-related activities.

Why Is Wellness So Important?

Addressing and maintaining your personal wellness can lead to:

- Higher self-esteem and self-confidence
- Decreased risk of depression and anxiety
- Decreased risk of chronic diseases
- Decreased risk of injuries and accidents
- Increased level of energy
- Increased awareness of personal needs
- Increased control of body weight

■ Changing Your Wellness Behavior

After taking the Wellness Evaluation (Exercise 1), you should have an idea of which aspects of your wellness behavior need improvement. Maybe you are not getting enough sleep, need to stop smoking, or need to eat healthier. Changes such as these may not happen overnight, and you'll need persistence, dedication, and an effective plan for changing your behavior. Your plan should include the following steps:

1. **Choose your target behavior.** Do not try to change several behaviors at once. You may want to try to quit smoking, start jogging, and get to sleep earlier all in the same week. It's more important to choose one behavior to ensure success.

2. **Monitor your behavior.** Start by defining and recording the behavior before you change it. It may be helpful to use a journal or notebook to monitor your behavior. If you want to improve your diet, for example, you should record everything you eat for three consecutive days.

3. **Analyze your data.** After you have recorded your behavior, analyze the results for patterns. Look closely for when, where, and why you engage in that behavior. Pay close attention to connections between your feelings and the situations in which you engage in this behavior.

4. **Set Specific, Measurable, Achievable, Relevant and Timely goals (SMART).** Consider breaking your ultimate goals into smaller, more specific goals. If your goals are more manageable, you will be more likely to stick to them. Consider implementing your behavior change for a lifetime. Behavior change that is slow and steady is more likely to result in a permanent change.

5. **Devise a strategy for success.** Formulate a detailed plan to change your behavior. Brainstorm environmental cues that may trigger the behavior. Consider the barriers that may keep you from reaching your goal. For example, if your goal is to stop smoking, consider what keeps you from stopping. Maybe your friends smoke, or you smoke when you are hungry. Plan for things that may get in your way and devise a strategy for combating these barriers. Carefully plan rewards for achieving your target behavior after you have accomplished your goal.

6. **Make a personal contract.** Once you have set your goals and have planned for potential barriers, it is important to make a contract with yourself. Include a goal statement, the time frame for reaching the goal, your plan for achieving the goal, your rewards for accomplishing the goal, and your signature. Consider having a friend or family member witness you signing the contract to provide support and encouragement.

■ Balancing Your Diet

Eating a variety of foods in moderation is the key to a balanced diet. Most college students have a difficult time eating healthy because of the lifestyles they lead. Most students eat excessive amounts of sugar and fat and very little protein or fiber. By eating healthy, you will have more energy for your academic and personal lives.

UNCW offers one dining hall, eight other dining locations, and three convenience stores. Wagoner Hall is the main dining hall for the UNCW campus. You will find all-you-can-eat dining, featuring an exhibition station, a produce market with vegetarian and vegan options, a bakery, an Italian kitchen, a grill, a sandwich shop, and a "home cooking" station that has food just like Mom makes! The Hawk's Nest is set up like a mall food court, showcasing individual locations such as Jolé Molé (Mexican), The Tuscan Oven (pizza and breadsticks), Hawk Wok (Asian), Varsity Grill (hamburgers, hot dogs, American fare), Tsunami (sushi), Freshëns, Salad Creations, Chik-fil-A®, and Quiznos®. Other locations around campus include grab-and-go spots such as the Courtside Snack Shop, Schoolhouse Cafe, and Fair Trade Market, Java City at Randall Library, The Landing, Einstein Bros. Bagels, and Sammy's Caribbean Café.

Tips for Eating On and Off Campus

There are several things you can do to eat healthy on a budget.

Living on campus:

- Try eating regular meals in Wagoner Hall or the Hawk's Nest instead of buying snacks.
- When buying snacks, choose healthy snacks such as fruit.
- If you find choosing healthy foods to be difficult, ask the Food Service Manager in the cafeteria or food court for tips.
- Eat fried foods in moderation. It's tempting to eat at Chik-fil-A or the Varsity Grill often. Try choosing a healthier option, like Salad Creations, when eating in the Hawk's Nest.
- Try to eat a balanced meal whenever possible.

Living off campus:

- Plan a menu for the week that features well-balanced meals.
- Look at the grocery store's advertisements before shopping for the best prices.
- Don't go to the grocery store when you are hungry.
- Always shop with a grocery list. Plan your meals and snacks ahead of time to avoid buying junk food.
- Read the labels. Look closely at serving sizes, calories, and fat grams on food labels.
- If you need to eat on campus or at a fast-food restaurant, try to choose a healthy option.
- When shopping on a budget, store brand foods are usually less expensive, though equal in quality.

Eating Healthy at Fast-Food Restaurants

Fast food is convenient and moderately priced. For college students with fast-paced lifestyles, fast food can be very appealing. However, you should avoid fast food as a

frequent choice for meals. Most fast food is loaded with excess sodium, fat, and calories. Whether you live on or off campus, consider the following tips when eating at a fast-food restaurant:

- Try baked or broiled foods instead of deep-fried foods (i.e., grilled chicken sandwiches or flame-broiled burgers).
- Avoid jumbo or "super sized" portions.
- Choose a side salad instead of fries.
- Try reduced-fat dressing on your salads.
- Drink water instead of soda.
- Choose a thin-crust pizza with vegetables instead of a deep-dish pizza loaded with meat and cheese.

Dieting

Many college students try a variety of fad diets. You may lose weight with a fad diet, but it is difficult to maintain the weight once you have lost it. It is more effective to lose weight by modifying your diet and exercising. Here are a few myths about dieting:

Dieting Myths

- **Eating fat-free foods will make you lose weight.** Many fat-free foods are higher in calories than regular foods. You may eat more to try to get the satisfaction you get from eating foods with fat.
- **You should deny all cravings.** Denying your cravings for certain foods can lead to binge eating. Sometimes it can be better to eat a small amount of the food that you are craving than to deny your craving for it.
- **Don't eat after 8:00 p.m.** The time at which you eat doesn't matter. Your body digests foods the same no matter what time it is. The problem is that most people choose unhealthy options late at night, such as pizza, ice cream, or chips.
- **Don't eat between meals.** Eating smaller meals with snacks in between is actually healthier than eating three large meals. You actually need food every three to four hours to avoid overeating. Try eating three meals with two to three healthy snacks in between.

■ Eating Disorders

Many college students attempt to attain the "perfect body." In fact, many college students believe that "thinner is better," basing their self-esteem on their body weight. Having unrealistic ideas about your body can lead to psychological distress along with several life-threatening disorders.

A growing number of college students are experiencing eating disorders. All three eating disorders discussed here—anorexia nervosa, bulimia nervosa, and binge eating disorder—have one common feature: all stem from dissatisfaction with body image and body weight.

Anorexia Nervosa

Anorexia is a quest for thinness typically characterized by a loss of 12–15 percent of normal body weight. Anorexics often claim to "feel fat" or "look fat" even though they are severely underweight. This intense fear of being fat leads to a distorted way of thinking about the body, self-starvation, over-exercising, and an absence of menstrual cycles. Almost 95 percent of diagnosed cases of anorexia are women; however, anorexia is becoming more common in men. Anorexia is life-threatening and can lead to depression, suicide, amenorrhea (absence of menstruation), hypertension, heart failure, and other cardiovascular disorders.

Bulimia Nervosa

Bulimia nervosa is characterized by recurrent episodes of binge eating followed by purging. During a binge, a bulimic may consume anywhere from 1,000 to 60,000 calories in a few hours. The binge is typically characterized by eating sweet-tasting foods in a secretive and planned situation. This is followed by an attempt to remove the food from the body by purging using laxatives or vomiting. Bulimics feel a loss of control over their eating during the binge period and cannot stop eating or limit how much they eat. This habit of binge eating and purging is usually a way of coping with emotions, stressful situations, or a major life change. Bulimia nervosa can cause serious health problems such as tooth decay, esophagus damage, depression, liver and kidney damage, and menstrual irregularities. Bulimia is difficult to recognize because most of the time bulimics conceal their eating habits and maintain a normal body weight.

Binge Eating Disorder

Binge eating disorder is characterized by uncontrolled eating patterns. You may be able to tell if a friend has a binge eating disorder if they eat more rapidly than normal, eat when they are not hungry, or eat until they are uncomfortably full. Binge eating is typically followed by feelings of guilt, depression, and shame. Binge eaters rarely eat because of hunger. Instead, they eat to cope with stress, conflict, or difficult emotions. Binge eaters are usually overweight and have a higher risk of developing depression and anxiety disorders.

Do You Know Someone with an Eating Disorder?

If you know someone who has an eating disorder, there are several things you can do to help. First, you should contact the Counseling Center located on Westside Hall's second floor, 910.962.3746. Listed below are more tips that should help you handle the situation:

- Educate yourself about eating disorders and their risks.
- Check out resources available on campus.
- Don't be afraid to ask for professional advice.
- Speak with your friend in the presence of other friends or family members.
- If you are going to talk with your friend, write down the specific concerns you have.
- Avoid giving simplistic advice.
- Express your support and understanding by emphasizing your friend's strengths.
- Expect your friend to refuse your help.
- If the situation is not life-threatening, and your friend continues to reject help, do not force it. Approach your friend again at another time.
- Call 911 or campus police at 962-2222 if the situation is an emergency.

■ Depression

During your first year at UNCW, you will face many changes and new challenges. These changes may be difficult to handle. Some students experience depression while in college.

Depression is more than just having a bad day; it is a serious disorder. Depression is characterized by:

- Persistent feelings of sadness and hopelessness
- Decreased or increased appetite and weight
- Loss of pleasure in usual activities
- Difficulty sleeping or oversleeping
- Restlessness and irritability
- Decreased energy
- Inability to concentrate
- Thoughts of suicide or death

Individuals suffering from depression may experience only a few of these symptoms. If you are concerned about yourself or a friend, contact a professional immediately. You can contact the Counseling Center located on Westside Hall's second floor or call 910.962.3746.

■ Sexual Behavior

Making health-conscious decisions about sex is an important component of wellness. Good decisions will reduce your risk of sexually transmitted diseases and unwanted pregnancy. Many UNCW students abstain from sexual behavior. It is possible to be intimate with another person without engaging in intercourse. However, if you choose to have sex, it is essential that you protect yourself from sexually transmitted diseases and/or an unwanted pregnancy.

To reduce your risk of contracting a sexually transmitted disease, you need to use a condom during all forms of sexual activity, including both oral and anal sex. By not using a condom, you are greatly increasing your chances of contracting a sexually transmitted disease.

Common contraception choices to prevent an unwanted pregnancy include hormonal contraceptives and condoms. Condoms used consistently and correctly when having sex also help to protect against STDs. Before using a form of contraception, it is important that you consider the possible side effects, advantages, disadvantages, and cost. Whatever method of contraception you choose, make sure you use it properly and consistently. A variety of birth control methods, including oral contraceptives (the pill), Depo-Provera (the shot), Nuva-Ring, and Ortho-Evra (the patch) are available by prescription. Since alcohol and drugs affect your decision-making skills, avoid mixing alcohol or drugs with sex.

Sexually Transmitted Diseases

Sexually transmitted diseases (STDs) are very common on college campuses nationwide. STDs can be spread through sexual contact with another person, including oral, anal, and vaginal sex. In some instances, STDs can be contracted through the infected blood of another person. There are two basic forms of STDs: bacterial and viral. Bacterial STDs include chlamydia, gonorrhea, and syphilis and can usually be treated with an antibiotic. However, if you contract a viral STD, you will carry the virus for the rest of your life. Viral STDs include genital warts (also referred to as human papillomavirus or HPV), genital herpes, hepatitis B, and HIV. There are treatments to relieve symptoms of viral STDs; however, there are no cures for viral STDs. Don't assume that condoms are 100 percent effective in reducing your risk of getting STDs. Some STDs, such as genital warts (HPV), can be spread by simple skin contact. If you have been exposed to an STD, there are several warning signs. They include a painful sore or wart around your genitals, a burning sensation during urination, unusual discharge, bleeding during intercourse, itching and tingling around the genitals, and yellowing of the skin (jaundice). Many of the most common STDs on college campuses, such as chlamydia, have few symptoms.

If you think that you have contracted an STD, you should seek help immediately. You can see a physician at the Student Health Center on the second floor of Westside Hall or phone 910.962.3280 for an appointment. The information you share with your physician is kept strictly confidential. It is important to get treated once you have a symptom. Once you have been diagnosed with an STD, do not engage in sexual activity until the STD is gone in order to protect your partner from the STD. Be honest with your current partner(s) and encourage testing. If your partner is not treated, you may contract the STD again. The highest rates of STDs are found in adolescents (ages 10–19) and young adults (ages 20–24). One in four Americans has or will be infected with an STD, according to the American Social Health Association. According to the Planned Parenthood Federation, the U.S. has the highest rate of STD infection in the industrialized world.

Sexual Assault

Sexual assault or abuse is any sexual activity undertaken without consent. This could include your inability to give consent because of drug or alcohol use, or being forced to engage in sexual activity. Sexual assault is a violation of North Carolina state law and the UNCW Code of Student Life. The National College Health Risk Behavior Survey, conducted in 1995, found that one out of every five college-age women report being forced to have sexual intercourse. Sexual assaults are rarely committed by strangers. In fact, 85 percent to 92 percent of sexual assault cases involve victims who know the offender (Rape in America: A Report to the Nation, 1992).

Three things have to be in place for a sexual assault to occur: a potential victim, a potential perpetrator, and an environment conducive to an assault. Limiting alcohol and drug consumption, avoiding situations where you feel uncomfortable, and paying attention to nonverbal cues a person may give you may offer some protection. Regardless of the circumstances, sexual assault is never the victim's fault.

Victims of sexual assault react in a number of ways. The most important thing to do if a friend is sexually assaulted is to believe them and offer support. If a person wants to report a sexual assault, the UNCW Police has outlined these procedures:

- Go to a safe place as soon as you can.
- Immediately call 911.
- Do not change your clothing. If you do, put your clothing in a paper bag (not plastic) and take it with you to the hospital.
- If you are sexually assaulted, go to a hospital.
- Do not clean your body or clothes. Try to preserve all physical evidence.
- Do not disturb or alter the crime scene.

UNCW CARE: Assault Response & Education

Westside Hall, second floor, 962.CARE or 512.4821 (24/7)
Support and confidential consultations about abuse or stalking

Off-Campus Resources

Wilmington City Police	911 or 343.3600
Rape Crisis Center	392.7460 or 392.7408
Domestic Violence Shelter and Services	343.0703
Sheriff's Department	341.4200
Wilmington Health Access for Teens	790.9949
New Hanover Regional Medical Center	343.7000
Cape Fear Hospital	452.8100
Rape Victim Assistance Program	1.800.826.6200
Coastal Horizons Rape Crisis Center	392.7460

■ Campus Safety

UNCW University Police can be contacted anytime at 962.2222.

Call Boxes

Almost 100 emergency call boxes have been strategically placed throughout the campuses of UNCW. These call boxes are available as a convenient means to communicate with the University Police Department. Whether you need an escort, assistance jump-starting/unlocking your car, or directions or are experiencing a true emergency, call boxes are available for your use. To activate the box, press the button on the front and wait for an answer to come from the box. When talking, press the button and speak clearly into the speaker of the box.

Although UNCW has taken precautions to ensure your safety, there are additional safety precautions you can take to protect yourself:

- Stay in well-lit public areas.
- Know the person or people you are with.
- Be aware of your surroundings.
- Lock your residence hall room or apartment and your car at all times.
- Look in and under your car before you get in.
- Walk in groups of three or more.
- If you feel uncomfortable in a situation, leave.
- Act immediately if you are assaulted in any way.

■ Rape Aggression Defense (RAD)

RAD is a course developed for women only that has established standards of acceptability for female self-defense. It teaches tactics and techniques that are hands-on and realistic in nature. This course is taught by certified instructors and comes with a workbook and a lifetime membership in the RAD system. Classes are scheduled two times a semester. Special classes can be requested by interested groups. For more information about RAD, contact C. T. Deacon at the University Police Department at 910.962.2222.

■ Exercise 1: Wellness Evaluation

The following evaluation will give you an idea of how your wellness lifestyle compares to the recommended wellness lifestyle. Using the scale provided, rate each statement below. Add up your score for each section.

Rating Scale:
1 = never   2 = seldom   3 = sometimes   4 = usually   5 = always

Physical Wellness

I eat a well-balanced diet.   _____

I do not smoke, drink, or use drugs.   _____

I get approximately six to eight hours of sleep each night.   _____

I exercise three to five times each week for 20–30 minutes.   _____

Emotional Wellness

I manage stress well in my life.   _____

I rarely experience emotions such as anger, jealousy, or hatred.   _____

I feel positive about myself and my life.   _____

I share my thoughts and feelings with a friend or a family member.   _____

Spiritual

I have a clear purpose in life.   _____

My values guide the decisions I make in life.   _____

I am able to easily forgive others.   _____

Personal reflection is important in my life.   _____

Interpersonal or Social

I verbally communicate well with others.   _____

I am able to develop close, intimate relationships with others.   _____

I care deeply for my friends and family members.   _____

I get involved in campus and community activities.   _____

Intellectual

I am open to the ideas of others.   _____

I think critically and question what I learn.   _____

I enjoy new opportunities and experiences. _____

I consider myself to be a creative person. _____

Environmental or Planetary

I spend time outdoors enjoying nature and my environment. _____

I protect myself from sun exposure. _____

I take steps to recycle products such as paper, plastic, and aluminum. _____

I avoid inhaling secondhand smoke. _____

Total score on all six dimensions of wellness _____

Rate your score:

120–100 Excellent

99–80 Good

79–60 Average

59 and below Needs Improvement

■ Alcohol, Tobacco, and Drugs

CROSSROADS Office

Hours: Monday–Friday 8:00 a.m.–5:00 p.m.
Location: Westside Hall, second floor

CROSSROADS, Substance Abuse Prevention and Education Programs, is dedicated to the advancement of thoughtful and healthy decision-making regarding the use of alcohol, tobacco, and other drugs. We believe that an engaged learner has the ability to make thoughtful decisions through access to the most current information available and a critical examination of beliefs and cultural expectations about substances in our lives.

CROSSROADS encourages legal accountability and personal responsibility in all choices involving alcohol, tobacco, and other drugs. We believe that the availability and utilization of early intervention services is essential to support students, as well as services for recovering and impacted students.

CROSSROADS aims to encourage, support, and be integral in the creation of an environment that encourages healthy behaviors through positive social norms, academic engagement and responsibility, a vibrant co-curricular life, and consistent enforcement of campus and community policies.

CROSSROADS recognizes that engagement with the Wilmington community on all of these levels is essential in achieving our goals as a campus and fulfilling our mission as a university. CROSSROADS programming will fall under one or more of the following program directions:

- Early identification and intervention for individual students
- Impacting individuals for behavior change
- Campus-wide collaboration on creating a healthy environment
- Connection to community to create healthy environments for current and upcoming students

■ Alcohol

Alcohol abuse is the number one problem facing college students today. The National Institute on Alcohol Use and Alcoholism lists alcohol as the most commonly used and abused drug in the U.S. and the leading cause of death among people between ages 15 and 24 due to automobile crashes and other injuries. Alcohol use is also linked to many cases of campus violence, vandalism, unwanted sex and pregnancy, low grades, and drop-out rates among college students. If you are under 21 years of age, it is illegal for you to consume alcohol.

Consider the following statistics from the American Council for Drug Education (1998) concerning alcohol use on college campuses:

- 159,000 of today's first-year college students will drop out of school next year because of alcohol or drug-related problems.
- 300,000 of today's college students will eventually die of alcohol-related causes such as drunk-driving accidents, cirrhosis of the liver, cancer, and heart disease.
- Nearly one-quarter of all college students report bombing a test or project because of the aftereffects of alcohol or other drugs.
- One night of heavy drinking can impair your ability to think abstractly for up to 30 days.

- In the last five years, the number of emergency room admissions for alcohol poisoning on campus communities has jumped 15 percent.
- 60 percent of college women diagnosed with an STD were drunk at the time of infection.
- At least one in five college students abandon safe sex methods they would normally use while sober when they are drunk.

In the 2003 UNCW Substance Abuse Survey:

- 67 percent of students have had one or more alcoholic drinks in the last two weeks
- 48.9 percent of UNCW students have had five or more drinks on any one occasion in the last two weeks (slightly below the national average of 49.7)

While drinking is an activity that is often associated with being in college, 25 percent of college students on the national level abstain from using alcohol. High-risk drinking, which is a form of alcohol abuse, is common on college campuses. Binge drinking is a form of high-risk drinking and is defined as having five drinks in a two-hour period for men and four drinks in a two-hour period for women. Frequent binge drinkers are more likely to engage in unprotected sex, drive drunk, violate campus ordinances, get injured, miss class, fall behind in school work, and argue with friends.

Physical Effects of Alcohol Use

For alcohol consumption, "one drink" refers to one 12-ounce can of beer, a 5-ounce glass of wine, or one 1.5-ounce shot of 80 proof liquor. Any one of these drinks can have instant physical effects on your body. When you consume alcohol, it is immediately absorbed into your bloodstream. Once the alcohol is absorbed into your blood, it affects nearly every system in your body. Alcohol can have several behavioral effects on your body, including loss of normal mental function, impairment of reaction time, physical imbalance when standing or walking, loss of vision, hearing, taste, smell, and overall control of your body. Chronic abuse of alcohol can cause damage to your liver (cirrhosis) and increase your risk of developing cancer and cardiovascular disease. Your blood alcohol concentration (BAC) is the primary factor that determines the effects of alcohol on your body. Your age, weight, heredity, sex, and amount of body fat, as well as the type of drink and the amount of food in your system, determine your blood alcohol concentration.

During the LAST year, have you experienced the following due to your drinking and drug use?

- *Had a hangover—65 percent*
- *Performed poorly on a test or project—16.9 percent*
- *Felt nauseated or vomited—56.1 percent*
- *Drove a car while under the influence—27.1 percent*
- *Done something I later regretted—35.8 percent*
- *Experienced memory loss or blackout—24.6 percent*
- *Had unplanned or unprotected sex—18.9 percent*
- *Had financial problems—16.3 percent*
- *Physically injured self—10 percent*
- *Passed out—19.1 percent*
- *Had alcohol poisoning—2.5 percent*
- *Had sexual intercourse when you normally would not have—14.2 percent*

From the 2003 UNCW Substance Use Survey

Complete Exercise 1, a short quiz on alcohol consumption, at the back of the chapter.

Drink Responsibly

If you choose to drink alcohol, it is essential that you drink responsibly. Drinking responsibly means keeping your BAC low and your behavior under control.

Responsible Behavior—Low-Risk Drinking

- Drink slowly and space out your drinks
- Eat before and while drinking to slow your body's rate of alcohol absorption
- Set an alcohol limit before you start drinking
- Alternate alcoholic beverages with non-alcoholic beverages
- Do everything possible to prevent an intoxicated friend from driving

Irresponsible Behavior—High-Risk Drinking

- Guzzling alcohol
- Relying on alcohol for a means of relaxation
- Drinking alcohol because you observe others drinking
- Drinking and driving

DWI/DUI is an abbreviation of driving while under the influence of intoxicants (alcohol) or of any substance or substances which impair driving ability. Other substances can include illegal drugs, prescription drugs, inhalants such as glue, gasoline, spray paint, etc., and/or over-the-counter medications. North Carolina's DUI law states that it is illegal to drive with a blood or breath alcohol content of 0.08 or higher.

In the last year, when given the option of driving after drinking, what did you do instead (check all that apply)?

- *Stopped and waited to sober up—46.9 percent*
- *Called for a ride—53.5 percent*
- *Stayed where I was—54.1 percent*
- *Took public transportation—21.2 percent*
- *Walked—30 percent*
- *Gave keys to someone else—40.3 percent*
- *Used a designated driver—70.5 percent*
- *Drove under the influence—23.6 percent*
- *Rode a bike—4.4 percent*
- *Rode with a driver who had been drinking—027.7 percent*

From the 2003 UNCW Substance Use Survey

■ Tobacco

Smoking is hazardous to everyone's health, both smokers and non-smokers. According to the U.S. Surgeon General, smoking is the leading cause of preventable death in the United States. Using tobacco is widespread throughout college campuses. Tobacco is available in several forms, including cigarettes, cigars, pipes, chewing tobacco, clove cigarettes, and snuff. All forms of tobacco contain nicotine, which is a psychoactive drug that can cause addiction. Withdrawal symptoms from tobacco include muscle pain, headaches, insomnia, and irritability. The use of tobacco causes negative effects on nearly every part of your body. Short-term tobacco use can cause loss of appetite, chronic bronchitis, hoarseness, stomach pain, and impaired vision. Long-term tobacco use is more serious and can cause:

- Cardiovascular disease (including heart attacks, stroke, and hypertension)
- Cancer (including lung, mouth, colon, liver, and esophagus)
- Tooth decay, gum disease, ulcers, and discolored teeth and fingers
- Stillbirths, infertility, and low birth weight of children

Secondhand smoke can cause as many problems as actually choosing to smoke a cigarette or chew tobacco. The Environmental Protection Agency estimates that people who work or live among smokers increase their risk of developing lung cancer by 24–50 percent. Secondhand smoke presents a particularly significant risk for children. Secondhand smoke is linked to the development of bronchitis, pneumonia, and asthma in children. Many people who smoke in college see themselves as social smokers and believe they will be able to quit after they graduate. This is not always the case. Many social smokers sadly discover that they are addicted. Another reason to avoid using tobacco products is the cost. On average, smoking a pack per day costs an average of $1,280 per year.

In the 2003 UNCW Substance Abuse Survey:

- 30.7 percent of students reported smoking cigarettes in the last 30 days.

Have you seen this logo around campus?

This logo embodies the spirit of the Campus Tobacco Coalition's efforts to reduce secondhand smoke exposure on campus.

85 percent of UNCW students believe that non-smokers should not have to walk through smoke to get into campus buildings.

Illegal Drugs

The use and abuse of illegal drugs occur in all educational, income, and age groups in the U.S. Drug use is common on college campuses nationwide. There are a variety of drugs available on college campuses, including marijuana, cocaine, heroin, amphetamines, and hallucinogens.

Marijuana is the most widely used illegal drug in America. 37 percent of college students reported using marijuana in the last year. Symptoms of using marijuana include mood swings, impaired thinking, increased appetite, staggering, aggressive behavior, and euphoria. It is possible to become intoxicated just by being in the same room with a marijuana smoker. Some common physical signs that may indicate someone is using marijuana are extreme redness of the eyes, an increase in appetite, and a dry mouth.

In the 2003 UNCW Substance Abuse Survey:

■ 25.5 percent of students reported using marijuana within the last 30 days.

Club drugs have become a part of popular culture in the U.S., turning up in dance clubs and bars at an alarming rate. Research indicates that club drugs cause serious health problems and even death. If they are used in combination with alcohol, the risk of illness and death is increased significantly.

Ecstasy (or MDMA) is taken in pill form and can cause damage to brain cells, memory loss, and physical impairment. Typical effects can seem positive at first, including a sense of euphoria, overly affectionate behavior, boosted energy, enhanced mental and emotional clarity, and sensations of lightness or floating. In large doses, ecstasy is very dangerous. It can cause increased heart rate, blood pressure, and body temperature, along with depression (following the high), anxiety, trouble with sleeping, great potential for overdose, dehydration (most common cause of death), heatstroke, and hallucinations. Users often feel so disconnected from their bodies that they may not be able to monitor physical symptoms and avoid possible dangers. Ecstasy alters serotonin levels in the brain, and researchers have found that chronic use can lead to long-term or permanent damage to those parts of the brain critical for thought, memory, and pleasure. Some side effects can occur weeks after taking the drug, such as confusion, depression, sleep problems, anxiety, and paranoia.

LSD, or acid, is a hallucinogen that can be taken in pill, liquid, or solid forms. LSD causes an increase in heart rate, nausea, chills, and numbness. Nationally 4 percent of students reported using LSD last year.

Rohypnol, also known as the date rape drug, is colorless, odorless, and tasteless. Rohypnol is used as a recreational drug in the rave scene. Rohypnol is rapidly absorbed by the body. Within 15–30 minutes after ingestion, the victims become confused, feel drunk, and appear to others as if they are drunk. Alcohol and other drugs increase absorption and effects. The full effect of the drug typically peaks between one and two hours after ingestion. Rohypnol can cause amnesia for up to eight hours after one dose.

GHB, another common club drug, is a colorless, odorless liquid that is usually tasteless but can be salty. GHB acts as a sedative with effects beginning within 15–30 minutes after ingestion. In lower dosages, users often appear to be drunk, experiencing decreased inhibitions and a sense of calmness. In higher dosages, it can cause sedation, drowsiness, nausea, muscle stiffness, respiratory problems, seizures, loss of consciousness, coma, or even death. Symptoms with overdose often include a three- to six-hour loss of consciousness and poor memory of events, usually remembering only "glimpses" of what has happened. Perhaps the greatest danger with GHB is that potency varies due to home production—so a dose that gets someone high one week could kill that person the next.

■ Pharmaceutical Drugs

"Pharming" is the use, misuse, or abuse of prescription drugs not prescribed for the person taking them. Usually, they are used for recreational purposes or to "self-medicate" for a legitimate health problem. People who "pharm" often take more than one medication at a time. The prescription drugs that are most commonly abused fall into three main categories:

■ Opioids—Most often prescribed to treat pain (such as OxyContin or Vicodin)
■ Depressants—Used to treat anxiety and sleep disorders (such as Valium)
■ Stimulants—Often prescribed to treat the sleep disorder narcolepsy, attention deficit hyperactivity disorder (ADHD), and obesity (such as Ritalin and Dexedrine)

Why Do People Use/Abuse Prescription Drugs?

People may be more likely to use prescription drugs than illegal drugs for a number of reasons including availability, cost, previous experience, and safety based on the belief that these are not "real" drugs. People may not feel that they are really doing drugs, since pharmaceuticals are FDA-approved. They may also believe prescription drugs to be safer than street drugs.

What Are the Risks?

Pharmaceuticals are legal drugs, but they are legal only for the person they are prescribed for. Using someone else's medication is simply not safe. Pharmaceuticals are not over-the-counter drugs because they are to be used only under the care of a medical provider. People who use or abuse prescription drugs often combine these drugs with alcohol or other drugs. When drugs are combined, they often produce what is known as a multiplication effect exaggerating the side effects of the drugs. Because most prescription drugs alter brain chemistry, the effects can be very unpredictable.

- A recent survey conducted on campus indicated that the most-used illicit prescription drugs among UNCW students are Ritalin, Adderall, and Strattera, followed by Xanax, Vicodin, Codeine, Percocet/Percodan, and OxyContin.

Ritalin

One of the most abused pharmaceutical drugs among college students is **Ritalin**. More than eight tons of Ritalin are consumed annually in the U.S. Ritalin is more potent than cocaine or amphetamines milligram for milligram, with longer-lasting effects. Most abusers crush the pills and snort it like cocaine. Snorting Ritalin provides a shorter, more powerful high, producing a mild euphoria that lasts about 30 minutes. Snorting Ritalin can cause open sores, nosebleeds, and the eventual deterioration of the nasal cartilage. Ritalin should not be mixed with antidepressants or over-the-counter cold medicines containing decongestants. Antidepressants may enhance the effects of a stimulant. Stimulants in combination with decongestants may cause blood pressure to become dangerously high or lead to irregular heart rhythms.

Short-Term Risks

- A large single dose of any opioid can cause severe respiratory depression that can lead to death.
- High doses of a stimulant such as Ritalin may result in dangerously high body temperatures and an irregular heartbeat.
- You risk cardiovascular failure or lethal seizures with the use/abuse of stimulants.

Long-Term Risks

- Tolerance for the drugs. Tolerance means that users must take higher doses to achieve the same initial effects.
- Physical dependence and addiction. The body adapts to the presence of the drug, and withdrawal symptoms occur if use is reduced or stopped.

Legal Risks

Most of these pharmaceutical drugs are Schedule II or III narcotics, which can result in serious federal penalties when misused. Depending on quantity, location of transfer, and the age of the recipient, the felony can be punishable by a fine of up to $10,000 and a prison term of up to 45 years.

Are You or a Friend Addicted?

A drug, alcohol, or tobacco addiction can have serious social and medical effects. Addiction can cause problems with academic or job performance, difficulties with relationships, and serious health issues. If someone becomes addicted, the dependence may become a central part of this person's life. The following are a few indicators of an addiction:

- Losing control of behavior
- Craving the drug
- Developing physical tolerance to the drug
- Experiencing withdrawal when stopping use
- Neglecting important school, social, or work-related tasks
- Using the drug continuously while denying a problem exists
- Spending more time than originally expected using the drug

Getting Help

Addiction is a disease that progresses through predictable stages. It takes a trained health professional, often a doctor specializing in addiction medicine, to make an accurate diagnosis and prescribe the most appropriate treatment. Alcohol and/or drug treatment programs should offer a variety of treatment practices that meet individual needs. Programs may include inpatient, residential, outpatient, and/or short-stay options. For more information on resources in the community, contact CROSSROADS: Substance Abuse Prevention and Education Program, Second Floor, Westside Hall, or call 910.962.4136.

Recovery at UNCW

12-step meetings on campus:

- Alcoholics Anonymous: Closed meeting. Mondays at noon in CROSSROADS suite, Second Floor, Westside Hall

AA meetings within walking distance of campus:

- Sundays at 7 a.m.; Mondays, Wednesdays, Fridays at 12 noon: Intergroup (open/discussion), 5001 Wrightsville Ave.
- Mondays at 8 p.m.: Sobriety Unlimited (closed/Big Book/Beginner/Step Study/Discussion), Wesley Methodist Church, 1401 S College Rd.
- Tuesdays at 8 p.m.: Welcome Group (closed/beginner/discussion, big book), St. Matthew's Lutheran Church, 612 S College Rd.
- Saturdays at 8 p.m.: Welcome Group (open/step, open/traditions, open/discussion), St. Matthew's Lutheran Church, 612 S College Rd.

NA meetings within walking distance of campus:

- Mondays at 8 p.m.: Phoenix (closed/discussion/beginner), St. Matthew's Lutheran Church, 612 S College Rd.
- Mondays and Wednesdays at 8 p.m.: Bring Your Own Book II (open/literature/day care), Church of the Servant, 4925 Oriole Dr.
- Fridays at 8 p.m.: Phoenix (closed/discussion/literature), St. Matthew's Lutheran Church, 612 S College Rd.

Exercise 2: Alcohol Quiz

How much do you know about alcohol? Circle true or false for each question below.

1. Alcohol depresses the central nervous system.   True   False

2. Taking aspirin increases your tolerance to alcohol.   True   False

3. A standard mixed drink has three times the alcohol in one can of beer.   True   False

4. Eating a heavy meal will slow down the rate at which alcohol affects a person.   True   False

5. Taking a hot shower or drinking coffee will not help sober you up.   True   False

6. The male and female bodies respond to alcohol in the same manner.   True   False

7. Consuming alcohol will warm you up in cold weather.   True   False

8. Sexual performance is enhanced when drinking.   True   False

Answers

1. **True.** Alcohol depresses your bodily functions, affecting your respiration and heart rate.

2. **False.** Aspirin has no effect on your blood alcohol concentration level. In fact, certain painkillers (such as Tylenol) can cause liver damage if taken with alcohol.

3. **False.** One mixed drink has approximately the same amount of alcohol as a 12-ounce can of beer.

4. **True.** Food in the stomach slows down the rate at which alcohol affects your body.

5. **True.** Only time will sober you up.

6. **False.** Women tend to respond more quickly to alcohol because of their smaller body size.

7. **False.** Alcohol widens your blood vessels, causing more heat to be lost from your body when drinking. As a result, drinking alcohol can increase risk of hypothermia in cold environments.

8. **False.** Alcohol decreases your ability to function sexually and is linked to a reduction of the male hormone testosterone.

◼ Exercise 3:

1. Complete the e-Chug self-assessment on the CROSSROADS webpage. The Alcohol *eCHECKUP TO GO* (e-CHUG) is a brief self-assessment that will provide you with accurate and detailed information about:

   - ◼ Your personal risk patterns
   - ◼ Your individual level of alcohol tolerance
   - ◼ Your unique family risk factors
   - ◼ Harm reduction strategies
   - ◼ Helpful resources at University of North Carolina Wilmington and in our community

2. Complete the e-Toke self-assessment on the CROSSROADS website. This site is designed to give you personalized feedback on your marijuana use. Answering each question truthfully and accurately will give you helpful feedback regarding your individual pattern of marijuana use and how it might be affecting your personal relationships, your life and career goals, and your overall health and well-being.

References

Belote, G. A., & Lunsford, L. W. (1998). *The Freshman Year: Making the Most of College.* Dubuque, IA: Kendall/Hunt.

Copper, C. (2001). *Keys to Excellence.* Dubuque, IA: Kendall/Hunt.

CROSSROADS website. http://uncw.edu/stuaff/crossroads/index.htm.

Fahey, T. D., Insel, P. M., & Roth, W. T. (2001). *Fit & Well: Core Concepts and Labs in Physical Fitness and Wellness.* Mountain View, CA: Mayfield.

Haywood, D. H. (1999). Choosing wellness as a lifestyle. *UNCW: The Freshman Year.* Dubuque, IA: Kendall/Hunt.

Pfau, B., & Lizinger, M. E. (2000). *Creating Connections: A Four-Step Program for Managing Stress.* Dubuque, IA: Kendall/Hunt.

Seven Tips to a Good Night's Sleep. (2000). *iVillage Health News.* Location: http://www.allhealth.com.

Wellness Evaluation. (2002). Retrieved May 7, 2002, from http://www.naples.cc.sunysb.edu.

CHAPTER 12

Diversity
Appreciating the Value of Human Differences for Enhancing Learning and Personal Development

Learning Goals

The primary goal of this chapter is to show how experiencing diversity in college can promote your learning, personal development, and career success.

■ Activate Your Thinking

Complete the following "sentence starter":

When I hear the word "diversity," the first thoughts that come to my mind are . . .

■ The Spectrum of Diversity

As you may have already detected by the title of this chapter, diversity simply means "variety" or "difference." Thus, human diversity refers to the variety or differences that exist among people that comprise humanity (the human species). When we use the word "diversity" in this chapter, we will be referring primarily to *different groups* of humans. The relationship between humanity and diversity is represented visually in Figure 1.

The relationship between humanity and human diversity is similar to the relationship between sunlight and the spectrum colors. Just as sunlight passing through a prism reflects all the different groups of colors that make up the visual spectrum, humanity occupying planet earth reflects all the different groups of people that make up the spectrum of human diversity. As you can see in Figure 1, groups of people can differ from

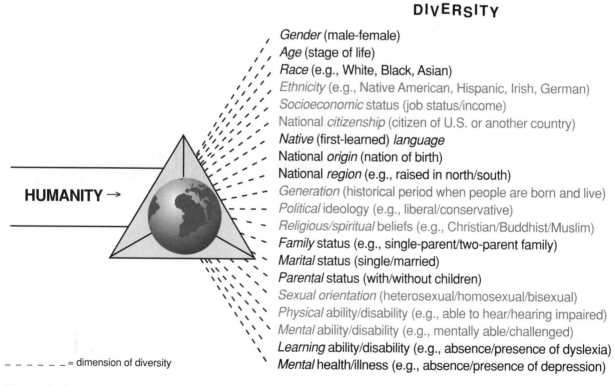

Figure 1 ■ Humanity and Diversity*

*This list represents some of the major dimensions of human diversity; it does not represent a complete list of all possible forms of human diversity. Also, disagreement exists about certain dimensions of diversity (e.g., whether certain groups should be considered races or ethnic groups).

one another in a wide variety of ways, including their physical features, values, beliefs, abilities, geographical locations, social backgrounds, and other personal dimensions.

Diversity has been viewed by some people to be a "political" issue. However, we view diversity as an *educational* issue—a learning experience that can have a powerful impact on an individual's college and career success. Since there have been different interpretations (and misinterpretations) about what diversity actually is, we would like to begin by clarifying some key terms that are essential to an accurate understanding of the meaning and value of diversity.

What Is Culture?

"Culture" can be broadly defined as a distinctive pattern of beliefs and values that develop among a group of people who share the same social heritage and traditions. Culture is the whole way in which a group of people has learned to live (Peoples & Bailey, 1998), which includes style of speaking (language), fashion, food, art, and music, as well as values and beliefs. Different cultures exist across different nations—often referred to as *cross-cultural* differences; and different cultures can exist within the same nation—commonly called *multicultural* differences. Thus, cultural

Culture is a distinctive pattern of beliefs and values that develop among a group of people who share the same social heritage and traditions.

© 2007 Jupiter Images Corporation

diversity may take the forms of *international* diversity and *national* (*domestic*) diversity. Although the terms "culture" and "society" are used as if they have the same meaning, they refer to different things. *Society* refers to a group of people who are organized under the same social system. For example, all members of American society are organized under the same system of government, justice, and education. On the other hand, culture is what members of certain groups of people in a society actually share with each other in terms of traditions and lifestyle (Nicholas, 1991). So, within the same society, multiple cultures can exist; hence, we use the term "multicultural society."

What Is an Ethnic Group?

An *ethnic group* (or *ethnicity*) refers to a group of people who share the same culture. Thus, culture refers to *what* an ethnic group shares in common, and ethnic group refers to the particular group of people *who* share a common culture. Major ethnic groups in the United States include Native Americans (American Indians), African Americans, Hispanic Americans (Latinos), Asian Americans, and European Americans. Ethnic subgroups also exist within each of these major ethnic groups. For example, Hispanic Americans include people who have cultural roots in Mexico, Puerto Rico, Central America, South America, etc.; Asian Americans include cultural descendents from Japan, China, Korea, Vietnam, etc.; and European Americans include descendents from Scandinavia, England, Ireland, Germany, Italy, etc. In the United States, European Americans are the *majority* ethnic group, meaning that the majority of the American population belongs to this ethnic group. Native Americans, African Americans, Hispanic Americans, and Asian Americans are considered to be ethnic *minority* groups.

Pause for Reflection

What ethnic group(s) do you belong to, or identify with? What common cultural values do you think are shared by your ethnic group(s)?

 LASSIC QUOTE
We are all the same, and we are all unique.

–Georgia Dunston,
African-American biologist and
research specialist in human genetics

The different cultures associated with different ethnic groups may be viewed simply as variations in the way groups of people express the same theme: being human. You may have heard the question: "We're all human, aren't we?" The answer to this important question is, "yes and no." Yes, we are all the same, but not in the same way.

One way to understand this apparent paradox is to visualize humanity as a quilt in which all humans are joined together by the common thread of humanity—we are all human beings; yet, the different patches that makes up the quilt represent diversity—the distinctive or unique cultures that comprise our common humanity. This quilt metaphor acknowledges the identity and beauty of all cultures. It differs from the old American "melting pot" metaphor—which viewed differences as something that should be melted down or eliminated, and the "salad bowl" metaphor—which suggests that America is a hodgepodge or mishmash of different cultures thrown together without any common connection. In contrast, the quilt metaphor suggests that the cultures of different ethnic groups can and should be recognized. Yet these differences may be woven together to create a unified whole—as in the Latin expression: "E pluribus Unum" ("Out of many, one"). This expression has become a motto of the United States, and you will find it printed on all its coins.

Personal Story

When I was 12 years old and living in New York, I returned from school one Friday afternoon, and my mother asked me if anything interesting happened at school that day. I mentioned to her that the teacher went around the room, asking students what we had for dinner the night before. At that moment, my mother began to become a bit agitated and nervously asked me: "What did you tell the teacher?" I said: "I told her and the rest of the class that I had pasta last night because my family has a tradition of eating pasta on Thursdays and Sundays." My mother then exploded and yelled back at me: "Why couldn't you tell her that we had steak or roast beef!" For a moment, I was stunned and couldn't figure out what I had done wrong or why I should have lied about eating pasta. Then it suddenly dawned on me: My mother was extremely embarrassed about being an Italian American. She wanted me to hide our family's ethnic background and make it sound like we were very "American." After this became clear to me, a few moments later, it also became clear to me why her maiden name was changed from the very Italian-sounding "DeVigilio" to the more American-sounding "Vigilis."

I never forgot this incident because it was such an emotionally intense experience. For the first time in my life, I became aware that my mother was ashamed of being a member of the same group to which every other member of my family belonged, including me. After her outburst, I felt a combined rush of astonishment and embarrassment. However, these feelings didn't last long because, in the long run, my mother's reaction actually had the opposite effect on me. Instead of making me feel inferior or ashamed about being Italian-American, my mother's reaction that day caused me to become more aware of, and take more pride in, my Italian heritage.

Although I have never forgotten this incident, I have since forgiven my mother, because I later learned why she felt the way she did. She grew up in America's "melting pot" generation—a time when different American ethnic groups were expected to melt down and melt away their ethnicity. They were not to celebrate diversity; they were to eliminate it.

—Joe Cuseo

What Is a Racial Group?

A *racial group (race)* refers to an ethnic group that also shares some distinctive physical traits, such as skin color or facial characteristics; however, there continues to be disagreement among scholars about what groups of people actually constitute a human "race," or whether totally distinctive races truly exist (Wheelright, 2005). Unlike an ethnic group, whose shared culture has been passed on through social experiences, a racial group's shared physical characteristics are those that they are born with and which have been passed on genetically. The United States Census Bureau (2000) identifies three races: White, Black, and Asian. Nevertheless, Anderson & Fienberg (2000) caution that racial categories are social-political constructs (concepts) and are not scientifically based.

Remember: There are no specific genes that differentiate one race from another. In other words, there is no way you could do a blood test or any type of "internal" genetic test to determine a person's race. Humans have simply decided to categorize people into "races" on the basis of certain external differences in physical appearance, particularly the color of their outer layer of skin.

 C **LASSIC QUOTE**
We have become not a melting pot but a beautiful mosaic.
—Jimmy Carter, thirty-ninth president of the United States and winner of the Nobel Peace Prize

The differences in skin color that exist among humans is likely due to biological adaptations that evolved among groups of humans. These differences helped them survive in different environmental regions where they were living and breeding. For instance, darker skin tones were more likely to develop among humans who inhabited and reproduced in hotter regions nearer the equator (e.g., Africans), where darker skin may have enabled them to adapt and survive in that environment. Their darker skin provided their bodies with better protection from the potentially damaging effects of the sun (Bridgeman, 2003) and better ability to use the sun's source of vitamin D (Jablonski & Chaplin, 2002). In contrast, lighter skin tones were more likely to develop among humans inhabiting colder climates more distant from the equator (e.g., Scandinavians) to allow their bodies to absorb greater amounts of sunlight because it was less plentiful and direct.

While humans may display racial diversity, the biological reality is that all members of the human species are remarkably similar. There is much less genetic variability among us than members of other animal species; in fact, approximately 98 percent of our genes are exactly the same (Bridgeman, 2003; Molnar, 1991). This accounts for all the similarities that exist among humans, regardless of what differences in color appear at the sur-

Answers: The emotions shown. Top, left to right: anger, fear, and sadness. Bottom, left to right: disgust, happiness, and surprise.

Photos © 2007 Jupiter Images Corporation and Top Middle Photo © Fred Goldstein, 2007. Used under license from Shutterstock, Inc.

Figure 2 ■ Humans all over the world display the same facial expressions when experiencing certain emotions. See if you can detect the emotions being expressed in the following faces. (To find the answers, turn your book upside down.)

face of our skin. For example, all humans have similar external features that give us a "human" appearance and clearly distinguish us from other animal species; we have internal organs that are similar in structure and function; and we have similar facial expressions for expressing our emotions (Figure 2).

CLASSIC QUOTE

Every human is, at the same time, like all other humans, like some humans, and like no other human.

—*Clyde Kluckholn, American Anthropologist*

Other human characteristics that anthropologists have found to be shared across all groups of people in every corner of the world include storytelling, poetry, adornment of the body, dance, music, decoration of artifacts, families, socialization of children by elders, a sense of right and wrong, supernatural beliefs, explanations of diseases and death, and mourning of the dead (Pinker, 1994).

It is important to realize that human *variety* and human *similarity* exist side-by-side. For instance, humans all over the world communicate verbally via language; in fact, newborn babies in all cultures babble by using the same wide range of sounds. However, these babies will eventually speak only in the sounds of the language(s) they are exposed to in their particular culture and other sounds they used while babbling will eventually drop out (Oller, 1981). Thus, language is a characteristic that all humans share as part of their common humanity, but the variety of languages spoken by people around the world is a reflection and expression of their diverse cultural experiences.

It is also important to keep in mind that *individual* differences *within* the same group of people are *greater* than the average differences between different groups of people. For example, although we live in a world that is very conscious of differences between races, the fact is that physical differences (e.g., height and weight) and behavioral differences (e.g., personality characteristics) among individuals within the same racial group are actually greater than the average differences between different racial groups (Caplan & Caplan, 1994).

As you proceed through this chapter, keep in mind the following distinctions among humanity, diversity, and individuality:

- **Humanity**—we are all members of the *same group* (the human species).
- **Diversity**—we are all members of *different groups* (e.g., our gender and ethnic groups).
- **Individuality**—each of us is a *unique person* who is different from any person in any group to which we may belong.

Diversity and the College Experience

The ethnic and racial diversity of students is increasing in American colleges and universities. In 1960, Whites comprised almost 95 percent of the total college population; in 2005, the percentage decreased to 69 percent. At the same time, the percentage of Asian, Hispanic, Black, and Native American students attending college increased (Chronicle of Higher Education, 2003). Approximately 35 percent of today's 18- to 24-year-olds are non-white, making it the most diverse generation in American history (The Echo Boomers, 2004).

American colleges are also becoming more diverse in terms of gender and age. In 2000, the percentage of females enrolled in college was almost 66 percent, compared to 25 percent in 1955 (Postsecondary Education Opportunity, 2001). The percentage of students enrolled in college today that are 24 years of age or older has grown to 44 percent (Chronicle of Higher Education, 2003).

You are also likely to find students on your campus from different nations. From 1990 to 2000, the number of international students attending American colleges and universities increased by over 140,000 (Institute of International Education, 2001).

© Stockbyte

The ethnic and racial diversity of students in American colleges is increasing.

TUDENT PERSPECTIVE

"I am very happy with the diversity here, but it also frightens me. I have never been in a situation where I have met people who are Jewish, Muslim, atheist, born-again, and many more."

—First-year student (Erickson, Peters, & Strommer, 2006)

Colleges and universities often intentionally recruit students with different cultural experiences and geographical backgrounds in order to create a campus environment that enriches the variety and quality of your learning experience. Thus, your campus may be the ideal environment for experiencing diversity. The college experience can provide you with the time, the place, the variety of people, and the quality of educational resources (courses, programs) needed to learn the most about and from diversity.

As a first-year student, this may be the first time in your life that you are a member of a community that includes so many people from such a variety of backgrounds. In fact, students report more experience with diversity during their first year of college than at any other time in the college experience (Kuh, 2002). So, this year may be the prime time for you to capitalize on the diversity around you and take full advantage of its many educational and personal benefits.

Pause for Reflection

1. What diverse groups do you see represented on your campus?

2. Are there groups on your campus that you did not expect to see, or to see in such large numbers?

3. Are there groups on your campus that you expected to see, but do not see, or see in smaller numbers than you expected?

■ Advantages of Experiencing Diversity

Diversity Increases the Power of a Liberal Arts Education

An effective liberal arts education should liberate or free you from the "tunnel vision" of an egocentric (self-centered) viewpoint and enable you to move outside yourself and see yourself in relation to the world around you. There is simply no way you can gain this global perspective without understanding human diversity. If we could reduce the world's population to a village of precisely 100 people, with all existing human ratios remaining the same, the demographics would look something like this:

The village would have 60 Asians, 14 Africans, 12 Europeans, 8 Latin Americans, 5 from the United States and Canada, and 1 from the South Pacific.

51 would be male, 49 would be female

82 would be non-white; 18 white

67 would be non-Christian; 33 would be Christian

80 would live in substandard housing

67 would be unable to read

50 would be malnourished and 1 dying of starvation

33 would be without access to a safe water supply

39 would lack access to improved sanitation

24 would not have any electricity (and of the 76 that do have electricity, most would only use it for light at night)

 7 would have access to the Internet

 1 would have a college education

 1 would have HIV

 2 would be near birth; 1 near death

 5 would control 32 percent of the entire world's wealth; all 5 would be citizens of the United States

33 would be receiving—and attempting to live on—only 3 percent of the income of "the village"

(Source: *State of the Village Report* by Donella H. Meadows, originally published in 1990 as "Who lives in the Global Village?" and updated in Family Care Foundation, 2005.)

 LASSIC QUOTE

It [liberal arts education] shows you how to accommodate yourself to others, how to throw yourself into their state of mind, how to come to an understanding of them. You are at home in any society; you have common ground with every class.

—*John Henry Newman, English Cardinal and educator*

Another perspective that should be developed as part of your liberal arts education is a *national* perspective, which involves understanding and appreciating your own nation. To appreciate the United States as a nation is to appreciate human diversity. Today, the United States is more ethnically and racially diverse than at any other time in its national history, and it will continue to grow more diverse throughout the twenty-first century (Torres, 2003). In 1995, about 75 percent of America's population was White; by 2050, it will shrink to about 50 percent (U.S. Census Bureau, 2004).

Because of this increasing diversity, "multicultural competence"—the ability to understand cultural differences and to interact effectively with people from different cultural backgrounds—has become an important liberal arts skill that is critical for success in today's world (Pope et al., 2005).

Just as the different subjects you take in the liberal arts curriculum opens your mind to multiple perspectives, so does experience with people from different backgrounds. Exposure to the different perspectives of people with different cultural experiences serves to expand your consciousness; it stretches your perspective and liberates you from viewing the world through the narrow perspective of a single culture—your own.

One cultural viewpoint cannot provide a complete understanding of any issue because it represents a one-sided viewpoint that is likely to be partial to its particular vantage point (Elder & Paul, 2002). Obtaining a wide range of cultural perspectives allows you to detect the partiality and weaknesses of partial viewpoints, but also allows you to combine their particular strengths to form a multi-sided perspective that is more comprehensive and balanced.

One of the major divisions of the liberal arts curriculum is the humanities. Courses in this division of knowledge focus on understanding humanity—the common elements of the human experience that are shared by all human beings.

Remember: *By learning about diversity (our differences), we simultaneously learn more about what we have in common—our shared humanity.*

LASSIC QUOTE

The mind is like a parachute; it works best when it is open.

—*Anonymous*

Experiencing diversity not only enhances your appreciation of the unique features of different cultures, it also provides you with a larger perspective on the universal aspects of the human experience that are common to all people, no matter what their particular cultural background happens to be.

Pause for Reflection

List three human experiences that you think are universal, i.e., that are experienced by all human beings in all cultures.

1.

2.

3.

Diversity Promotes Self-Awareness

Learning from people with diverse backgrounds and experiences also serves to sharpen your self-awareness and self-understanding by allowing you to compare and contrast your life experiences with people whose life experiences differ sharply from your own. This *comparative perspective* can give you an important reference point, putting you in a better position to see more clearly how your unique cultural experiences have influenced the development of your personal beliefs, values, and lifestyle. When students around the country were interviewed about their diversity experiences in college, many of them reported that these experiences enabled them to learn more about themselves. Some said that their interactions with students from different races and ethnic groups produced "unexpected" or "jarring" self-insights (Light, 2001).

Diversity Strengthens Development of Learning and Thinking Skills

Just as the quality of your physical health and performance are improved by consuming a varied and balanced diet of foods from different food groups, the quality of your mental performance is improved by helping yourself to a balanced diet of ideas obtained from different groups of people. Experiencing their rich variety of cultural perspectives nourishes your mind with good "food for thought." Research consistently shows that we learn more from people who are different from us than we do from people who are similar to us (Pascarella, 2001; Pascarella & Terenzini, 2005). This result is probably best explained by the fact that when we encounter what is unfamiliar or uncertain, we are forced to stretch beyond our mental comfort zone to actively compare and contrast it to what we already know in order to understand it (Acredolo & O'Connor, 1991; Nagda, Gurin, & Johnson, 2005).

Keep in mind that learning is strengthened when it takes place in a social context that involves human interaction. As some scholars put it, human knowledge is "socially con-

CLASSIC QUOTE

The more eyes, different eyes, we can use to observe one thing, the more complete will our concept of this thing, our objectivity, be.

—*Friedrich Nietzsche,*
German philosopher

structed"—it is built up through interaction and dialogue with others (Bruffee, 1993). According to these scholars, our thinking is largely an "internal" (mental) representation of conversations we have had with other people (Vygotsky, 1978). So, the nature and quality of our conversations with others affects the nature and quality of our own thinking. If we have multiple conversations with humans from very different backgrounds, then the nature of our thinking becomes more diverse and complex. In contrast, when we restrict the diversity of people who we interact with, we artificially restrict the range and complexity of our thought—by limiting the variety of lenses or angles we can use to view issues and solve problems.

Research on first-year college students shows that students who experience the highest level of exposure to different dimensions of diversity (e.g., interactions and friendships with peers of different races, or participating in multicultural courses and events on campus) report the greatest gains in:

■ thinking complexity—the ability to think about all parts and all sides of an issue (Gurin, 1999),
■ reflective thinking—the ability to think deeply (Kitchener et al., 2000), and
■ critical thinking—the ability to think logically (Pascarella et al., 2001).

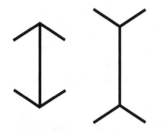

Figure 3 ■ Optical Illusion

Lastly, experiencing diversity can enhance your ability to think *creatively*. Just as experiences with academic disciplines (subjects) can equip you with different thinking styles and strategies that may be combined to generate new ideas, so do experiences with different dimensions of diversity. Although a major advantage of culture is that it helps bind people together, it can also blind people from other perspectives. Since culture shapes the way we think, it can cause groups of people to view the world solely through their own cultural frame of reference (Colombo, Cullen, & Lisle, 1995). Diversity experiences supply us with different thinking styles that can help us think outside the boundaries of our own cultural framework. These experiences also help us to be aware of our perceptual "blind spots" and to avoid the dangers of group think—the tendency for tight, like-minded groups of people to think so much alike that they overlook the flaws in their own thinking—which can lead to poor choices and faulty decisions (Janis, 1982).

Optical illusions are a good illustration of how our cultural perspectives can blind us or cause us to misperceive things. For instance, compare the length of the two lines in Figure 3.

If you perceive the line on the right to be longer than the line on the left, welcome to the club. Virtually all Americans and people from Western cultures perceive the line on the right to be longer. Actually, both lines are equal in length. (If you don't believe it, take out a ruler and check it out.) However, people from non-Western cultures who live in environments with circular architecture rather than buildings with lines and corners, do not make this perceptual error (Segall, Campbell & Herskovits, 1966).

The key point underlying this optical illusion is that our cultural experiences shape and sometimes distort our perceptions or interpretations of reality. We think we are seeing things objectively or "as they really are," but we are often seeing things subjectively from our limited cultural vantage point. Being open to people from different backgrounds who perceive the world from different cultural vantage points opens up our range of perception and helps us overcome our cultural blind spots. As a result, we can see and think about the world around us with greater clarity and balance.

© 2007 Jupiter Images Corporation

The people who live in these circular huts would not be fooled by the optical illusion in Figure 3.

Diversity Enhances Career Preparation and Success

Learning from diversity also has a very practical benefit: It better prepares you for the world of work. Whatever career you may choose to enter, you will likely find yourself working with employers, employees, co-workers, customers, and clients from diverse cultural backgrounds. America's workforce is now more diverse than at any other time in its history, and work today takes place in a global economy that involves greater economic interdependence among nations (e.g., international businesses), more international trading (imports/exports), more multinational corporations, more world travel, and more effective worldwide communication—due to advances in the World Wide Web (Dryden, & Vos, 1999; Smith, 1994). Consequently, employers of college graduates have begun to place higher value on job candidates with international knowledge and foreign language skills (Fixman, 1990; Office of Research, 1994).

C **LASSIC QUOTE**

When all men think alike, no one thinks very much.
    —*Walter Lippmann, distinguished journalist, and originator of the term, "stereotype."*

Successful career performance in today's diverse workforce requires sensitivity to human differences and the ability to relate to people from different cultural backgrounds who work in the United States and across different nations (National Association of Colleges & Employers, 2003; Smith, 1997). One national survey of business leaders and policymakers revealed that they want college graduates to have more than just "awareness" or "tolerance" of diversity; they want graduates to have actual *experience* with diversity (Education Commission of the State, 1995). Today's world truly has become a "small world," and your success in it will be enhanced if you gain a multicultural and cross-cultural perspective.

Diversity Stimulates Social Development

Experiencing diversity also promotes your social development. When you interact with people from a variety of groups, you widen your social circle by expanding the pool of people with whom you can associate and develop relationships. As the old American proverb goes, "Variety is the spice of life." Or, as the French might say: "Viva la difference!" (Long live difference!)

LASSIC QUOTE

Empirical evidence shows that the actual effects on student development of emphasizing diversity and of student participation in diversity activities are overwhelmingly positive.

—*Alexander Astin,*
What Matters in College

Just as the quality of your dining experiences are enriched by the range and variety of ethnic foods you can choose from to stimulate your taste palate, so too can the quality of your learning experiences be enriched by the range and variety of ethnic groups with which you can choose to interact. In fact, research indicates that students who have more diversity experiences in college report higher levels of satisfaction with their college experience (Astin, 1993).

■ Blocks to Experiencing Diversity

Although there are multiple benefits associated with diversity, there are also some human tendencies that can interfere with or block us from experiencing diversity and reaping its benefits. Three of these potential stumbling blocks are *stereotyping*, *prejudice*, and *discrimination*.

Stereotyping

The word stereotype is a combination of two root words: "stereo" (to look at in a fixed way) and "type" (typical). It is the tendency to view individuals of the same type (group) in the same (fixed) way. In effect, stereotyping ignores or disregards a person's individuality; instead, all individuals who share a similar group characteristic (e.g., race or gender) are viewed as having similar personal characteristics—as in the expression: "You know what they are like; they're all the same." If virtually all members of a stereotyped group are judged or evaluated in the same way, this results in *prejudice*.

Pause for Reflection

1. Have you ever been stereotyped, based on your appearance or group membership? If so, how did it make you feel and how did you react?

2. Have you ever unintentionally perceived or treated someone in terms of a stereotype rather than as an individual? What assumptions did you make about that person? Was that person aware of, or affected by, your stereotyping?

Prejudice

The word "prejudice" literally means to "pre-judge." It represents a judgment, attitude, or belief about another person or group of people, which is formed before the facts are known. Stereotyping and prejudice often occur together because individuals who are placed in a stereotyped group are commonly pre-judged in a biased (slanted) way. When this bias is negative, it is referred to as *stigmatizing*—associating inferior or unfavorable traits with people who belong to the same group. Although, technically, prejudice may be either positive or negative, the term is most often used to refer to negative pre-judgment or stigmatizing, which is the way it will be used in this chapter.

Someone with a prejudice toward a group typically avoids contact with individuals from the stigmatized group. Thus, the prejudice continues because there is little or no chance for the prejudiced person to have positive experiences with a member of the group that could contradict or disprove the prejudice. Thus, a vicious cycle is established in which the prejudiced person avoids contact with the stigmatized group, and this lack of contact keeps the prejudice going by not allowing any opportunities for it to be contradicted.

A prejudice can also remain intact because facts that contradict it are often ignored through the psychological process of *selective perception*—the tendency for the prejudiced person to see what he or she *expects* to see (Hugenberg & Bodenhausen, 2003). This results in the prejudiced person choosing to pay attention to information that is consistent with the prejudice and "seeing" that information, while ignoring or overlooking information that contradicts the prejudice. Have you ever noticed that fans rooting for their favorite sports team tend to focus on and "see" the calls or decisions of referees that go against their own team, but do not seem to notice or react to calls that go against the other team? This is a classic, everyday example of selective perception. It could be said that selective perception changes the process of "seeing is believing" into "believing is seeing." Even if a contradictory piece of information happens to slip through the prejudiced person's attention filter, it is likely to be dismissed as an "exception to the rule," or as an exception that "proves" the general rule (Aronson, et al., 2005).

Selective perception can also be accompanied by *selective memory*—the tendency to remember only information that is consistent with the prejudice, while forgetting information that is inconsistent or contradictory (Judd et al., 1991). It is possible for the psychological processes of selective perception and selective memory to operate *unconsciously*, so the prejudiced person may not be fully aware that they are using them or that they are resulting in prejudice (Baron, Byrne, & Brauscombe, 2006).

Whether prejudice is conscious or unconscious, the bottom line is that it can cause a person to minimize or cut off interaction with a whole group of people. As a result, the prejudiced person fails to experience and profit from the particular dimension of diversity (e.g., ethnic, racial, or national) that members of the stigmatized group have to offer. Worse yet, the person's prejudice can lead to acts of *discrimination* against members of the stigmatized group.

Discrimination

Literally translated, the term discrimination means division or separation. While prejudice is an attitude or belief, discrimination is an *action* taken toward another individual, which results in that person receiving different treatment. So, it could be said that discrimination is prejudice put into action.

"Hate crimes" represent an extreme form of discrimination. These are crimes motivated solely by prejudice against members of a stigmatized group—for example, damaging their personal property or physically assaulting them (e.g., "gay bashing"). Hate crimes are acts of discrimination that are committed consciously and maliciously. However, just like prejudice, some forms of discrimination can be very subtle and may take place without people being fully aware that they are discriminating. For example, there is some evidence that white, male college professors tend to treat female students and students from ethnic or racial minority groups differently than they do males and non-minority students. In particular, females and minority students tend to:

- receive less eye contact from the instructors,
- be called on less frequently in class,
- be given less time to respond to questions asked by instructors in class, and
- have less contact with instructors outside the classroom (Hall & Sandler, 1982, 1984; Sedlacek, 1987; Wright, 1987).

In the vast majority of these cases, the discriminatory treatment that these students received was subtle and not done consciously or deliberately by the instructors (Green, 1989). Nevertheless, these unintended actions are still discriminatory, and they may send a message to these students that their ideas are not worth hearing, or that they are not as capable as other students (Sadker & Sadker, 1994).

Pause for Reflection

Have you noticed classroom teaching behaviors or strategies used by instructors that clearly treated all students equally and promoted appreciation of student diversity?

What did these instructors do?

 LASSIC QUOTE

Let us all hope that the dark clouds of racial prejudice will soon pass away and the deep fog of misunderstanding will be lifted from our fear-drenched communities, and in some not too distant tomorrow the radiant stars of love and brotherhood will shine over our great nation.
—*Martin Luther King, Jr., civil rights activist and clergyman*

Personal Story

Being African American and living in southeastern Kentucky, the heart of Appalachia, did not provide for the grandest of living styles. Even though my father worked twelve hours a day in the coal mines, he earned only enough pay to supply staples for the table. Our family also worked as tenant farmers to have enough vegetables for my mother to can for the winter and to provide a roof over our heads.

My mother was a direct descendent of slaves and moved with her parents from the deep south at the age of seventeen. My father lived in an all-black coal mining camp, into which my mother and her family moved in 1938. My dad would say to me, "Son, you will have opportunities that I never had. Many people, white and black alike, will tell you that you are no good and that education can never help you. Don't listen to them because soon they will not be able to keep you from getting an education like they did me. Just remember, when you do get that education, you'll never have to go in those coal mines and have them break your back. You can choose what you want to do, and then you can be a free man."

My father lived through a time when freedom was something he dreamed his children might enjoy someday, because before the civil rights movement succeeded in changing the laws, African Americans were considerably limited in educational opportunities, job opportunities, and much else in what was definitely a racist society. My father remained illiterate because he was not allowed to attend public schools in eastern Kentucky.

In the early 1960s my brother, my sister, and I were integrated into the white public schools. Physical violence and constant verbal harassment caused many other blacks to forgo their education and opt for jobs in the coal mines at an early age. But my father remained constant in his advice to me: "It doesn't matter if they call you n_____; but don't you ever let them beat you by walking out on your education."

Being poor, black, and Appalachian did not offer me great odds for success, but constant reminders from my parents that I was a good and valuable person helped me to see beyond my deterrents to the true importance of education. My parents, who could never provide me with monetary wealth, truly made me proud of them by giving me the gift of insight and an aspiration for achievement.

—Aaron Thompson

■ Causes of Prejudice and Discrimination

There is no single or definitive answer to the question of what causes people to be prejudiced and to discriminate against other groups of people. However, research indicates that the following factors can play an influential role.

The Influence of Familiarity and Stranger Anxiety

Research has repeatedly demonstrated that when humans encounter things that are unfamiliar or strange, they tend to experience feelings of discomfort or anxiety. In contrast, what is familiar tends to be more accepted and better liked (Zajonc, 2001).

When we encounter people who are not familiar to us, experiencing at least some feeling of discomfort is a natural human tendency that probably occurs automatically. In fact, these feelings may be "wired into" our bodies because it was once important to the survival and evolution of our species (Figure 4). When we encountered strangers in our primitive past, it was to our advantage to react with feelings of anxiety and a rush of adrenaline, known as the "fight or flight" response, because those strangers may have been potential predators who were about to threaten or attack us. This evolutionary response may also explain why "stranger anxiety" is a very normal part of human development during infancy. Between about 8 and18 months of life, virtually all infants when seeing a stranger will react with anxiety (increased heart rate, breathing, crying) (Papalia & Olds, 1990).

Familiarity and stranger anxiety may contribute to prejudice by causing members of the same group to favor members of its own group and to be "on guard" to defend them from members of other groups who are less familiar or strange (Aronson, et al., 2005). Members of minority groups are less familiar to the majority group because they are fewer in number. Also, members of minority groups are less likely to have regular contact with members of the majority group because they are less likely to live in the same area (e.g., the same neighborhood), due to residential segregation of racial and ethnic groups, which is still common today (Massey, 2003; Tienda & Cortes, cited in Nagda, Gurin, & Johnson, 2005). Thus, members of the majority group may view minority group members as "unfamiliar," and this lack of familiarity may automatically trigger nega-

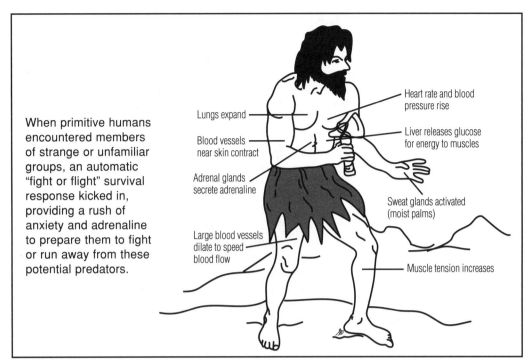

When primitive humans encountered members of strange or unfamiliar groups, an automatic "fight or flight" survival response kicked in, providing a rush of anxiety and adrenaline to prepare them to fight or run away from these potential predators.

Lungs expand

Blood vessels near skin contract

Adrenal glands secrete adrenaline

Large blood vessels dilate to speed blood flow

Heart rate and blood pressure rise

Liver releases glucose for energy to muscles

Sweat glands activated (moist palms)

Muscle tension increases

Figure 4 ■ "Fight-or-Flight" Reaction

tive feelings of uncertainty and anxiety. These negative feelings may then become associated with the minority group, which can lead to negative prejudices toward that group.

Pause for Reflection

Prejudice can be subtle and only begin to surface when the social or emotional distance between members of different groups grows closer. Rate your level of comfort (high, medium, low) with the following situations.

Someone from another racial group:

1. *going to your school*	high	medium	low
2. *working in your place of employment*	high	medium	low
3. *living on your street as a neighbor*	high	medium	low
4. *living with you as a roommate*	high	medium	low
5. *socializing with you as a personal friend*	high	medium	low
6. *being your most intimate friend or romantic partner*	high	medium	low
7. *being your partner in marriage*	high	medium	low

For any item you rated "low," why do you think it received that rating?

The Tendency to Categorize People

Humans have a tendency to put groups of people into mental categories in order to organize their complex social world and make it simpler to understand (Jones, 1990). While this is a normal human tendency, it can lead to stereotyping members of other groups, which blinds us to their individuality. It also can contribute to prejudice because we tend to create categories of *in*-groups ("us") and *out*-groups ("them"). One negative consequence of this tendency is that it can lead to *ethnocentrism*—the tendency to view one's own culture or ethnic group as the central or "normal" in-group and other cultures as less important or "abnormal" out-groups. This tendency can, in turn, lead to prejudice and discrimination toward people with cultural backgrounds that differ from our own.

Our cultural experiences can affect our judgments and conclusions about what is perceived as socially acceptable or "normal." For instance, in American culture, it may be socially acceptable for males to tell others of their achievements or accomplishments; however, in English and German cultures, such behavior is likely to be perceived as immodest or immature (Hall & Hall, 1986). Failure to appreciate cultural differences can lead to ethnocentric thinking, which fails to consider that groups of people may have attitudes and behaviors that are different but equally acceptable or "normal" when viewed from the perspective of their respective cultures. Ethnocentric thinking is a form of simplistic, dualistic (black-white) thinking that can lead to the conclusion that the way things are done by the in-group ("us") must be "right," and the behavior of out-groups ("them") must be "wrong."

Group Perception

Research studies show that humans are more likely to see members of groups that they do not belong to as more similar to each other in attitudes and behavior than members of their own group (Baron, Byrne, & Brauscombe, 2006). For instance, individuals perceive people older than themselves as being more alike in their attitudes and beliefs than members of their own age group (Linville, Fischer, & Salovey, 1989).

One explanation for this tendency to see members of other groups as being more alike than members of our own group is that we have more experience with members of our own group, so we have more opportunities to observe and interact with a wide variety of individuals within our group. In contrast, we have less experience with members of other groups, so the variety of individuals we have had contact with is narrower, perhaps leading us to conclude that the individual differences among them are narrower, i.e., they are more alike in attitudes and behavior than members of our own group. This effect can be so strong that we often fail to detect differences in the faces of individuals who are members of groups that we're unfamiliar with, i.e., "They all seem to look alike" (Levin, 2000). A dramatic example of this tendency is the case of Lenell Geter, an African-American engineer, who spent over a year of a life sentence in prison for a crime he didn't commit. Four of five non-black witnesses misidentified him for another black man who actually committed the crime and was later apprehended.

Majority Group Members' Attitudes

Research shows that if negative behavior occurs at the same rate among members of both majority and minority groups (e.g., the rate of criminal behavior in both groups is 10 percent), members of the majority group are more likely to develop negative attitudes (prejudice) toward the minority group than their own group (Baron, Byrne, & Brauscombe, 2006). For example, it has been found that whites in the United States tend to overestimate the crime rates of African-American men (Hamilton & Sherman, 1989).

One possible explanation why the negative behaviors of minority group members are more likely to produce negative views of their group is the tendency for majority group members to better remember instances of negative behavior associated with members of the minority group. Since minorities are more likely to be seen as different or distinctive, their behavior is more likely to stand out in the minds of majority group members, which makes it more likely that these negative behaviors will be remembered (McArthur & Friedman, 1980). Since these negative behaviors are more likely to be retained in the minds of the majority group, they are more likely to negatively influence their view of the minority group, thus increasing the possibility of prejudice.

Although prejudice on the part of the majority group toward minority groups has led to the most extreme form of discrimination and domination (Baron, Byrne, & Brauscombe, 2006), any group can become a target for prejudice. (See pages 254–255 for a snapshot summary of the many different groups of people that have been the target for prejudicial theories and beliefs.) Members of a minority group can also be prejudiced toward the majority group, as illustrated by the student perspective in the margin.

Group Membership and Self-Esteem

Self-esteem—how you feel about yourself—can be influenced by group membership. If people think that the group they belong to is superior, it enables them to feel better about themselves (Tafjel, 1982). In other words, "My group is superior, and since I belong to it, I am superior." This type of thinking is even more likely to occur when an individual's self-esteem has been threatened or damaged as a result of some personal frustration or failure. When this happens, the person whose self-esteem has been threatened or damaged can boost it by stigmatizing or putting down members of another group (Rudman & Fairchild, 2004), or by blaming them and making them the "scapegoat" (Gemmil, 1989). For example, they might say, "If it weren't for 'them,' we wouldn't have this problem." Probably the most extreme example of "scapegoating" in human history took place in Nazi Germany, where Jews were blamed for the country's economic problems and became targets of the Holocaust. Studies have shown that when times are tough (e.g., when unemployment is high) and people are frustrated, prejudice and discrimination tend to increase (Aronson, et al., 2005).

Although the causes of prejudice are still not completely understood, we can help guard ourselves against it by remaining aware of the five tendencies discussed in this section, namely:

1. The tendency to favor familiarity and fear strangers;
2. The tendency to mentally categorize people into "in" and "out" groups;
3. The tendency to perceive members of other groups as more alike than members of our own group;
4. The tendency for the attitudes of majority group members to be more influenced by negative behaviors committed by members of minority groups than members of their own (majority) group; and
5. The tendency to build our self-esteem through group membership.

Snapshot Summary   **Box 1**

Stereotypes and Prejudiced Belief Systems about Group Inferiority

As you read this list, make a note next to each item indicating: (a) whether you've heard of this form of stereotype or prejudice, and (b) whether you've observed or experienced it.

Ethnocentrism: *considering one's own culture or ethnic group to be "central" or "normal," and viewing cultures that are different as "deficient" or "inferior."*

> *For example, claiming that another culture is "weird" or "abnormal" for eating certain animals that we consider unethical to eat, even though we eat certain animals that they consider unethical to eat.*

Racism: *prejudice or discrimination based on skin color.*

For example, Cecil Rhodes (Englishman and empire builder of British South Africa), once claimed: "We [the British] are the finest race in the world and the more of the world we inhabit the better it is for the human race."

Apartheid: *a strict system of racial separation and discrimination against non-white people, which was once national policy in South Africa.*

Classism: *prejudice or discrimination based on social class, particularly toward people of low socioeconomic status.*

> *For example, focusing only on the contributions made by politicians and wealthy industrialists to America, while ignoring the contributions of poor immigrants, farmers, slaves, and pioneer women.*

Nationalism: *excessive interest and belief in the strengths of one's own nation without acknowledgment of its mistakes or weaknesses, and without concern for the needs of other nations or the common interests of all nations.*

> *For example, "blind patriotism" that blinds people to the shortcomings of their own nation, and views any questioning or criticism of their nation as being disloyal or "unpatriotic." (As in the slogan, "America: right or wrong!")*

S TUDENT PERSPECTIVE

"I would like to change the entire world, so that we wouldn't be segregated by continents and territories."

—College sophomore

Regionalism: *prejudice or discrimination based on the geographical region of a nation in which an individual has been born and raised.*

> *For example, a northerner thinking that all southerners are racists.*

Xenophobia: *extreme fear or hatred of foreigners, outsiders, or strangers.*

For example, someone believing that all immigrants should be kept out of the country because they will increase the crime rate.

Anti-Semitism: *prejudice or discrimination toward Jews.*

> *For example, the mass murdering of Jews in Nazi Germany.*

Religious Bigotry: *stubborn and total intolerance of any religious beliefs that are different from one's own.*

> *For example, people who believe that members of their own religion are "favored" or "chosen" by God and will be saved, while those of other religious faiths are sinners and will (or should) be punished.*

Terrorism: *intentional acts of violence against civilians that are motivated by political or religious prejudice.*

For example, the September 11th attacks on the United States.

Ageism: *prejudice or discrimination based on age, particularly toward the elderly.*

For example, believing that all "old" people are bad drivers with bad memories.

Ableism: *prejudice or discrimination toward people who are disabled or handicapped.*

For example, avoiding interaction with handicapped people because of anxiety about not knowing what to say or how to act around them.

S **TUDENT PERSPECTIVE**

"Most religions dictate that theirs is the only way, and without believing in it, you cannot enter the mighty kingdom of heaven. Who are we to judge? It makes more sense for God to be the only one mighty enough to make that decision. If other people could understand and see from this perspective, then many religious arguments could be avoided."

—*First-year student*

Sexism: *prejudice or discrimination based on sex or gender.*

For example, believing that no one should vote for a woman president because she would be too "emotional."

Heterosexism: *belief that heterosexuality is the only acceptable sexual orientation.*

For example, using the phrase, "You're so gay" as an insult or put down; or believing that gays should not have the same legal rights and opportunities as heterosexuals.

Homophobia: *extreme fear and/or hatred of homosexuals.*

For example, people who create or contribute to anti-gay Web sites.

■ Strategies for Making the Most of Diversity

We can learn the most from diversity by taking each of the following three steps:

1. Self-reflection,
2. Personal action, and
3. Interpersonal interaction.

Each of these steps represents a progressively higher level of involvement with diversity, so the higher you go, the more you will learn.

C **LASSIC QUOTE**

A fanatic is one who can't change his mind and won't change the subject.
—*Winston Churchill, Prime Minister of the United Kingdom during World War II, and Nobel Prize winner in Literature*

Self-Reflection: Gaining Self-Awareness and Developing Diversity Tolerance

The first step to learning from diversity is to develop self-awareness about our attitudes toward diversity, particularly awareness of any stereotypes and prejudices we may have that are biasing our perceptions of, or behaviors toward, different groups of people. At

By writing a constitution that failed to grant female citizens the right to vote, America's founding fathers forgot their mothers (along with all other women) and provided a very vivid example of sexism.

the bare minimum, we want to behave in a way that demonstrates tolerance or acceptance of diversity.

As previously mentioned, research indicates that prejudice and discrimination can occur unconsciously or unintentionally (Baron, Byrne, & Branscombe, 2006). Listed below are some specific strategies for increasing your conscious awareness of attitudes and feelings about diversity.

Keep a journal or diary of your personal reflections on diversity.

Studies show that students learn most effectively from diversity experiences when they take time to reflect on these experiences, particularly when they record these reflections in writing (Lopez, et al., 1998; Nagda, et al., 2003). If you decide to reflect on your diversity experiences, it might be useful to keep the following questions in mind:

- What type of feelings or emotions did you experience?
- When and where did you experience these feelings? (What was the situation or context?)
- Why do you think you felt that way?

Becoming aware of our subtle and sometimes subconscious prejudices is the first step toward eliminating them. Reducing prejudice not only benefits those who are the targets of prejudice, it also benefits those who reduce their own prejudice. Research indicates that people who are less prejudiced report more satisfaction with their lives (Feagin & McKinney, 2003)—perhaps because they are more open to social experiences and less distrustful or fearful of the people around them (Baron, Byrne, & Branscombe, 2006).

Pause for Reflection

Have you ever been prejudiced against a certain group of people?

If you have, what was the group, and why do you think you held that prejudice?

LASSIC QUOTES

Stop judging by mere appearances, and make a right judgment.
—*The Bible, John 7:24*

You can't judge a book by the cover.
—*Hit record, 1962, by Ellas Bates, a.k.a., Bo Diddley (Note: a "bo diddley" is a one-stringed African guitar.)*

Consciously avoid preoccupation with physical appearances.

Go deeper and get beneath the superficial surface of appearances to view people in terms of *who* they really are and how they really act, not in terms of how they look. Remember the old proverb: "It's what's inside that counts." Judge others by the quality of their personal character, not by your familiarity with their physical characteristics.

Personal Story

When I was a new college student at a large university in the south, I encountered a student who talked loudly, had her ears pierced all around the lobes, and used words my mom never allowed me to use. At first, I was turned off by these differences, but I was also absolutely intrigued by her. It appeared that other students were too, because she seemed to be "together" and very cool. I'm ashamed to admit it, but it took me the whole year to realize that my way was not necessarily the right way (it was just more familiar), and her way was not really wrong or deficient (it was just different).

—*Viki Sox Fecas, Program Manager for Freshman and Pre-Freshman Programs and co-author of this text*

LASSIC QUOTE

The common eye sees only the outside of things, and judges by that. But the seeing eye pierces through and reads the heart and the soul, finding there capacities which the outside didn't indicate or promise.
—*Samuel Clemens, a.k.a., Mark Twain; writer, lecturer, and humorist*

Make a conscious attempt to perceive people as individuals—not as group members, and form your impressions of them on a case-by-case basis—not by using a "general rule."

This may seem like an obvious and easy thing to do, but remember, research shows that there is a natural tendency for humans to consider members of another group as being more alike (or all alike) than members of our own group (Taylor, 2006). Thus, we may have to deliberately fight off this grouping or "lumping together" tendency and consciously focus on each person's individuality.

Personal Action: Learning about Diversity by Acquiring Knowledge of Different Cultures

While self-awareness is an important first step toward learning from diversity, we also need to step outside ourselves and make an active attempt to learn about other social groups and cultures. Our perception of reality is a blending of fact (objectivity) and our interpretation (subjectivity)—which is shaped and molded by our particular cultural perspective (Paul, 1995). Viewing issues from different cultural perspectives allows you to perceive "reality" and see "truth" from different vantage points, which advantages your thinking by making it more comprehensive and less ethnocentric.

Thus, to think in a balanced and unbiased fashion, we need to acquire knowledge about the diverse groups that make up our social environment and how their experiences may be different from our own. In order to acquire this knowledge, we must first acknowledge that diversity exists. It means not being blind to, or in denial about human differences, and it is more than simply saying, "We're all human, so let's get over our differences and move on." This comment ignores the fact that different groups of people have had very different life experiences and continue to face different challenges. More importantly, it denies their group identity, which is an important element of their self-concept and self-esteem.

> **Remember:** Don't let cultural differences get in the way of potentially rewarding relationships. The more opportunities you create to learn from others who are different from yourself, the more opportunities you will create to learn about yourself.

Someone who merely tolerates diversity (level 1) might say things like, "Let's just get along," "live and let live," or "to each his own." Learning about diversity (level 2) involves taking a step beyond diversity tolerance to the higher level of diversity *appreciation*—becoming interested in the cultures and experiences of different groups of people and wanting to learn more about them. Listed below are some strategies for taking this second step.

To increase your understanding and empathy for the experiences of members of another group, imagine yourself as a member of a different group, and attempt to visualize what the experience might be like.

Better yet, see if you can place yourself in the position or situation of someone from that group. For instance, ride in a wheelchair to experience what it is like for someone who is physically disabled, or wear blinders to experience what it's like to be visually impaired.

Incorporate diversity into your work on course assignments.

If you have a choice about what topic to do research on in a particular course, consider choosing a topic relating to diversity; or, consider discussing the diversity implications of whatever topic you may be writing or speaking about (e.g., use multicultural or cross-cultural examples as evidence to illustrate your points).

Take courses that cover material relating to diversity.

You can actively plan to do this by reviewing your college catalog for course descriptions and identify courses that are designed to promote understanding or appreciation of multicultural diversity within the United States or cross-cultural diversity across different nations.

Strongly consider taking a foreign language course.

This will not only benefit you educationally, but it should also benefit you professionally because employers of college graduates are placing increasing value on employees who have foreign language skills (Fixman, 1990; Office of Research, 1994).

Participate in co-curricular activities on campus that relate to diversity.

You can actively plan to do this by reviewing your student handbook for co-curricular programs, student activities, or student clubs that promote diversity awareness and appreciation. Planning in advance to attend some of these programs may be easy to do, because they often coincide with annually scheduled "national" weeks or months, such as Black History Month, Women's History Month, Latin Heritage Month, and Asian American Month.

Studies indicate that taking diversity courses and participating in co-curricular programs helps to reduce unconscious prejudice (Blair, 2002) and strengthens mental development

(Pascarella & Terenzini, 2005). Furthermore, what you learn in these courses and programs can provide you with the preparation and confidence to move on to the next step—direct interaction with people from diverse backgrounds.

Interpersonal Interaction: Learning through Interaction and Collaboration with Members of Diverse Groups

Through formal courses and programs, you can learn about diversity. However, you can also learn through diversity experience—direct, first-hand interaction with people from diverse groups and backgrounds. Studies show that learning is maximized when students step beyond just learning about diversity through reading and attending lectures to actually experiencing diversity by interacting with others from diverse groups (Nagda et al., 2003). Such interpersonal experiences move you from the level of multicultural or cross-cultural awareness to a higher level that involves intercultural interaction. This represents a significant increase in your level of involvement with diversity. It is almost like the difference between learning about a foreign country by taking a class or reading about it and actually traveling to the country, interacting with its natives, and immersing yourself in its culture.

© STOCKBYTE

Cultivating relationships with others from diverse groups increases your awareness and comfort level when interacting with those from different cultural backgrounds.

This third step involves actively seeking out interaction with members of diverse groups of people who can contribute to your learning and who can learn from you. It requires being open to interaction, dialog, and cultivation of personal relationships with individuals from diverse groups. If you have taken the previous step and learned about different cultures, you may now be more confident about interacting with people from different cultural backgrounds. However, your comfort level with this level of involvement may depend on how much experience you have had with diversity prior to college.

Pause for Reflection

How would you rank the amount or variety of diversity you have experienced in the following settings?

1. The neighborhood in which you grew up

2. The places where you have worked or been employed

3. The high school you attended

4. The college or university you now attend

Which setting had the most and least diversity? What do you think accounts for this difference?

CLASSIC QUOTE

All that is necessary is to take an interest in other persons, to recognize that other people as a rule are much like one's self, and thankfully to admit that diversity is a glorious feature of life.

—*Frank Swinnerton,*
British novelist and literary critic

If there is diversity on your campus that you have had little previous exposure to, seeking out and initiating interaction with members of unfamiliar groups may not come easily or naturally for you. On the other hand, if you have had little or no prior experience with diverse groups, you also have the most to gain from experiencing the diversity that is now available on your campus. Research on human learning consistently shows that new experiences that differ from an individual's prior experiences are those that tend to produce the greatest learning and the greatest gains in mental development (Piaget, 1985; Acredolo & O'Connor, 1991).

Even if you had experience living in diverse environments prior to college, you may not have experienced the particular types or dimensions of diversity that exist on your campus, or you may have not yet developed the most effective ways for interacting with and learning from members of diverse groups. Whatever your prior experience with diversity may be, look at the diversity on your campus as a new educational opportunity. Consider it to be a campus resource, and capitalize on this social resource to promote your educational and personal success.

Listed below is a series of strategies for increasing the quantity and quality of your interaction with members from diverse groups on campus.

Intentionally create opportunities for interaction and conversation with students from diverse groups.

"I have a love of words, too."

Fight off the natural tendency to associate only with people who are similar to you. One way to do this is by placing yourself in situations where you are close enough for conversation to take place with individuals from diverse groups. Research indicates that meaningful interpersonal interactions and friendships are more likely to develop among people who are within close distance to one another (Latané, et al., 1993). So, make an intentional attempt to create this condition. For example, in class, sit near a student from another country; or, at lunch, sit near a student from a different ethnic or racial group.

Keep in mind that the definition of discrimination is giving unequal treatment to different groups of people. If we interact solely with members of our own group and separate ourselves from members of a group who are different than us, we are treating these two groups unequally. This qualifies as discrimination, even if we are not doing it maliciously or consciously.

Make an earnest attempt to learn the names and interests of students from diverse groups.

This will enable you to establish early, personal rapport that can serve as a foundation for further interaction and deeper conversation. Pay particular attention to interests that you may have in common, because shared interests can provide a source of interesting conversation, and perhaps, lead to the development of a long-term friendship.

Consider spending some time at the multicultural center on your campus, or join a campus club or organization that is devoted to diversity awareness (e.g., international student club).

This will enable you to make contact with members of groups other than your own, and clearly sends a message to them that you are interested in doing so, because you have taken the initiative to visit them on "their turf."

Participate in a multicultural or cross-cultural retreat sponsored by your college.

A retreat setting can provide a comfortable environment for getting to know people at a personal level, without the everyday interference and distractions that take place on campus.

Become involved in volunteer or community service activities that may allow you to work in diverse communities or neighborhoods.

Research suggests that college students who participate in volunteer experiences report significant gains in learning and leadership development (Astin, et al., 2000).

Attempt to locate and participate in an internship in a company or organization that will allow you the opportunity to work with people from diverse backgrounds and cultures.

This will not only provide you with a good learning experience, it will also improve your preparation and qualifications for career entry after college. Surveys of employers indicate that they value college graduates who have actual "hands on" experience with diversity (Education Commission of the States, 1995).

If possible, participate in a study abroad program that allows you to live in another country and interact directly with its natives.

In preparation for this international experience, take a course in the language, culture, or history of the nation to which you will be traveling.

Take advantage of the Internet to "chat" with students from diverse groups on your campus, or with students in different countries.

Electronic communication can be a more convenient and more comfortable way to initially interact with members of diverse groups with whom you have had little prior experience. After you've communicated successfully online, you may then feel more comfortable about communicating in person.

Deliberately seek out the views and opinions of students from diverse backgrounds.

For example, ask students from different backgrounds if there was any point made or position taken in class that they would strongly question or challenge. Seeking out divergent (diverse) viewpoints has been found to be one of the best ways to develop critical thinking skills (Kurfiss, 1988).

Join or form discussion groups with students from diverse backgrounds.

You can experience diverse perspectives by joining groups of students who may be different from you in terms of such characteristics as gender, age, race, or ethnic group. When ideas are generated freely in groups comprised of people from diverse backgrounds, a powerful "cross-stimulation" effect occurs, whereby one group member's idea often triggers different ideas from other group members (Brown et al., 1998).

You might begin by forming discussion groups of students who are different with respect to one characteristic but similar with respect to another. For instance, join a group of students of your gender but who differ with respect to race, ethnicity, or age. This strategy can give your diverse group some common ground to build on, as well as increase their awareness that humans who are members of different groups can, at the same time, be members of the same group—and share similar experiences, needs, or concerns.

> **Remember:** Including diversity in your discussion group not only increases its social variety, it also increases the quality of the group's thinking. Diverse discussion groups allow each member to access the different perspectives and thinking styles of people with different background experiences.

For instance, older students may have more life experience for younger students to draw upon and learn from, while younger students may bring a fresh, idealistic perspective to group discussions with older students. Also, males and females tend to contribute different thinking styles to group discussions. Studies show that males are more likely to be "separate knowers" who have a greater tendency to "detach" themselves from the concept or issue being discussed so they can analyze it, whereas females are more likely to be "connected knowers" who have a stronger tendency to relate personally to concepts and connect them to their own experiences. For example, when confronting a poem, males are more likely to ask themselves, "What techniques can I use to analyze it?" In contrast, females are more likely to ask themselves, "What is the poet trying to say to me?" (Belenky, et al., 1986, p. 101). It has also been found that females generally adopt a more collaborative style during group discussions and are more likely to collect ideas of others in a group-learning situation, whereas males are more likely to adopt a competitive approach and debate the ideas of others (Magolda, 1992).

Pause for Reflection

How would you define teamwork?

What do you think are the key factors that make study groups or group projects successful?

Form collaborative learning teams.

A learning team is much more than a discussion group; it moves beyond discussion to collaboration—whereby teammates rely on each other as part of a united effort to reach a shared goal.

Studies show that interpersonal contact between members of different ethnic and racial groups, which takes place while they work collaboratively to achieve a common goal, tends to reduce racial prejudice and promote interracial friendships (Allport, 1954; Amir, 1976). This may be due to the fact that when these individuals from diverse groups work collaboratively on the same team, they become members of the same group. Thus, they all become members of the "in group," with no one being an "outsider."

Take Action Now!   **Box 2**

Tips for Teamwork: Creating Successful Collaborative Learning Groups

1. **Teammates should have a common goal.**

   To help your team identify and work toward a common goal, plan to produce a final product that can serve as visible evidence of the group's effort and accomplishment (e.g., a completed sheet of answers to questions, a list or chart of specific ideas, or an outline). This will help keep the team focused and moving in a common direction.

2. **Teammates should have equal opportunity and individual responsibility for contributing to the team's final product.**

   For example, each member of the team should have equal opportunity to participate during group discussions and should be responsible for contributing something specific to the team's final product—such as a different perspective (e.g., national, global, or ethical) or a different form of thinking (e.g., application, synthesis, evaluation).

3. **Teammates should work interdependently—that is, they should depend on or rely upon each other to achieve their common goal.**

   Similar to a sports team, each member of the learning team has a specific position and role to play. For instance, each member of the team could assume a different role, such as:

   - *manager—who assures that the team stays focused on their goal and doesn't get off track,*
   - *moderator—who assures that all members have equal opportunity to contribute,*
   - *summarizer—who identifies what the team has accomplished and what remains to be done, or*
   - *recorder—who keeps a written record of the team's ideas.*

4. **Before beginning their work, teammates should take some time to interact informally with each other to develop a sense of team identity and group solidarity.**

   For example, take some "warm up" time for teammates to get to know each other's names and interests before tackling the learning task. Teammates need to feel comfortable with each other in order for them to feel comfortable about sharing personal thoughts and feelings, particularly if the team is comprised of individuals from diverse backgrounds.

5. **Teamwork should take place in a friendly, informal setting.**

   The surrounding atmosphere can influence the nature and quality of interaction among members of the group. People are more likely to work openly and collaboratively with others when they are in a social environment that is warm and friendly. For example, a living room or a lounge area would provide a more informal and friendlier atmosphere than a classroom or library.

6. **Learning teams should occasionally change membership so that each member gets an opportunity to work with different individuals from other ethnic or racial groups.**

   If someone with a prejudice toward a certain ethnic or racial group has the experience of working on multiple teams, which include different individuals from the same racial or ethnic group, the prejudiced person is less likely to conclude that any positive experience was due to having interacted with someone who was an "exception to the rule."

When contact between people from diverse groups takes place under the above conditions, it can have the most powerful effects on diversity appreciation and team learning. Working in teams under these conditions is a win-win situation: Prejudice is decreased, and at the same time, learning is increased.

References: Amir (1969); Allport (1979); Aronson, Wilson, & Akert (2005); Cook (1984); Sherif et al. (1961); and Wilder (1984).

The greatest gains in reducing prejudice and improving relationships among members of different ethnic and racial groups take place when collaboration occurs under the six conditions described in Box 2. Research also indicates that these are the same conditions that are most likely to produce the largest gains in learning among team members (Slavin, 1995; Johnson, et al., 1998).

At the conclusion of collaborative teamwork and group discussions, take some time to pause and reflect on the social interaction that took place.

Ask yourself questions that cause you to think back on the ideas that emerged from diverse members of the group and think about what impact these ideas had on you. For instance, after group discussions you could ask yourself the following questions:

- What major differences did you detect among group members during your discussion?
- What major similarities in viewpoints or background experiences did all group members share?
- Did the discussion cause you to reconsider or change any ideas you previously held?

Take a leadership role with respect to promoting diversity.

There are a variety of ways in which you can demonstrate diversity leadership, such as those listed below.

- During group discussions, take on the role of a moderator, who ensures that the ideas of people from minority groups are included, heard, and respected.

For example, encourage and reinforce the contributions of students who may be reluctant to speak up because of their minority status. Putting members with diverse cultures on the same team may serve to reduce prejudice, but only if each member's cultural identity and perspective is sought and acknowledged, not ignored or abolished (Baron, Byrne, & Brauscombe, 2006).

- Serve as a community builder by identifying similarities or recurring themes you see across the ideas and experiences of students from varied backgrounds.

LASSIC QUOTE
The nation's future depends upon leaders trained through wide exposure to that robust exchange of ideas which discovers truth out of a multitude of tongues.
—*William J. Brennan, former Supreme Court Justice*

For example, all humans live in communities, develop relationships, have emotional needs, and undergo life experiences that affect their self-esteem and personal identity. So, be on the lookout for patterns of unity that underlie diversity.

Diversity without unity allows for no sense of community and can lead to feelings of group separation and divisiveness, because we fail to detect the deeper similarities that lie beneath our more obvious differences. We need to dig more deeply to find the common ground from which our differences grow. By raising your fellow students' consciousness of the common or universal themes that bind different groups of people together, you can help ensure that highlighting diversity will not heighten divisiveness.

> **Remember:** *Diversity represents variations on the common theme of humanity. Although people have different cultural backgrounds, they are still cultivated from the same soil—they are all grounded in the common experience of being human.*

- ■ Take a stand against prejudice or discrimination by constructively expressing your disagreement with those who make stereotypical statements or prejudicial remarks. You may avoid risk by saying nothing, but your silence may be perceived by others to mean that you agree with the person who made the remark. A number of studies have shown that when a person in a group observes others making prejudiced comments, that person's prejudice can increase, perhaps due to the pressure of group conformity (Stangor, Sechrist, & Jost, 2001). On the other hand, if a prejudiced person sees that his views are out of line with others, particularly others who are liked or respected, the person's prejudice can be reduced (Baron, Byrne, & Brauscombe, 2006). So, by taking a leadership role and not remaining silent when people make prejudiced remarks, you may not only help reduce that one person's prejudice, you may also reduce the prejudice of others who heard the remark.

- ■ Take the initiative in forming friendships with members of diverse groups. These friendships not only enrich your social life, they can also help reduce prejudice among members of your own group. Research indicates that when people see a member of their own group develop a positive relationship with someone from a group that they are prejudiced against, their prejudice tends to decline (Paolini, et al., 2004).

> **Remember:** *When you take a leadership role in modeling appreciation of diversity and combating prejudice in others, you are taking a stand for social injustice and for the ethical principle of equity—equal opportunity and impartial treatment of all people.*

CLASSIC QUOTE

Americanism is a question of principles, of idealism, of character: it is not a matter of birthplace or creed or line of descent.

—Theodore Roosevelt, American soldier, president, and Nobel Prize winner

Furthermore, you are demonstrating responsible citizenship by doing something good for your community and, ultimately, your country. Let us not forget that the United States is a nation that was originally built and developed by members of diverse immigrant groups, many of whom left their native countries to escape different forms of prejudice and discrimination, and to experience the freedom of equal opportunity in America (Levine, 1996).

As a democracy, the United States is a nation that is built on the foundation of individual rights and freedom of opportunity, which are guaranteed by its constitution. When the personal rights and freedom of fellow citizens are threatened by prejudice and discrimination, the political stability and survival of any democratic nation is threatened.

Diversity and democracy go hand-in-hand; by appreciating the former, you preserve the latter.

Pause for Reflection

Turn back to the diversity spectrum on page 236 of this chapter and look over the list of groups that make up the spectrum. Do you notice any groups that are missing from the list that should be added, either because they have distinctive cultures or because they have been targets of prejudice and discrimination?

■ Summary and Conclusion

CLASSIC QUOTE

A progressive society counts individual variations as precious since it finds in them the means of its own growth. A democratic society must, in consistency with its ideal, allow intellectual freedom and the play of diverse gifts and interests.

—*John Dewey, U.S. educator, philosopher, and psychologist*

The growing diversity in America and on American college campuses represents a social resource that we can intentionally capitalize on to promote our personal development. By seeking out and learning from diversity, rather than separating ourselves from it, we gain a more complete understanding of our nation and our world; we sharpen our self-awareness and self-insight; we learn to think with greater complexity and creativity; we acquire cultural knowledge and intercultural communication skills that are relevant to career success; and we enrich our social lives by increasing the variety of human beings with whom we interact, network, and develop relationships.

Last, but certainly not least, diversity is an opportunity to develop your personal character and leadership. By serving as a moderator, mediator, and community builder, you assume the role of a leader who helps to build bridges of unity across islands of diversity.

Remember: By being open to diversity and opposed to prejudice and discrimination, you also demonstrate character. You become a role model whose actions visibly demonstrate to others that diversity has both educational and ethical value and that it's not only the smart thing to do, but also the right thing to do.

■ Learning More through Independent Research

Web-Based Resources for Further Information on Diversity

Learn more about current issues relating to prejudice and discrimination by exploring the information provided at the following two Web sites.

Tolerance.org

This is the site of an educational and public service organization for people interested in fighting bigotry in America and creating communities that value diversity. It tracks hate groups, hate crimes, hate Web sites, and hate music, and it supplies research-based strategies for promoting social justice on campus and in the community. You can subscribe to a free newsletter that provides updates on the latest social, educational, and legal news relating to bigotry and diversity.

If you visit this site, try taking one of the *Hidden Bias Tests* that have been developed by psychologists at Harvard, the University of Virginia, and the University of Washington.

Amnesty.org

This is the Web site of Amnesty International (AI), which is a worldwide organization of people who are committed to preserving human rights. While Tolerance.org is a national organization, AI is an international movement that includes almost 2 million members from over 150 countries in every region of the world. Many of these people have very different political and religious beliefs, but they share the common concern and goal: to prevent violation of human rights. Its Web site includes strategies for protecting and promoting human rights, and information on how you can join this organization or its local volunteer groups.

If you visit this site, consider reading AI's *Universal Declaration of Human Rights*, which has been translated into more than 300 different languages for worldwide use.

■ Diversity Self-Awareness

Further your diversity self-awareness by completing the following four exercises.

1. Diversity Spectrum

    We are members of different groups at the same time, and our membership in these groups can influence our personal development and self-identity. In the figure below, the shaded center circle represents yourself, and the six non-shaded circles represent six different groups that you belong to, which you feel have influenced your personal development.

    Fill in these circles with the names of those groups to which you belong that have had the most influence on your personal development. You can use the diversity spectrum that appears on the first page of this chapter to help you identify different groups. Do not feel you have to come up with six groups to fill all six circles. What is most important is to identify those groups that you think have had significant influence on your personal development or identity.

    After you identify these groups, take a moment to reflect on the following questions:

    a. Which one of your group memberships has had the greatest influence on your personal identity and why?

    b. Have you ever felt limited or disadvantaged by being a member of any group(s)?

    c. Have you ever felt that you experienced advantages or privileges because of your membership in any group(s)?

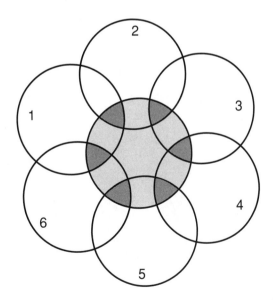

2. When Have You Felt Different?

Describe an experience in your life when you felt that you were different from, or didn't fit in with, the majority of people around you.

Why did you feel that way? How do you think members of the majority felt about you?

3. Questions about Other Groups or Cultures

Write down, in question form, anything that you have wondered about people from a particular group or culture that is different than your own.

Would you feel comfortable approaching and posing these questions to someone from this group or culture? Why or why not?

4. Personal Experience

Have you ever been the personal target of prejudice or discrimination?

What happened? Who was involved? How did you feel?

■ Case Study

Hate Crime: Racially Motivated Murder

Jasper County, Texas, has a population of approximately 31,000 people, 80 percent of whom are White, 18 percent Black, and 2 percent are of other races. The county's poverty rate is considerably higher than the national average, and its average household income is significantly lower. In 1998, the mayor, president of the Chamber of Commerce, and two councilmen were Black. From the outside, Jasper appeared to be a town with racial harmony, and its Black and White leaders were quick to state there was racial harmony in Jasper.

However, on June 7, 1998, James Byrd, Jr., a 49-year-old African-American male, was walking home along a road one evening and was offered a ride by three White males. Rather than taking Mr. Byrd home, Lawrence Brewer (31), John King (23), and Shawn Berry (23), three individuals linked to white-supremacist groups, took Mr. Byrd to an isolated area and began beating him. They then dropped his pants to his ankles, painted his face black, chained Mr. Byrd to their truck and dragged him for approximately 3 miles. The truck was driven in a zigzag fashion in order to inflict maximum pain on the victim. Mr. Byrd was decapitated after his body collided with a culvert in a ditch alongside the road. His skin, arms, genitalia, and other body parts were strewn along the road, while his torso was found dumped in front of a Black cemetery. Medical examiners testified that Mr. Byrd was alive for much of the dragging incident.

While in prison awaiting trial, Lawrence Brewer wrote letters to King and other inmates. In one letter, Brewer wrote: "Well, I did it and am no longer a virgin. It was a rush and I'm still licking my lips for more." Once the trials were completed, Brewer and King were sentenced to death. Both Brewer and King, whose bodies were covered with racist tattoos, had been on parole prior to the incident, and they had previously been cellmates. King had spent an extensive amount of time in prison where he began to associate with White males in an environment where each race was pitted against the other.

As a result of the murder, Mr. Byrd's family created the James Byrd Foundation for Racial Healing in 1998. On January 20, 1999, a wrought iron fence that separated Black and White graves for more than 150 years in Jasper Cemetery was removed in a special unity service. Members of the racist Ku Klux Klan have since visited the gravesite of James Byrd, Jr. several times, leaving stickers and other markers that have angered the Jasper community and Mr. Byrd's family.

Sources: *San Antonio Express News*, September 17, 1999, *Louisiana Weekly*, February 3, 2003, *Houston Chronicle*, June 14, 1998, Two Towns of Jasper, PBS.

■ Reflection and Discussion Questions

1. What social factors (if any) do you think led to the incident?

2. Could the incident have been prevented? If yes, how? If no, why not?

3. What do you think will be the long-term effects of this incident on the town?

4. How likely do you think it is that an incident such as this could occur in your hometown or near your college campus?

5. How would you react if it did happen?

CHAPTER 13

Stress
Accentuate the Positive

Everyone knows when he or she is experiencing stress, and each one of us can discuss various stressors that confront us each week. A **stressor**, according to Hans Selye, is anything that produces tension in your life, which may be of a physical nature (e.g., starvation brought on by a drought in east Africa, restricted access to a friend's house caused by a broken leg in a cast) or a psychological nature (e.g., being involved in interpersonal conflict, being frustrated in a second attempt to pass a required course). Of these two categories, it seems that psychological stressors are forever present, even in the best of times, for most students. Psychological stressors confront us all regardless of how healthy, powerful, or rich we are, although these stressors differ in the degree to which they "stress us out."

Stress often arises when we have choices to make. In most cases we would rather deal with selecting between two goods than two evils, but conflict can be experienced when one is selecting between two attractive outcomes. Such an **approach-approach** type of conflict might involve having to select between two high-paying jobs after graduating from college. While approach-approach conflicts are unlikely to end like the one in the example known as "Buridan's ass," where a donkey caught between two equally attractive piles of hay dies from being unable to decide which pile to eat, conflict is conflict, and even selecting between two desirables can be stressful.

Memories concerning our struggle to choose between two evils seem to be vivid and lasting. For example, a person choosing between taking out a student loan with a high interest rate or asking his or her parents for additional help knowing they can ill afford the assistance is in this situation. Having two dreadful choices is commonly referred to as being caught "between a rock and a hard spot." The person is experiencing an **avoidance-avoidance** type of conflict. No matter what the cause, psychological frustration can be profoundly stressful and may even cause us to respond aggressively. We might scream at our roommate or even become physically violent in extreme cases of stress.

If asked, all of us could easily list stressful events or periods in our life (e.g., death of a pet, moving from one school or town to another, loss of a close family member through death, divorce of parents, loss of some prized possession, enrolling in college classes for the first time). Stress can be defined as a personal experience of physical or mental strain that results in numerous physiological changes (e.g., heart-rate increases, increase in the force of one's heartbeat, digestive disturbance, blood-vessel constriction, elevated blood pressure, noticeable sweating, rise in muscle tightness). In this chapter we will discuss the causes and symptoms of stress and how you can develop effective ways to cope with stress.

What Is Stress Exactly?

The items listed on the assessment tool developed by Holmes and Rahe help us understand what the term stress encompasses in everyday language. Simply stated, **stress** is a reaction to the various things that happen to us, both negative and positive. Interestingly, while most of us readily think of negative events as stress-provoking (e.g., jail term, death of a close friend, being fired at work), in reality events that are very positive in nature can also be stressful (e.g., change in residence, vacation, marriage). Even though we might be able to cite exceptions, in the vast majority of cases one's wedding day is a joyful event marked by celebration. Marriage also introduces many changes for both people involved. Issues can range from who pays for which day-to-day living expense to the "correct" way to squeeze toothpaste from a tube. Changes associated with marriage can generate a lot of stress.

A meaningful and useful way to conceptualize stress is given in the following formula.

Stress = Number of Resources − Number of Changes

Thus, high levels of stress are due to changes exceeding resources, and low levels of stress are due to resources exceeding changes.

Holmes and Rahe's list of stressful events covers a wide range of the adult life span, although several of the items would not apply to many undergraduates. In a college environment one would expect to find certain changes not listed by Holmes and Rahe to be just as stressful as those listed. These could include dropping or being withdrawn from a class with a "W," receiving a $20 ticket from campus police for a parking violation, changing from one major to another, not being able to enter a major because of one's grade point average, being withdrawn from a course with a "WF," joining a sorority or fraternity, transferring to another college (leaving this college or coming to this college as a transfer student), failing a course in one's major with a "favorite" professor, first dismissal from college, and being accused of academic dishonesty. In the above equation, note that the word "change" is important. Frequently we are forced to deal with changes that wear us down physically and psychologically because we lack the necessary resources at the time to cope. Our store of coping resources can fluctuate. Remember the last time when you had the flu and experienced a drop in your ability to cope with the demands placed on you?

Not all change is bad; in fact, there is evidence to suggest that we need a certain amount of change to maintain our physical and psychological balance. Psychologists and other researchers once studied the effect of relatively unchanging surroundings (referred to as sensory deprivation studies). Participants were required to wear blindfolds or the equivalent, to stay still by lying down in soundproof rooms or large containers, to have their arms restrained in special devices to avoid experiencing tactile sensations, and so forth. The effects were profound in some cases; some participants even reported hallucinations. While too much change is bad, too little can also be bad. Apparently, too few external changes result in the body creating self-induced changes (hallucinations). But we are all individuals, and it is important to recognize that individuals differ in how much change they can tolerate.

■ Psychological Hardiness and Personality Differences

In *Man in Search of Meaning*, Victor Frankl describes how an individual can confront a truly unusual degree of change (incarceration in a concentration camp) and not only survive but come out stronger as a result. Perspective is very important in explaining outcomes, and we all differ in the degree to which we like change, or seek change in our lives. Some people seem to be revitalized by changes, and some even seek out high-pressure positions because of the constantly changing demands. Many presidents of the United States likely fall into this category of stress-hardy individuals. People such as Jimmy Carter, Elizabeth Dole, John Glenn, Hillary Clinton, Dianne Feinstein, George W. Bush, and Christine Whitman who are serving or have served in high-profile positions in politics probably all possess a high level of psychological hardiness. For example, when Senator Feinstein was asked whether she would consider running for president, she said:

> *I've been the first [woman] four times now: once as president of the Board of Supervisors [in San Francisco], as mayor, as the first gubernatorial candidate in my state, the first woman Senator from my state. What I've learned is there is a testing period that goes on—particularly in an executive capacity. I think it [takes someone] with the ability to run a campaign well, put together a platform that resounds with the American people and someone with the stamina, the staying power, the determination and enthusiasm to carry it off. (Ciabattari, 1999, p. 6)*

Psychological hardiness is reflected in individuals who like and seek change and challenges, possess a clear focus or goal, and perceive themselves as having control.

Stressful events can be short in duration (e.g., writing a speech) or long (e.g., a difficult job with a lot of responsibilities), but it is not always the magnitude of the event that determines how well we cope. The same stressors might be tolerable for one person but overwhelming to another. Our personal level of psychological hardiness is very important. Salvatore Maddi and Suzanne Kobasa (1994) studied executives in stressful situations, primarily due to an organization undergoing reorganization with the possibility of lost employment. Such periods of reorganization are associated with ill health (increases colds, influenza, backaches, and migraine headaches). Maddi and Kobasa found that some individuals were not as susceptible to the reorganization stressor. These resilient individuals were able to maintain a sense of control over most events encountered in life. The psychologically hardy displayed few of the effects found in others. The researchers found that the psychologically hardy (PH) possess

- An open attitude toward change, assessing *change as a challenge* rather than a threat to one's self.
- *A high degree of commitment* to what the person is involved in. This commitment is tied to goals and objectives. Subjects low in commitment tended to display evidence of being alienated from work, people, and things.
- *A sense of control over most events* rather than a sense of helplessness. High PHs are convinced they can influence the course of their future. In their eyes, effort makes a difference at work, in school, and in relationships. Low PHs felt they had little if any power to influence outcomes. For this latter group, outside forces controlled their future.

One of the lessons to be learned from the work of Maddi and Kobasa is that individuals confronted with stress can meet it head on (take active steps) or let the situation roll over them (take a passive approach). In the latter case, the person does not see the situation as a challenge, but rather as a threat beyond his or her control. In some cases, rather than being able to call upon a sense of commitment to sustain them during a difficult period, individuals low on hardiness worry and try to escape; they may deny what is occurring or even blame others. The following list summarizes the differences between high PH and low PH.

High PH	Low PH
Sees a challenge	Sees a threat
Commitment	Alienation
Active coping	Passive coping
Seeks change	Avoids change
Feels invigorated	Feels helpless

Martin Seligman (1995) has coined the term **learned helplessness**. Specifically, Seligman used the term to refer to situations where a person (or animal, since a lot of studies in this area use animal subjects) acts in a helpless manner if exposed to situations that are harmful or painful *and cannot be avoided*. The unavoidability of these situations seems to inhibit learning how to escape a harmful or painful situation in the future—a situation that could be avoided. In one early study on learned helplessness, dogs were placed in one of two treatments. Those in treatment A were confined to a harness and given electric shocks without any possibility of escape. Those in treatment B were exposed to the same exact conditions except if the animal struggled it could escape. Treatment A led to the dogs becoming less competitive, less aggressive, and less able to escape painful situations in the future. Treatment B resulted in dogs who were more competitive, aggressive, and better capable of escaping painful situations in the future. Other animal experiments on mice and rats produced animals in the learned helplessness group who were less active, displayed greater difficulty learning, and gave up sooner when confronted with challenges. Human participants in similar studies were found to be affected adversely in terms of problem-solving ability.

In general, from the numerous studies conducted it appears that some humans, due to certain experiences in and outside the academic world, "learn to be helpless." The effects of learned helplessness follow.

- The ability to effectively solve problems is reduced. A drop in motivation, energy, and the will to struggle and survive occurs.

- Learning becomes much more difficult. People ignore or seem unable to profit from information.
- An elevation of emotional or physical distress occurs. Individuals are likely to show outward signs of anxiety and depression. If conditions are not altered, the person may become sick or develop an illness (similar to Holmes and Rahe's findings that also uncovered a relationship between stressful conditions and illness).

Finally, an individual's personality type influences how much stress the person may experience. For example, while anxiety can be a symptom of stress and anxiety levels vary from day to day and week to week (called state anxiety), individuals also display somewhat consistent patterns (called trait anxiety). Charles Spielberger (1972) identified these two categories and uncovered some interesting findings. While the announcement of an important test can be expected to alter one's level of state anxiety, individuals differ in how much it affects them. These differences are related to the personality of the individual. Individuals with low trait anxiety usually seem calm and laid-back, while individuals with high trait anxiety typically seem high-strung and are frequently worried. Keep in mind that anxiety is not in and of itself bad—it serves to motivate us to study. Both high-anxiety and low-anxiety individuals may experience performance problems but for different reasons; in the former case, the high level of anxiety hinders processing of information, and in the latter, there is too little anxiety to motivate the person to study adequately.

Another type of personality that has been linked to stress is the **Type A personality**. Type A personalities are stress generators, creating stress in addition to what is placed on them from the outside. Type A personalities are driven to work (often working long hours, weekends), very goal conscious (frequently thinking of goals that need to be achieved and tasks that need to be completed), and find it very difficult to relax. This type of person always seems to be in a rush and may tend to finish others' sentences. Type A personalities find it very difficult to settle for less than perfection. Behind the wheel of a car, Type A personalities are likely to become agitated or angry because other drivers are "moving too slow," preventing the Type A from getting to his or her destination. The advantage of being a Type A is achievement (higher grades); the disadvantage is poor health (they tend to be more susceptible to heart attacks).

■ Prolonged Stress and Impairment of Functioning

Clearly, stress can be generated in many different ways, and we know from Holmes and Rahe's work that high levels of stress can result in illness and dysfunction. Does this happen overnight? The good news is no. The effects tend to accumulate over time, which means we have a period of time to take action to prevent the worst-case scenario from occurring. According to Hans Selye, when responding to stress, we go through a series of stages called the General Adaptation Syndrome (GAS).

Stage 1: Alarm (Fight/Flight)

Stress leads to physiological changes in your body (e.g., heart rate and respiration increase, adrenaline levels rise, and digestive functions drop). The body is gearing itself up to take action. The person prepares to either *"fight or take flight,"* that is, run from a perceived danger.

Stage 2: Resistance

Our "fight or flight" response has its origins in our early history as humans two million or more years ago. The problem is we are no longer literally fighting or running from saber-toothed tigers. We can neither punch the rude, unreasonable professor nor run out of his required class. Often we must stay put and endure the stressors in our life and suffer the consequences (in the twenty-first century the "fight or flight" response we are physiologically and mentally prepared to carry out is no longer appropriate in many situations). When we are stuck between fight and flight, the physiological changes that occur in the alarm stage still occur but at a lower level. But this level is still strong enough to wear us down psychologically and physically.

Stage 3: Exhaustion

At this point our resources are low and physical deterioration can set in (possibly contributing to conditions such as heart disease, hypertension, asthma, colitis, and, according to some researchers, ulcers and some forms of cancer). These diseases of adaptation or psychosomatic illnesses are the result of the person being blocked from reacting to a problem in a manner that can reestablish his or her equilibrium.

Too much adrenaline is associated with a drop in white blood cells, which impacts the immune system. For many students, prolonged stress results in symptoms such as fatigue, boredom, less restful sleep, loss of appetite (or eating much more), agitation, and becoming prone to making mistakes and having accidents. It has been estimated that over 45% of headaches are stress related.

■ What Can Be Done?

Many students (and nonstudents) respond to stress in self-defeating ways, by using drugs and alcohol, withdrawing from the things that are important but cause stress, and using psychological defenses such as denial, projection, or fantasizing. In fact, there are many things that can be done to relieve and prevent stress. Here are several suggestions that we have found effective and relatively easy to apply.

Everyday Techniques for Reducing Stress

Check your gauges (psychological/emotional, behavioral, and physical). Periodically stop and determine how much stress you are experiencing. Is it high or low? Whatever the level is, is the stress having a negative impact on your academic performance, your personal life, or your ability to just enjoy life? Sometimes such self-examination leads to the awareness that there are some unnecessary sources of stress in your life. For example, perhaps an acquaintance is always putting you down in subtle ways but denies doing so; no one should go through life maintaining such an association. If confronting the person does not change the situation, it is probably better to break off the relationship.

Feed yourself psychologically and emotionally. Read that book you have wanted to get to, listen to your favorite music, go to a movie or the local mall, start a hobby, or get involved in a community service such as Habitat for Humanity. It is important to take time to get away. While a stressed-out student may find it difficult to find the time to get away, such time-outs can replenish one's depleted energy and help break the cycle of lingering stress (i.e., GAS).

Feed yourself physiologically and behaviorally. Exercise. Spend 30 minutes three times a week. Take advantage of the college exercise facility if one is available; play tennis, racquetball, handball, basketball, and learn mountain climbing. Joining a team also helps to establish a support system. If you are on a tight schedule and cannot take time to travel somewhere, walk or run a mile or more a day near your residence (walk or run with a trusted partner so you are not out alone), or ride a bike on campus and climb the stairs in a campus building rather than riding the elevator. Not only is health improved by exercise, but exercise has been proven to reduce stress levels. Of course, adequate sleep and good nutrition are necessary ingredients in managing anxiety and stress.

Breathe deeply. During periods of stress take a moment to close your eyes. Breathe in two or three times in a slow and deep manner, allowing your stomach to rise as you breathe in. Slowly exhale through your lips. Increasing one's oxygen level in this manner can help relieve stress.

Divert your attention. Waiting for the professor to distribute a test to the class or to be called on to make a presentation can elevate your anxiety and stress level. Instead of sitting there thinking negative thoughts ("I am not sure I am prepared"), bump the negative thoughts aside with a pleasant image (visualize your favorite vacation spot) or focus on an available image (the tree outside the window that is swaying in the breeze). A simple refocusing from negative thoughts to something more pleasant in nature has been found to reduce anxiety and stress.

Visualize success. When feeling anxious due to some stressor (e.g., a major course paper that is due), visualize yourself as being successful. Visualize the various steps necessary in a task and actually picture yourself being successful each step of the way. A student teacher might go to the classroom where he or she will be teaching and go through the lesson plan without students there. He or she might use the chalkboard, read from the text, and so forth, all the while imagining a positive outcome. Such an activity has proven to be effective in reducing one's level of anxiety and stress.

Apply environmental engineering tactics. Make your apartment, dorm room, or house a relaxing environment. Decorate the walls with favorite posters or pictures, place objects around that elicit pleasant memories or feelings, purchase a tropical fish tank, which can help to create a soothing environment. Have a place that can be your place to escape to and fill it with items that make you feel good.

Techniques for Periods of High Stress

During periods of high stress we typically find it much more effective to develop an ongoing routine that involves cognitive restructuring, muscle relaxation, meditation, or sequential imagery. Such techniques are intended to be learned and practiced on a regular basis.

Cognitive Restructuring. Sometimes students are aware they are their own worst enemy because of negative self-talk. These are messages that a person repeats to himself or herself that negatively affect both performance and quality of life. Both test-anxious and non-test-anxious students say negative things to themselves (e.g., "I am going to fail this test!"), but test-anxious students make such remarks much more frequently and tend to believe them more. Albert Ellis, the creator of rational emotive behavior therapy, has had considerable success in having people tackle their stress-producing thoughts using an A-B-C approach to modifying behavior.

   A = activating event, which can be thought of as the stressor ("I have an important test Tuesday"). The event in and of itself is not the problem; it is how we perceive the event that is crucial.

   B = belief about the activating event. If my belief is that I will fail the test, then I will experience unnecessary stress.

   C = consequence. If I perceive myself as failing, I will experience stress and thus become anxious and not perform at my optimum level. We can alter the process at point B by forcefully injecting more positive thoughts to push out the self-defeating ones we have come accustomed to speaking silently to ourselves.

Ellis emphasizes that our irrational thinking generates a great deal of stress that simply does not reflect reality. This view is captured in the story of the man who discloses the following when reflecting back about his long life: "I am an old man who has had many worries in my life, few of which ever came true."

Imagery. Imaging exercises can also break the cycle of negative self-talk but do so with images, not words. For example, a person may practice sequentially going through a certain set of positive images for 10 minutes or longer. During a period of stress (e.g., waiting for a test to be distributed in class), the person can call upon one of the images used to reduce anxiety on the spot.

An example of imaging exercise follows. Read over the following images and then close your eyes and imagine the scene described.

> It is a beautiful spring day.
> Out my window I can see a crystal-clear, deep-blue sky.
> Almost as in a dream I go to my front door and step outside.
> There is a gentle breeze.
> The smell of flowers and the sound of singing birds are very pleasant.
> I walk out onto the fresh, green grass.
> I slowly kneel down and decide to lie back on the fresh, spring grass.
> The temperature is just right.
> I start to daydream about a trip to my favorite beach.
> I see myself on the beach and the sun is not too bright, just nice and warm.
> The water is a beautiful aqua color that I can see through to the bottom.
> The sand on the beach is a beautiful white, and coconut trees are spread out up and
>   down the beach.
> I start to walk on the beach.
> The sound of the waves is very soothing.
> The saltwater smell is refreshing.
> I stop when I notice a seashell embedded in the sand. It has many bright colors.
> Reds.
> Yellows.
> Blues.
> I bend over and pick up the beautifully colored shell.
> The feel of the water-worn shell is comforting.
> The sun is going down and is near the horizon.
> I sit down on the sand to watch the sun set.
> It is a beautiful sunset with various shades of reds, and I feel warm and at peace.
> A deep sense of peace flows over me, and I have no fears or worries.
> I return from my imaginary trip feeling both very relaxed and revitalized, as if I just
>   enjoyed a long, restful sleep from which I open my eyes and feel great and
>   optimistic about the world.

Deep Relaxation. For this exercise it is recommended that you practice approximately 20 minutes per day for about two weeks to master the technique. In a quiet, disturbance-free location, you are to go through the following muscle groups, tensing and relaxing them. The technique teaches a person, without going through the whole procedure, to quickly scan the body in approximately 10 seconds to locate pockets of muscle tension, which are then relaxed. The resulting state of relaxation can bring about a significant reduction in anxiety and stress allowing the person to focus his or her attention without having negative thoughts intrude. Keep in mind that when practicing this technique, you should not strain any part of the body that has been injured or is recovering from injury.

Lie back in a bed (or on the floor). Place a pillow under your head. After taking three deep breaths as described earlier, do the following:

Close your eyes.

Clench both your fists. Study the tension.

Relax the fingers of your hands and study the difference.

Enjoy the feeling of just lying there relaxed.

Again, clench both hands tighter and tighter. Study and focus on the tension you created in this part of your body.

Allow yourself to become relaxed all over.

Bend your elbows. Feel the tension created by bending your elbows. Dwell on the tension. Get to know how the tension feels in this part of the body.

Allow yourself to become very relaxed all over.

Become more and more relaxed. Imagine that you are so relaxed that you are sinking into the surface beneath you.

Straighten your arms out. Feel the tension created by pushing your arms straight out.

Now relax your arms and let them find their own place.

Wrinkle your forehead. Examine how the wrinkles feel and picture how they look. Now relax. Let the wrinkles go and picture in your mind the way your forehead now looks without the wrinkles.

Squeeze your eyes shut. Experience the tension you created using your eyes. Relax your eyes.

Relax all over.

Stay as relaxed as possible for about a minute.

Relax.

Relax.

Now clamp your teeth together. Study the tension created by biting your teeth together. Tension is being created in the jaws. Picture in your mind how the muscles in this area are tight.

Relax.

Now press your head back—push back on the pillow. Now stop and allow your body to become comfortable all over. Picture your body melting into the surface of the bed (or floor). Your body is so relaxed it is sinking down.

It is like you are a big rag doll just lying there.

Relax.

Move your head down so it is now against your chest. Study the tension that this movement created.

Relax.

Bring you shoulders up. Study the muscle tension created when you try to touch your ears with your shoulders.

Relax.

Now pull in your stomach, tighter and tighter. Now relax.

Relax.

Create a small arch in your back. Feel the tension in your muscles when you arch your back. Relax and allow your back to settle into a comfortable position as you do when you go to sleep at night.

Point your toes up toward the top of your head. Maintain this for 20 seconds. Now relax.

Relax.

Point your toes away from the top of your head. Maintain this position for about 10 seconds. Now relax.

Relax.

Raise one leg. Keep the leg up until the tension starts to become uncomfortable. Now lower that leg.

Relax.

Now lift the other leg. Keep it up for about the same length of time. Okay, now relax.

Become as relaxed as you are capable of becoming. Release all the muscle tension in your body. Relax more and more until you reach a very relaxed state—a very, very deep state of relaxation.

Lie there in a relaxed state for a while.

Now *imagine* getting up (*do not move*—just imagine getting up.) Notice the change in muscle tension even when you just picture in your mind that you are getting up.

Go back to a deep state of relaxation. Let any tension you find pour out of your body as if you were a bucket with many, many holes and the tension is water.

After about a minute permit yourself to come out of your relaxed state. You will feel refreshed upon getting up from where you were lying.

Meditation. There are various meditation techniques that can be used. A basic ingredient is to clear one's mind of thoughts and to concentrate on breathing. For example, as a person breathes in, he or she should count *one* for the *breath in*, *two* for the *breath out*, *three* for the next *breath in*. Continue all the way to the number *ten*. The trick is not to allow stray thoughts or images to occupy your mind. If this occurs, you must start over with the number one. It sounds easy—it is not. Try this exercise. It will take a period of practice (sometimes a long period) before you can reach the number ten without some sort of intrusion into your mind. Emptying one's mind is difficult.

In part, meditation is a way to slow us down. The mind is sometimes described as "a bunch of monkeys jumping from tree to tree," a metaphor to reflect how cluttered our mind can be with all the thoughts that enter its domain, disturbing its peace. As early as the 1970s, Herbert Benson and his colleagues at Harvard Medical School (see *The Relaxation Response*, 1975) found that by passively clearing the mind during meditation, oxygen requirements drop, heartbeat slows, blood pressure lowers, and we experience a mental and physiological calmness.

■ Sources

Barrios, B. A., Ginter, E. J., Scalise, J. J., & Miller, F. G. (1980). Treatment of test anxiety by applied relaxation and cue-controlled relaxation. *Psychological Reports, 46,* 1287–1296.

Benson, H. (1975). *The relaxation response.* New York: Morrow.

Ciabattari, J. (1999, January). Women who could be president. *Parade Magazine,* 6–7.

Ellis, A., & Grieger, R. (Eds.) (1977). *Handbook of rational emotive therapy.* New York: Springer.

Friedman, M., & Rosenman, R. H. (1974). *Type A behavior and your heart.* New York: Knopf.

Glauser, A., & Glauser, E. (2001). *Cultivating the spirit of mindfulness in counseling and psychotherapy.* Presentation made at the 2001 World Conference of the American Counseling Association, San Antonio, TX.

Maddi, S. R., & Hess, M. J. (1992). Personality hardiness and success in basketball. *International Journal of Sport Psychology, 23,* 360–368.

Maddi, S. R., & Kosaba, D. M. (1994). Hardiness and mental health. *Journal of Personality Assessment, 64,* 265–274.

Seligman, M. E. P. (1975). *Helplessness: On depression, development, and death.* San Francisco: W. H. Freeman.

Selye, H. (1953). *The Stress of Life.* New York: Knopf.

Spielberger, C. D. (Ed.). (1972). *Anxiety: Current trends in theory and research.* New York: Academic Press.

CHAPTER 14
Citizenship and Leadership

C ollege prepares you to earn a living. Ideally, it also prepares you for life. Whether in the workplace or as a citizen, leadership will be an enormous asset. You will face challenges that you cannot meet by yourself. You will need the assistance of others. You will have to lead.

The modern workplace is highly competitive, and leadership is a highly prized skill. The people who recruit college graduates to work for their organizations are on the lookout for can-do, results-oriented candidates. As you approach graduation in a few years and start interviewing for full-time employment, you will almost surely be asked about your leadership experiences: Did you hold an office in any organization? Did you chair any committees? Tell me about a time when you served on a committee which was responsible for an important project, and the work wasn't getting done. What did you do to help the committee accomplish its mission?

For most of our history as a nation, college was an option for only an elite few. Those privileged to attend were expected to be leaders. This obligation to serve society transcended professional success. College graduates were supposed to be civic leaders as well. Society still needs citizen leaders—individuals whose commitment to the common good is expressed through thoughtful, informed action. Our nation—and the entire world—requires statesmen and women, informed voters, social activists, and philanthropists at every level.

The 21st Century will pose enormous challenges: environmental, violence, public health, and economic inequities to list but a few. Because technology has made the world small, other people's problems are now our own. If urban youth are alienated and unemployed, their rage threatens us all. If the Mexican economy flounders, we get more illegal immigrants. If the Russian economy fails, we are faced with the prospect of a new regime that may be hostile toward the USA. Local pollution becomes international acid rain. Global warming affects the climate and shoreline of all nations.

John Donne wrote that "No man is an island." Ernest Hemingway reminded us that the bell tolls for each of us. So, why should you regard it as your obligation to make your school, your city, your country, and your world a better place? Because we sink or swim together. Citizenship is for the common good. Citizenship is also in your own interest.

Let us add that this is not an ideological position. It transcends liberal and conservative perspectives. Indeed this is one of the few principles upon which all our national leaders agree even though they may be divided as to just how to address the enormous challenges facing us. Conservative thinker William F. Buckley extolled the concept of voluntary national service in his recent book, *Gratitude: Reflections On What We Owe to Our Country*. President Clinton implemented a national service corps. So, whose job is it to be a better citizen? Yours and ours.

■ Leadership

In order to make a better world, we need better leaders. Citizenship requires leadership. So does professional success. If you can lead no one, your education is incomplete. True, you probably won't be President of the United States, a Four Star General, or the CEO of a major corporation. (But then, why not?) More likely, you will be a director, a teacher, or an entrepreneur. And you will almost certainly at some point chair a committee, head a project, propose an idea to neighbors or colleagues, or parent a child. Each and every one of these roles/activities requires you to lead. How do you do it, and can you learn the skills it takes?

The Components of Leadership

We believe there are at least six characteristics that make for successful leadership:

- ■ Vision: a sense of the future and its possibilities.

- Ethics and integrity: a commitment to think carefully about the public good and our own values when we act.
- Service orientation: the habit of working for others.
- Communication skills: the ability to say and write what we mean, simply and powerfully as well as the ability and commitment to listen with understanding to the concerns of others.
- Self awareness: the ongoing realization of personal strengths and weaknesses, of knowledge of interests, values, temperament, aspirations, and abilities.
- Teamwork in diverse groups: skills to accomplish common goals by working with others who bring a variety of experiences to the task.

Let's take a brief look at each.

VISION. Before you can lead someone to the promised land, you must be able to see it yourself—even if you haven't been there yet. Indeed, the greatest leaders are able to create the future by vividly imagining it. John Kennedy envisioned a man on the moon. Stephen Jobs envisioned a world in which we all use personal computers. Mary Kay envisioned a network of small business women who were also saleswomen creating a business juggernaut. Why couldn't your vision be greater still?

While we encourage you to dream big, we also know that not every business prospers, nor is every dream realized. Nor is every vision about changing the world. Sometimes it's about changing a small part of it—seeing the successful child in the troubled youth you mentor, seeing a team that wins by playing together, picturing a residence hall in which students are a community of learners.

A vision is related to the goals that together will make the vision a reality, but a vision isn't a goal or even a collection of goals. A vision is a portrait of a future you wish to create. Although it comes from your imagination, it is something you can describe vividly. It is something that you can see and so you can describe it to others. A vision can sustain you in tough times. It can compel others to work together in the service of that vision. It can unite, motivate, and provide a common direction.

Where do visions come from? How do you become visionary? We believe you can become more visionary, but like everything else, you acquire vision only by paying your dues. First, you must understand yourself. You must know YOUR values, interests, abilities, and goals. You must create YOUR mission before you can create one that others will buy into. Second, you must know the world around you. You cannot create a new world (or even a small part of it) without first understanding the present one. You need to know the field or domain in which you would lead. You will also be well served to know something of the world beyond that field. True innovation often emerges from the synthesis of disparate ideas from seemingly unrelated fields. Ignorant, uninformed people are not likely to develop very useful, much less compelling visions.

Leaders face almost constant new challenges. They must come up with new strategies and techniques for coping with a world undergoing revolutionary change. While leaders must be grounded in solid, enduring values they must keep abreast of technical, scientific, and cultural changes. How can any business compete if it uses outdated information technology? How can medicine advance apart from genetic research? How can marketing executives sell new products if they don't know the mood of the public? Ted Turner, owner of a regional television station in Atlanta, read Alvin Toffler's *Future Shock* and envisioned an innovative way of communicating the news around the world. Eventually, his vision matured into a media empire revolving around CNN. In 1998, Turner was named man of the year by *Time Magazine.*

Probably the most important characteristic you can possess is an insatiable curiosity—a burning desire to learn. This desire must translate into action—reading, experimentation, involvement, reflection. You would be short-sighted to confuse going to college with acquiring an education. You would be a fool to pass up the education that's available to you while you're here. Moreover, right now is the time to cultivate the successful habits of the continuous, life-long learner. If you are not making quantum leaps in knowledge acquisition from here on out, you will be shortchanging yourself in the vision department and therefore in the domain of leadership.

Finally, the most compelling organizational visions resonate with constituents because the constituents had a role in developing the vision. Sometimes, this occurs indirectly because a leader knows her followers so well that she is able to incorporate their values and aspirations into a vision that resonates with the rank and file of the entire membership. On other occasions, leaders explicitly ask for input from members? What shall our strategy be? What should our organization look like a year from now?

ETHICS AND INTEGRITY. Before individuals will follow someone's lead, they must believe in that person. Leaders, therefore, must be true to their words. Their walk must match their talk. James Kouzes and Barry Posner, two of the most influential scholars of leadership today, argue that a leader's credibility with constituents is the absolute "sine qua non" of leadership. Why commit yourself to a cause to which the leader claims to be invested, but who behaves otherwise?

Ethics are important because leaders exert power. That power can be expended for good or evil. A dictator, such as Adolf Hitler, had many qualities that made him a powerful leader. He was able to mobilize large numbers of people to commit to a common cause. The cause to which he enlisted the German people, however, was based upon ethnocentrism. He led his people toward ignoble ends. His leadership caused death and suffering almost beyond imagining. While membership in the human race carries with it the responsibility to behave honorably, leaders must bear an even heavier responsibility. When they pursue the common good, society is enriched. When they do not, others will suffer.

Ethics are important because without them organizations cannot flourish. Customers do not want to buy from a company they don't trust. Customers won't come back to a store

that sells faulty products. Organizations perceived to be unethical may not last very long. Members of an organization will form a culture that is based upon the practices of its leadership. If managers, directors, vice-presidents, and CEOs lie to their employees and fail to keep their promises, the employees soon start lying to management. As deceit and petty politics rise, morale and productivity plummet. This is true whether the organization is a giant multinational corporation, a local high school, or a college fraternity.

There is inevitably an ethical component to leadership. Think of great leaders, and you think of honorable men and women. This doesn't mean our greatest leaders were saints, but they are remembered as having a firm moral center. It's not enough to have good ideas and charisma. You must have a coherent set of values. Your actions must match your words. If people don't know where you stand, they will not want to back you. If people doubt your word, why in the world would they want to follow you?

SERVICE ORIENTATION. We usually think of charismatic leaders by virtue of their ability to deliver stirring public speeches. While inspirational speech-making is a useful leadership skill, research conducted by Jay Conger and Rabindra Kanungo reveals that constituents will commit to a leader's cause only when the leader is perceived as serving organizational ideals rather than merely self interest. Moreover, those leaders were regarded as more charismatic when they were perceived as serving the organization and its members.

Robert Greenleaf's name is synonymous with "servant leadership." He was profoundly influenced by reading Herman Hesse's *Journey to the East* in which the leader of the journey is initially mistaken by his fellow travelers as a "mere servant." Eventually, the travelers come to realize that this humble servant is the glue that holds the group together, maintains their safety, and keeps them headed in the right direction.

You can intimidate some people into following your lead, but people follow out of fear only so long as you have some power over them. Most of us do not typically have that sort of positional power over those whom we would influence. If you want to be an effective leader of a student organization, you will be effective because you are somehow able to connect with members who volunteer their time and energy. Even in the business world, the best managers and executives know that their best staff members are, in essence, volunteers. Top employees can always get good jobs somewhere else.

The best leaders motivate people to *want* to follow them. How do you get people to want to? Communicating a compelling vision certainly helps, but others won't even consider your vision unless they're convinced you have their well-being at heart. Think about some leader whom you would gladly follow through thick or thin. Chances are, you believe this person respects you, cares about you, desires your success. The best leaders exude concern for their colleagues and constituents.

You demonstrate concern for those whom you would lead by being considerate, by understanding them, and by encouraging them. While your first image of a leader might be some take-charge person giving an inspiring speech, you must learn to listen if you want others to listen to you. Good leaders are empathic: they can see things from the other person's perspective. The very best leaders understand others deeply, grasping what events mean to their followers. Because good leaders know their followers well, they know what resources are needed in order for the followers to complete their missions. Much of a good leader's energy is devoted to preserving the well-being and morale of every member of the organization and of securing the resources to enable members to do their jobs. A true leader, then, serves the organization and its members.

Servant leaders, then, are committed to their followers and to their organization's ideals. Ideas are cheap. Let us amend that. Ideas—even good ones—without the commitment and dedication to turn them into action are cheap. Many a lofty vision has died because the person who dreamed it did not invest the blood, sweat, and tears to make that vision a reality.

Think back on when someone wanted you to work for a cause. Did the captain ask you to sacrifice for the good of the team, but (s)he never passed the ball? Didn't make you very committed to the team, did it? Did the president of your organization ask you to work Saturday morning at the fund raiser, but (s)he slept in? Maybe next time you'll sleep in too. Leaders who aren't committed to serving their organization and its members soon have no one to lead.

Commitment starts in the heart. It is feeling passionately about something. Commitment, however, always boils down to action. It is standing up for your ideas. It is working long and hard without complaining to turn ideas into reality. So, how do you get committed? How do you kindle passion in your heart for something beyond yourself? How do you become a servant leader?

If nothing fires you up, we suspect you're avoiding life rather than living it. If you are a young adult just out of high school, you probably enjoy more freedom in your life than you have ever had or ever will have. You can spend your time playing computer games, watching TV, and taking naps. Or you can immerse yourself in academic and extracurricular life. You can join a professional society, start a small business, or work for Habitat for Humanity.

Sometimes, motivation fires you up to take action, but if nothing motivates you, we urge you to act anyway. Once you start thinking, doing, and serving, enthusiasm will follow. In a recent discussion on leadership, a number of fraternity and sorority officers revealed to me (Bill) what they thought most held their organizations back. Too many of the members didn't want to get involved, didn't want to assume responsibility for improving things, didn't want to stick their necks out. They were waiting for the other members to fix things. The following story, created by the prolific Anonymous, neatly captures this problem.

"Four people named Everybody, Somebody, Anybody, and Nobody met to accomplish an important task. Everybody was sure Somebody would do it. Anybody could have done it, but Nobody did it. Somebody got angry about that, because after all, wasn't it Everybody's job? Everybody thought that Anybody could do it, but Nobody realized that Everybody wouldn't do it. It ended up that Everybody blamed Somebody when Nobody did what Anybody could have done."

COMMUNICATION SKILLS. OK, you have a great idea—an idea that is positively visionary. It's almost certain that you will need help to make your vision a reality. How do you get others to buy into your vision? Throughout this book we've emphasized the importance of communication skills. In order to lead you must communicate your vision to the people whom you want to help you. Not only must you paint a clear picture, you must persuade others to make a commitment to work with you towards the realization of your vision.

This is partly a "public speaking" issue. Can you stand up in front of a group and speak confidently and sincerely? Can you do this before a handful, a dozen, a roomful, a thousand? Speaking effectively before a group may intimidate or even terrify you, but it is a VERY useful skill. Among the activities that most executives claim to like is speaking before large groups.

This doesn't mean that you have to be a declaimer of olympian proportions in order to be a leader. Some people are more persuasive one to one. If you saw the movie, *Malcolm X*, you may recall the lengthy conversations Malcolm had with the inmate instrumental in his conversion. The other inmate rarely raised his voice. Nor were his words flowery. But he spoke from the heart and convinced Malcolm to work for a much larger cause than himself.

In the business world, would be leaders are encouraged to master the art of the "parking lot speech." Everybody is busy, and the only time you have to sell your idea to a colleague may be in the minute or so when you meet in the parking lot on the way to or from the office. For students, the analog is the "walk to class speech." You run into somebody whose support you need, and you have just minutes together on your way to History class. Can you boil down your ideas so they are clear and simple, yet still persuasive before you reach the classroom?

If you are not sure of your persuasive abilities, work to improve them. Consider some of the following ways to improve this essential skill:

- Take a class in public speaking
- Attend an assertiveness workshop
- Participate in a sales seminar or workshop
- Volunteer to give a committee's report to the group-at-large
- Join an organization such as Toastmasters
- Run for office in an organization
- Try out for a part in a play

The written word is also an important tool for those who would lead. George Washington had Thomas Paine's words disseminated to every member of his army. These words helped to create a common understanding of why the revolutionary soldiers were fighting and increased their commitment to that cause. An executive with experience in both the public and private realm recently underscored to me the importance of writing clearly. Almost every day in the workaday world, you must write reports, memos, letters, summaries, and proposals. Your success hinges partly on how well you write. Moreover, if you write poorly, you leave a tainted track record. The only knowledge of your work that the CEO possesses might be your proposal. If it's laced with grammatical errors, misspelled words, and awkward phrasing, it is unlikely that your proposal will find favor. It is even less likely that your star will rise in the organization.

Communication is, of course, a two-way street. You must receive information from others as well as dispense it. Listening with sensitivity for the deeper meanings and emotions behind the words of others is vital for leaders. As one saying goes: humans have one mouth and two ears. This is nature's way of reminding us that we should spend twice as much time listening as speaking. Listening is crucial for leaders for a variety of reasons. Through active listening, a leader can learn about the concerns of the members of an organization. By listening attentively, a leader demonstrates concern for those members and thereby motivates them. By listening, a leader can get ideas which will influence the very direction an organization takes.

SELF AWARENESS. As a leader, your biggest resource is yourself. Does it not, therefore, make sense to know as much as possible about this resource—strengths and weaknesses, beliefs and values, skills and abilities. If you understand your weakness in public speaking, you can work on improving that skill. You can also delegate that responsibility to another member of your team who will better express your organization's perspective. I once had a very bright assistant who was blind to his inability to communicate in plain English to an unsophisticated audience. On several occasions, he mistakenly assumed he had persuaded his audience to buy his ideas when the only thing he had convinced them of was that he couldn't speak simply and clearly.

We urge you to cultivate a clearer self-understanding while you are in college. If self awareness is valuable for every person who will be educated, it is crucial for those who will lead. We suggest that psychological tests are one useful means of self-exploration. In fact, it is routine for individuals entering management training and leadership development programs to be given a battery of tests. Extensive feedback is provided to the trainee by a skilled clinician. Further feedback is provided by other trainees and trainers to corroborate the testing. It is commonplace for employees in many organizations to receive 360 degree feedback—feedback from bosses, colleagues, subordinates, and even customers. The purpose of all this feedback: to promote self-awareness.

Warren Bennis, in *On Becoming a Leader*, states that to "know thyself" is to understand clearly the differences between the way you define yourself and the way others define you. Leaders create change. Since not everyone likes change, those who interact with leaders may define them quite differently than would the leaders themselves. Some will assume a woman lacks the toughness to lead. Others will assume that a person of color possesses insufficient talent for leadership. There are countless ways that constituents can dismiss someone's leadership—too new to the organization, the wrong age, from the wrong part of the world, from the wrong social class. It is the leader's firm sense of self that will enable that person to perform in the face of such resistance.

It is not just that leaders know themselves, however; it is that they constantly try to improve themselves. Leaders use their self awareness as a springboard for recreating themselves. When they discover deficiencies, they work to overcome them. They read, they train, they study successful leaders, they seek out the experiences which will enable them to grow.

TEAMWORK IN DIVERSE GROUPS. Think back for a moment on some of your experiences as a member of a sports team, a member of a committee, or one of a team charged with completing a project. It is highly likely that you can recall some team member who was domineering, self-absorbed, inattentive, unfocused, argumentative, or irresponsible. Remember how frustrated you felt, how disheartening it was to have to cope with this character. You could have won the game, but Chris let everybody down because of poor practice habits. You could have had an outstanding organization which consistently got first-rate results, but Pat held the entire organization back because of a giant ego. Perhaps the group was able to compensate for the counter-productive member, but it made it harder for everyone else.

Managers and corporate recruiters are quite aware of the importance of teamwork. Business and management writers have covered many organizational success stories that were powered by effective teams. Katzenbach and Smith, in *The Wisdom of Teams*, cite a number of examples: Motorola was able to design and manufacture the world's leading cell phone. Ford became the most profitable American automobile company through teamwork. Teams are critical to 3M's ongoing success. The Desert Storm military victory over Iraq could not have been accomplished without the extraordinary teamwork it took to move 300,000 people, 100,000 vehicles, and 7,000,000 tons of equipment, fuel, and supplies. In Harlem, the first Little League in forty years was introduced through the efforts of a group of citizens working together. Glenn Parker surveyed fifty-one companies and reports in *Team Players and Teamwork* that effective teamwork consistently resulted in greater productivity, more effective use of resources, and better problem solving.

Student organizations are no different. Fraternities and sororities, sports clubs, and professional societies are less successful without teamwork. No officer wants to take on new members who impede group progress. Therefore, you must be a team player in order to succeed in today's world. Team skills are crucial for your professional success. They are also necessary for your success as a student and as a developing leader.

In *The Breakthrough Team Player*, Andrew DuBrin lists skills and attitudes that make for effective teamwork including:

- Assuming resonsibility for problems
- Willingness to commit to team goals
- Ability to see the big picture
- Belief in consensus
- Willingness to ask tough questions
- Helping team members do their jobs better
- Lending a hand during peak workloads
- Rarely turning down a co-worker request
- Openness to new ideas
- Recognizing the interests and achievements of others
- Active listening and information sharing
- Giving helpful criticism
- Receptiveness to helpful criticism
- Being a team player even when personally inconvenienced

In other words, the more fully human you are, the better a team player you will be, and the better a leader you will be. Needless to say, this is an ongoing life-long process of learning and development.

Not only must you collaborate, you will be called upon to collaborate effectively with people who are very different from yourself. In fact, much of the power of teamwork comes from combining the contributions of diverse talents and perspectives. The increasing complexity of today's business world requires such "alchemy." Better decisions are generally made by groups of diverse people. Moreover, in a global economy, you will be expected to work with people from all over the world.

Think of an outstanding football team. It is comprised of many talented athletes pulling together for a common cause. Perhaps the star is the quarterback. However talented that quarterback, the team would not be as effective if it were comprised of eleven outstanding quarterbacks. None would have the weight or strength to play on the line. They would probably not have the speed to play tailback, receiver, or in the defensive secondary. A successful sports team requires not just talent, but different kinds of talent. The same is true of a corporation. Scientists and engineers must be able to work together with accountants, managers, marketing specialists, and advertisers.

Most of us are more comfortable working with people like ourselves. Engineers like working with engineers and writers prefer the company of other literary types. Once you enter the workforce, however, you will be expected to collaborate with people whose skills and outlooks differ from your own. If accountants called all the shots, the company might never take any risks. If engineers called all the shots, aesthetics and design might suffer. If artists ruled, the new widgit might triumph aesthetically, but sink financially.

You must also be able to work with people whose race, religion, politics, and lifestyles are unfamiliar or, at any rate, different from your own. The American workforce of the future will be diverse. If you can't work with differences, your career will suffer.

■ Learning to Lead

We believe that learning to lead is imperative for every college student. Yet many students are notoriously indifferent to the leadership opportunities available to them. Leadership certainly requires careful reflection. Taking classes, attending speeches, and reading books about leadership can provide students with both insight and inspiration about their own capacity to lead. We believe, however, that leadership is a "contact sport." You learn by entering the fray. If you are not a member of an organization, if you never vote,

if you avoid participating in the governance of your residence hall—your commitment to learning to lead is questionable.

In order to get a college degree, you are required to take an array of courses, including core course, courses in a major, and a smattering of electives. Chances are, you are NOT required to study leadership either in the classroom or through your involvement in campus activities. You will be cheating yourself, however, and jeopardizing your career if you do not resolve to improve as a leader. Today's apathetic student is tomorrow's indifferent citizen whose very inactivity amounts to fiddling while society burns.

While we urge you to cultivate your capacity to lead, do not make the error of confusing a position or an office with true leadership. While chairing a committee, presiding over an organization, and joining campus organizations all provide excellent leadership developmental opportunities, none of these inevitably guarantees excellence. That comes from practicing the six habits we identified at the top of this chapter. Leadership then is about serving others and operating ethically. It is about envisioning how to make things better and communicating that vision effectively. Leadership is about understanding yourself and collaborating with all kinds of people. These are six skills which are as important as anything you will ever learn, and no matter how committed you are to cultivating them, you will never master them. Like most things in life that matter, learning to lead is a life-long process. It's time to get started!

Leadership Self Assessment

Vision

In order to be "visionary," you must first be well-informed. Today, that means being a continuous learner, both in school and on your own. How many of the following statements can you affirm?

_____ 1. I frequently read a daily newspaper.

_____ 2. I can name four political columnists of varying ideological points of view.

_____ 3. I frequently read a weekly news magazine.

_____ 4. I often watch a national news show on television.

_____ 5. I often read a business periodical (e.g., *Wall Street Journal, Fortune, Business Week*, etc.)

_____ 6. I follow the latest developments in science and technology.

_____ 7. I've been to a play within the past year.

_____ 8. I've seen a movie with subtitles within the past year.

_____ 9. I have read an unassigned work of literature within the past year.

_____ 10. I periodically read a professional or trade journal within my field of interest.

_____ 11. I attend meetings or conferences of a professional society.

_____ 12. I've learned some new computer skills within the past year.

_____ 13. I sometimes discuss my field of interest with others to find out more about it.

_____ 14. I have attended a serious concert/performance within the past year.

_____ 15. I occasionally watch television documentaries that cover history, science or current affairs.

_____ 16. I have eaten the food of at least six different countries within the past year.

_____ 17. I have friends and acquaintances of a variety of ethnic and religious backgrounds.

_____ 18. I can readily identify most countries on a world globe.

_____ 19. I understand some basic features of most major cultural groups throughout the world.

_____ 20. I have read a serious nonfiction book which was not assigned within the past year.

_____ 21. I know the basic tenets of each of the world's major religions.

What other actions do you take to indicate your commitment to continuous learning?

What do your responses reveal about your commitment to continuous learning? What do you need to do differently in the future?

■ Ethics and Integrity

Name an individual whom you judge to be high in integrity: _____

How long have you known this individual? _____

_____

How long did it take before you recognized the person's integrity?

_____

_____

What characterizes this person that spells integrity?

_____

_____

What actions does this person take that suggest integrity?

_____

_____

Can you identify a situation in which this person's integrity was tested?

_____

_____

How did (s)he handle the test?

_____

_____

Name an individual whom you judge to lack integrity: _____

How long have you known this individual? _____

How long did it take before you recognized the person lacked integrity?

_____

_____

What characterizes this person that spells weak integrity?

_____

_____

What actions does this person take that suggest weak integrity?

_____

_____

Can you identify a situation in which this person's integrity was tested?

_____

_____

How did (s)he handle the test?

_____

_____

In what related ways are you like the person with high integrity?

_____

_____

In what related ways are you like the person with weak integrity?

_____

_____

How will you increase your personal integrity?

_____

_____

■ Service Orientation

There are many ways you can serve others: through the political process, through philanthropic work, and through your demeanor in daily interactions. Check those items below which reflect YOUR personal behavior:

_____ 1. I'm registered to vote.

_____ 2. I vote in most elections.

_____ 3. I know who my congressman is.

_____ 4. I've worked in a political campaign.

_____ 5. I know the news well enough to be an informed voter.

_____ 6. I contribute money in support of my beliefs.

_____ 7. I contribute time in support of my beliefs.

_____ 8. I stay informed of the causes I'm committed to addressing.

_____ 9. I contribute money to the cause.

_____ 10. I contribute time and energy to the cause.

_____ 11. I'm a member of a group which serves the cause.

_____ 12. I avoid activities which harm the cause.

_____ 13. I compliment people when they succeed.

_____ 14. I congratulate people when they win an award.

_____ 15. I encourage people when they have setbacks.

_____ 16. I send notes or e-mail to encourage people.

_____ 17. I keep track of people's birthdays.

_____ 18. I send birthday cards to friends and acquaintances.

_____ 19. I give gifts or stage a surprise when a colleague achieves something big.

_____ 20. I work more for organizational goals than for personal glory.

Communication

_____ 1. I can be silent when others need to speak.

_____ 2. I can hear the feelings and meanings behind the words.

_____ 3. I can ask questions that encourage self-revelation.

_____ 4. I avoid criticizing other persons.

_____ 5. I convey my interest by eye contact and body language.

_____ 6. I ask questions in class.

_____ 7. I contribute to class discussions.

_____ 8. I offer my views during meetings.

_____ 9. If I disagree strongly during a meeting, I'll say so.

_____ 10. I can effectively report a committee's discussion back to the main group.

_____ 11. I can run a meeting effectively.

_____ 12. I know Robert's Rules of Order.

_____ 13. I can address a small group effectively.

_____ 14. I can hold a large group's attention when I speak.

_____ 15. I can make a strong case for my point of view.

If you're not satisfied with your persuasive skills, here are ten antidotes.

1. Prepare a meaningful question before class. Ask it during class.

2. Prepare a thoughtful observation before class. State it when appropriate during class.

3. Think about an issue likely to come up at your next meeting. Ask for the floor, and make your point.

4. Think about a perspective with which you're likely to disagree at the next meeting. Prepare a rejoinder. State your rejoinder at the next meeting.

5. Volunteer to speak for your committee.

6. Volunteer to run a committee meeting. Prepare an agenda, and stick to it.

7. Study Robert's Rules of Order.

8. Volunteer to speak before a small group on something that's important to you. Prepare thoroughly, and practice your speech.

9. Volunteer to speak before a large group on something that's important to you. Prepare thoroughly, and practice your speech.

10. Try to convince a friend or acquaintance to join you in some cause.

Self Awareness

It is difficult to assess yourself accurately. For example, answer the following question: Are you blind to your own faults? Even if you are, your blindness prevents you from knowing it. There are some habits that suggest an openness to self-examination that are worthy of cultivating, however. How many do you practice?

_____ 1. I read any critique of my work made by a professor and reflect on it.

_____ 2. I attempt to understand my personality survey scores in this class.

_____ 3. I solicit feedback from others about my performance.

_____ 4. I am willing to take some moderate risks in order to improve as a leader.

_____ 5. When others criticize me, I honestly try to weigh the validity of their remarks.

_____ 6. I compare my own skills to those discussed in this chapter.

_____ 7. When I read other leadership literature, I use the ideas to look at myself.

_____ 8. I can honestly identify some areas in which I need to improve myself.

_____ 9. I can honestly identify some areas of personal strength.

_____ 10. I use experiential activities in class and workshops to learn about myself.

Teamwork

_____ 1. I contribute my fair share on group projects.

_____ 2. When I disagree with other team members, I say so.

_____ 3. When forming a team, I try to select diverse talents.

_____ 4. I understand the stages of group development.

_____ 5. I understand how my personality best contributes to team performance.

Putting It All Together

Most of us will never head up a major corporation or hold a major political office. Nonetheless, we can exert leadership in many ways—by holding an office in a smaller organization, by speaking up at organizational meetings, by volunteering to handle a problem. Here are some ways you could stretch your leadership wings.

1. Identify an issue about which you have strong, unexpressed feelings in an organization to which you belong. Think about what you could say or do to strengthen the organization's stand on this issue. Craft a statement which you could make at a meeting. Imagine what it would be like to make the statement. What would the response of your fellow members be? Can you think of effective ways of responding to them? Pick an ally within the organization that you could share your views with. How does (s)he respond? Does (s)he have any suggestions for improvements? Are you accurately understanding the opposing point of view? Select a time when you will raise the issue and state your position. Go for it!

2. Identify a concern or a problem which you have. Then identify a person in authority who could address your concern. Think of a *reasonable* course of action which the authority could take to improve the situation. Make *sure* that the authority has the power to effect the change you recommend, that the action is cost-effective, that it will not cause undue damage elsewhere. Craft a recommendation you could make to the authority. Practice it with an ally. Make an appointment with the authority. When you meet, explain your concern, recommend your solution, and state your willingness to help implement the solution, if that's feasible.

3. Identify an office or position you would like to hold. It should be in an organization in whose goals you believe. Declare your intention to run for office. Or, if more appropriate, speak with current officers about your desire to assume a greater leadership role. If you run for office, secure the commitment of some friends who will help you. Get organized, plan a campaign, implement it. If the more likely route to power is through appointment, discuss your desire to serve on a particular committee or as a particular office holder. Explain why you think you can do the job. Ask for feedback and a commitment to be given the opportunity to lead.

4. Read some books and articles on leadership and citizenship.

5. Attend a leadership workshop.

6. Sign up for an academic class in leadership.

■ Post-Survey

1. **Gender**
   - ☐ Male
   - ☐ Female

2. **Age:** _____ (Please fill in)

3. Are you a transfer student?
   - ☐ Yes
   - ☐ No

4. **Ethnic Group**
   - ☐ White American
   - ☐ African American
   - ☐ Hispanic/Latino
   - ☐ Asian
   - ☐ Native American
   - ☐ Pacific Islander
   - ☐ Multiracial

5. **Classification:**
   - ☐ Freshman (0–29 hours)
   - ☐ Sophomore (30–59 hours)
   - ☐ Junior (60–89 hours)
   - ☐ Senior (90 hours and above)

6. Did you transfer from a community college?
   - ☐ Yes
   - ☐ No
   - ☐ Other (please list)

7. Where do you live?
   - ☐ Campus residence hall
   - ☐ Private home
   - ☐ Private apartment
   - ☐ Campus apartment
   - ☐ Greek housing

8. If you commute to and from campus, how long does it take to make the round trip?

- ☐ Do not commute
- ☐ Less than 1 hour
- ☐ 1–2 hours
- ☐ 3–4 hours
- ☐ More than 5 hours
- ☐ Other (please list)

	Strongly Agree	Agree	Neutral	Disagree	Strongly Disagree
9. My college education will enable me to attain my career and life goals.	☐	☐	☐	☐	☐
10. I feel that I am part of a social network on campus.	☐	☐	☐	☐	☐
11. I have decided on a major.	☐	☐	☐	☐	☐
12. I feel comfortable contacting my professors outside of class.	☐	☐	☐	☐	☐
13. I always feel prepared for class.	☐	☐	☐	☐	☐
14. I feel there is at least one university employee who cares about my welfare (i.e., instructor, advisor, staff member).	☐	☐	☐	☐	☐
15. I know what occupation I want to pursue.	☐	☐	☐	☐	☐
16. I am committed to completing my degree.	☐	☐	☐	☐	☐
17. I am involved in activities on campus.	☐	☐	☐	☐	☐
18. I know how to concentrate in class.	☐	☐	☐	☐	☐
19. I know my academic strengths.	☐	☐	☐	☐	☐
20. I know what resources are available to me as a student.	☐	☐	☐	☐	☐
21. I feel the climate at my college allows me to freely express my opinions and views.	☐	☐	☐	☐	☐
22. I ask for help from others when needed.	☐	☐	☐	☐	☐
23. I balance school and other responsibilities effectively.	☐	☐	☐	☐	☐
24. I have a clear picture of my long-term goals.	☐	☐	☐	☐	☐
25. I know how to study for different types of tests.	☐	☐	☐	☐	☐
26. I am confident in my ability to succeed.	☐	☐	☐	☐	☐